Contents

Political ideology today

This new textbook provides an introduction to political ideologies, the powerful and persuasive ideas which have motivated the actions of both political leaders and ordinary people.

Ian Adams begins by explaining the nature of ideology and the part it plays in political life, and then looks at each of the main ideologies in turn. He takes a broadly historical approach to show how each ideology has evolved as a tradition with a variety of sometimes conflicting forms. Liberalism, socialism, conservatism, Marxism, anarchism and fascism are all discussed, together with the New Right in the 1980s, and more recent developments in religious and sexual politics, environmentalism and animal rights. Adams shows that contemporary ideological thinking is thriving, despite the 'end of ideology' proclaimed after the capitalist West's triumph in the Cold War. He also discusses prospects for future ideological developments.

This book is designed to meet the needs of both A level and undergraduate students in politics, and is also suitable for the general reader wanting an introduction to political ideas.

Ian Adams is Senior Lecturer in Government at New College, Durham.

Politics today

Series editor: Bill Jones

Political ideology today

Ian Adams

Manchester University Press
Manchester and New York
Distributed exclusively in the USA and Canada by St. Martin's Press

Published by Manchester University Press
Oxford Road, Manchester M13 9PL, UK
and Room 400, 175 Fifth Avenue, New York, NY 10010, USA

Distributed exclusively in the USA and Canada
by St. Martin's Press, Inc., 175 Fifth Avenue, New York,
NY 10010, USA

British Library Cataloguing-in-Publication Data
A catalogue record for this book is available from the British Library

Library of Congress Cataloging-in-Publication Data
Adams, Ian, 1943–
    Political ideology today / Ian Adams.
    p.   cm.—(Politics today)
  ISBN 0–7190–3346–2.–ISBN 0–7190–3347–0 (pbk.)
  1. Political science.   2. Ideology.   3. Right and left (Political
science)   I. Title.   II. Series: Politics today (Manchester,
England)
JA83.A47   1993
320—dc20   92–40256

ISBN 0 7190 3346 2 *hardback*
ISBN 0 7190 3347 0 *paperback*

Photoset in Linotron Ehrhardt
by Northern Phototypesetting Co. Ltd, Bolton

Printed in Great Britain
by Bell & Bain Ltd, Glasgow

Acknowledgements

I would particularly like to thank Bill Jones and Richard Purslow for their help and encouragement, and above all for their patience. I would also like to thank Julia Henderson, whose careful reading of the text saved me from many errors and omissions.

Ian Adams

To Syd and Muriel

True political science is the science not of what is, but of what ought to be.

Abbé Siéyès, 'Economi politique', MS, 1772

1

Introduction

Only a few years ago the pattern of world politics seemed indefinitely fixed. There were two dominant 'blocs' of countries with each bound together by similar beliefs. The 'Western bloc' believed in liberal democracy and a government-managed welfare capitalism, while the 'Eastern bloc' believed in a version of Marxism called 'communism'.

In the last few years much has changed. Most spectacular has been the collapse of communist regimes in Eastern Europe in 1989, followed by the Soviet Union. Less striking, but still important, has been the development of new ideas in the more successful West, which is now more ideologically various as a result.

Some have argued that the West has simply won the Cold War, and we look forward to an era of ideological uniformity. But this is perhaps wishful thinking. For one thing, the ending of old rigidities in itself implies the possibility of greater variety. There are still communist regimes; there are former communist regimes that may evolve in any number of directions; there is a striking revival of nationalism in many areas; religious fundamentalism, particularly anti-Western Islamic fundamentalism, has made a considerable impact on world affairs in recent years which is unlikely to diminish; and within liberal democracies there are new ideological developments, including feminism and sexual politics and green politics. Meanwhile, new varieties of socialism, liberalism and other ideologies continue to evolve.

The world today is a fast-changing place ideologically. If we are to understand the modern world as we approach the twenty-first century we must know something about the nature and influence of these ideologies.

What is ideology?

Beyond the idea of a political doctrine, there is little agreement about the nature of ideology. Its essential elements; whether all political doctrines are ideological or only some, and if so which; how we decide whether doctrines are true or false, good or bad; are all questions that have generated many opinions and much heated debate.

Concepts of ideology

For most of its controversial career as a concept, the word 'ideology' has implied some kind of false thinking, something we could all well do without. As a consequence, most theories of ideology have been partisan, where theorists and followers of one political doctrine have tried to characterise other people's ideas as ideological. Thus Marx saw ideology as distortions of reality ('false consciousness') in the interests of a particular social class, usually the ruling class. Liberalism, for example, was the ideology of the bourgeoisie, which masked its exploitation and oppression of other classes. Marx's own theories were deemed scientific and therefore not ideological.

Liberals, on the other hand, usually associate ideology with what they call 'closed' systems of thought which purport to be absolute truth. Such thinking leads to the view that those people possessed of the truth must have power and that other people must not be allowed to stand in the way of truth and progress, which leads directly to totalitarianism. This is seen as contrasting with liberalism itself, which is open and tolerant and rational. Liberalism claims to be a set of sound philosophical principles, while doctrines like Marxism and Fascism are ideological.

Traditional conservatism (which liberals tend to regard as lacking in principle and only interested in power, rather than as ideological) tends to see ideology as any kind of politics driven by theory, that is, a politics based on some vision of how society ought to be and pursuing policies designed to make the vision a reality. This they believe to be a futile and dangerous way of approaching politics, and a way to which all doctrines, except conservatism, are prone. Conservative ideas by contrast are conceived of as being based upon experience and common sense and judicious caution; in other words, pragmatic rather than ideological.

One of the problems with these partisan views of ideology is that, apart from being manifestly self-serving, they each form part of a wider set of beliefs, so that it is difficult, for example, to subscribe to the Marxist view of ideology without being committed to the rest of Marxism as well.

Sociologists and other academics have tried to be more objective about the question, but they too tend to see ideology as a false kind of thinking from which we need to rid ourselves. However, recent years have seen a change of attitude. Increasingly, scholars, as well as politicians and journalists, have taken to using the word in a non-partisan, non-pejorative way, so that it means simply a set of political beliefs about how society ought to be and how to improve it, irrespective of whether those ideas are true or false or good or bad. This neutral concept also makes it easier to discuss the role of ideology in politics, and analyse its elements, without becoming involved in partisan disputes.

Ideology and politics

Politics is largely about reconciling conflicting views in order to come to collective decisions over what to do. Conflicting views arise because people's interests differ. People's values differ as well, and conflicts over values are just as important because we are not only concerned to do what will be effective, but also to do what is right. Individual values may be involved in particular issues, such as the rights and wrongs of abortion, or nuclear weapons, but there are also broader systems of ideas about how society should be run, what values – such as justice, equality or freedom – it should embody, and these are ideologies.

Although ideologies are concerned with large and distant questions about the best kind of society and the ideal way to live, they are also closely bound up with practical political activity. For example, some politicians may oppose a government proposal to privatise some aspect of the social services because, quite apart from technical considerations of efficiency or cost, they do not wish to see a society where people's welfare becomes a matter of private profit, with the danger that the worse off will end up with a poorer service or none at all. Other politicians may support the same proposal because they want to see a society where as much as possible is left to the free market, which they believe is a society that brings the greatest individual freedom, and therefore is a morally superior society to one where the state provides such things. It is these fundamental differences of what is right and what kind of society we should live in that ideology is concerned with above all.

Values and the ideal society

Ideology is first of all concerned with values; that is, how we ought to treat each other and live together in society. Ideologies offer rival visions of the 'good society', the morally best kind of society for human beings to live in. This is true of doctrines we may despise as morally contemptible. The Nazis, for example, saw a world in which the superior races ruled over the inferior as a just world, and as the right way for human beings to live.

All ideologies have a conception of an ideal society, which embodies the values that the ideology promotes. And this is not just what is the best society for some people in a particular time or place, but what is best for human beings as such. To have a view like this involves holding beliefs about human nature, such that only if human beings live in a certain way will they be fulfilled and their true potential flourish.

Thus, one ideology, classical liberalism, may see human nature as essentially selfish but rational and therefore see the ideal society as one where individuals have maximum freedom to pursue their own interests in competition with everyone else. Another ideology that is socialist may see people as essentially equal and co-operative, where selfishness and competition leads to a class-divided society which distorts human nature and prevents it flourishing. Yet another ideology, anarchism, may see human nature as spontaneously social, a nature that is distorted when some people have power over others, and a society where there is no government and nobody can dominate anybody else is the ideal society where humanity will develop fully. Perhaps only in certain forms of conservatism is it not essential that the ideal be different from the world we have.

If we have a picture of how the world ought to be then we have a means of evaluating our present world. We can measure it against the ideal and see how far it falls short. We can judge to what extent equality or freedom or justice or the right order of things is missing or denied or threatened.

Furthermore, if the world is not as the ideology would have it be, then there must be some reason why it is not so. Each ideology has its theory about why there is a difference between what is and what ought to be. Liberals tend to blame ignorance, irrational ideas and so forth. Socialists blame capitalism, while for anarchists the source of evil is the state. Conservatives, who tend to look more favourably at the world as it is, or their bit of it, have theories about how their ideal is threatened.

Finally, if we have a conception of the ideal way to live, the 'good society', and we have an evaluation of our present state, then we need a programme for getting from our present state to the ideal (or for defending the ideal we have). For some the need is to abolish capitalism, or abolish government, or create a society where everybody is in free competition with everyone else, or re-establish monarchy, or free the nation from foreign domi-nation, or regain a lost harmony with nature, or whatever it might be.

Thus, rather like religions, ideologies have a certain compre-hensiveness about their conception of the human condition. They offer all-embracing theories about human nature and the ideal society best suited to that nature, and why our present world falls short (if indeed it does) and how the better world can be created, or the present ideal defended. These elements all connect together to present a more or less coherent vision of human reality.

Belief, action and tradition

Ideologies, then, are guides to political action. They give us ideals to believe in, goals to strive for and tell us for what causes to fight. They thereby give the individual believer a sense of identity and a sense of purpose. One can see oneself as a liberal working for human rights, a nationalist working for one's country's freedom, a revolutionary socialist working to overthrow the capitalist system, or a woman challenging the power of patriarchy, all on behalf of part of humanity, and thereby working for the ultimate good of humanity as such.

Ideologies can tell us what policies to pursue, who are our friends and enemies, and why rival beliefs are at best wrong and dangerous. Ideologies can, therefore, inspire common action and satisfy our aspiration to create or preserve the best possible world in which all, or at least those most worthy, can find fulfilment.

However, an important point must be made here. The various elements of ideology only fit neatly together in the way just described when we look at particular versions of ideology. When we speak of socialism or conservatism or any of the major ideologies, we are speaking of broad traditions of thought made up of many such versions. These versions frequently conflict with each other and give rise to disputes about which is the true or authentic version, such as whether, for example, communism was 'true' Marxism or a distortion of it, or if anarcho-capitalism is authentic anarchism. To understand ideologies we need to see each tradition developed individually over time.

An historical approach

Readers of this book might reasonably complain that it might just as well have been called 'Political ideology yesterday'. There is certainly much in it about the past. But there are good reasons for this. In the first place, the ideological beliefs that prevail today are the outcomes of often long and complicated developments which need to be understood to some extent if we are to make sense of present complexities. For example, in Britain it could be argued that the Conservative party is to a considerable degree no longer inspired by conservatism; that pure liberalism is no longer the doctrine of the Liberal party; and that the Labour party has finally given up socialism. Unravelling confusing truths such as these requires a certain amount of historical perspective.

Secondly, while it is true that there have been recent developments in ideology, it is nevertheless still the case that the political beliefs of most people today were developed a century or more ago. The great creative phase of ideological construction was roughly the century following the outbreak of the French Revolution, and we are still to a large extent living off the intellectual capital of that period when the foundations of much of our present thinking were laid.

Thirdly, it is a mistake to regard ideological thinking as a body of accumulating knowledge or wisdom in the manner of science. In science, for the most part, present theories have replaced older ones because they were demonstrably superior, and it is not really necessary to be a good scientist to know what those discarded theories were. But political ideologies are not like this. They are broad traditions of thought, often with co-existing contradictory strands, that evolve and grow more according to what people find plausible at any one time, than in conformity to any set of rules determining truth or falsity. Consequently, ideas that are convincing at one time may come to seem outmoded and useless at another, but then may be revived with new vigour at yet another time. This is easy enough to illustrate with a couple of examples.

Probably the most dynamic and expanding ideological position of the last quarter of the twentieth century has been New Right free-market capitalism, of the kind with which Margaret Thatcher and Ronald Reagan were associated. This view is also sometimes called 'neo-liberalism' because it is essentially a revival of early nineteenth-century liberal thought, a version of liberalism that a mere twenty years ago seemed obsolete to most people interested in political ideas. Furthermore, the most distinguished philosopher connected with this movement, Robert Nozick, takes his inspiration from the ideas of the seventeenth-century philosopher John Locke.

A second example comes from socialism. Until recently, both democratic and revolutionary varieties were associated with the existence and development of a large bureaucratic state that controlled the economy and provided a variety of services on a massive scale. Such ideas have lost much of their attraction in recent years and socialists have been re-examining their tradition and looking again at older, nineteenth-century conceptions of socialist society based on greater power at a local level, conceptions of socialism that had long been discarded as irrelevant to the modern world.

Therefore we need to look back to make sense of our present ideological preoccupations. We need to be aware of the evolution of ideas in order to comprehend the various familiar and exotic species of ideology that inhabit the political world today. In this book, therefore, the various ideologies are presented in the order of their appearance on the political stage. Each ideology is described as a tradition of thought evolving over time, from origins to present influence.

The crucible of modernity

Ideological thinking is at least as old as the ancient Greeks, but if our concern is with the ideologies of today's world, then we must focus on those doctrines that have inspired modern political movements. In this sense the age we live in is still very much the age of the French Revolution, for as the historian Simon Schama has put it 'the Revolution had indeed been the crucible of modernity; the vessel in which all the characteristics of the modern world had been distilled' (*Citizens*, 1989, preface).

Before looking at individual ideologies we need to see why the French Revolution is so critical an event in the development of today's ideologies.

The French Revolution was a mighty cataclysm that changed the history of modern times as has no other single event. It came as one of a spate of revolutions which helped to create the modern world. There was the American Revolution and the industrial revolution, and even an intellectual revolution in the rise of Romanticism, but it is the French Revolution that is important politically. It was the point when politics was recreated and redefined and given a new vocabulary, and when modern politics was created.

It was the most self-conscious of revolutions. Unlike the Renaissance or industrial revolution, everyone knew it was a great revolution from the start, especially those engaged in it. They knew that they were taking part in momentous events, that they were changing the world, and that Europe could not be the same again. Everyone in the Western world, even the least educated, was transfixed by the turmoil in France.

There had of course been political revolutions before, most notably in England in the previous century and more recently in America. But England in the seventeenth century had been on the fringe of Europe, a great European war was going on at the same time in Germany, and in any case the old order was restored. The American rebellion was closer in time and politics, but America was perceived as a distant wilderness on the other side of the world.

By contrast to both of these, France was in many ways the leading country of Europe, the heart of European civilization, and possessed of the most majestic of monarchies. Paris was widely regarded as the leader of the arts and fashion, as well as the intellectual capital of Europe. It was against this background of eminence and splendour that the violence and fanaticism of the revolution was so extraordinary and startling. There had been nothing like it in European history.

It was because France was seen as the centre of European civilisation, the very home of reason, that the political and psychological shock and significance was so immediate and profound for everyone. At one blow it destroyed the sanctity of the established order of Europe that had prevailed hitherto, and which had been regarded as natural and inevitable, God-given and ultimately indestructible. The destruction of the political order, the massacre of the ruling aristocracy and the power of the Paris mob were almost beyond belief.

More important than the destruction of the old was the possibility of making the world anew, of making a fresh start based on reason and justice. It was a frightening time, but also a time of great hope, particularly before the Terror; the end of civilization or the beginning of civilization, according to your point of view. The hope of a new age was expressed by the young Wordsworth in the famous lines:

> Bliss was it in that dawn to be alive,
> But to be young was very heaven!
>
> . . . 'twas a time when Europe was rejoiced,
> France standing on the top of golden hours,
> And human nature seeming born again.

> (William Wordsworth, *The Prelude*)

When society and the frame of human existence no longer seemed divinely ordained or eternal, all things seemed possible. To the revolutionaries everything could be changed, everything re-made along rational lines.

The very measurement of space and time was refashioned with the metric system and the ten-month year (dividing things by ten was taken as self-evidently more rational than by any other number). Even a new religion of the Supreme Being, as the fount of reason, was inaugurated. This was claimed to be a rational religion, traditional Christianity being deemed based on myth and superstition. But perhaps most startling of all was the notion of remaking human nature, of reshaping humanity by political means.

Symbolising this apparent capacity to change the whole of life at will, the making and remaking of the French state went on with bewildering frequency. There was an extraordinary parade of political forms – from absolute to constitutional monarchy, to totalitarian democracy to military dictatorship – all telescoped into a few years. And we were given a new vocabulary with which to understand the world politically: 'left and right', 'popular sovereignty', 'national self-determination', and so on. In such an atmosphere, ideas of how society ought to be organized abounded. And in the ferment of ideas of the revolutionary period almost the whole range of modern ideologies was born: nationalism, socialism, conservatism, anarchism and feminism.

Only liberalism could be said to have had a previous history to this in a recognizably modern form, since it was deeply involved in the making of the Revolution itself. But until then it had been a largely Anglo-Saxon eccentricity, which had been taken up by a number of French intellectuals. The French Revolution universalized it, spreading liberal ideas through Europe and beyond, and developing new versions in the process. Liberalism is, therefore, the oldest of modern ideologies and it is with liberal ideas that we will begin.

This is followed by separate accounts of the clutch of ideologies that sprang to life during the French Revolution and its aftermath: conservatism, nationalism, socialism, anarchism and Marxism. The next major doctrine, fascism, was a twentieth-century development, though constructed out of predominantly nineteenth-century materials. This is also true of the next ideology dealt with, the New Right, which although very recent, is largely a revival of early liberal thinking. The next two chapters cover a series of recent developments that are curiously contrasting. 'New radicalism' deals with several doctrines that are genuinely new departures, in green ideas and various 'liberation' ideologies, while 'Religious fundamentalism' deals with ideas of far greater antiquity than any of the ideologies discussed. The book concludes with a discussion of the future of ideology, and the ideas of those who think that our first ideology, liberalism, has triumphed and that the age of ideological conflict, the age of the French Revolution, may be about to end.

2

Liberalism and democracy

Liberalism has been the most successful ideology of the modern world. The ideals of the Western world are largely liberal ideals. Indeed, with the collapse of communist regimes in Europe since 1989 it has been argued that there is no serious rival for the adherence of the majority of humankind in sight. However, it is only possible to make such a sweeping generalisation by interpreting the term 'liberalism' very broadly. For liberalism is not a single set of fixed beliefs, but a broad tradition of thought that has been evolving over more than three centuries in several different directions.

There are a number of things which most liberals would agree that liberalism stands for. Above all there is individual freedom or liberty. This in turn implies those things that will secure and enhance that liberty, including equality of rights, constitutional government, the rule of law and toleration. However, different versions of liberalism interpret freedom and its attendant values in different and sometimes conflicting ways, and also differ as to how these ideals are best pursued. To understand these differences we need to go back to liberalism's English roots.

Whigs and republicans

In many respects the Renaissance and Reformation mark the end of the Middle Ages. But in political and social thought, it was liberalism that eventually came to challenge the medieval outlook. It offered an alternative conception of humanity as essentially rational and capable of running its own affairs without the tutelage of church and king. Instead of the old natural hierarchy with everyone fixed in their God-given place, men were conceived of as being essentially equal, possessed of equal rights and equally capable of liberty and making up their own minds.

England was among the countries most affected by the social and intellectual changes of the time, and it was here, assisted by the catalyst of civil war, that liberal ideas gradually developed. It was later, in the eighteenth century, that these ideas reached a wider European and American audience, when they were assisted (especially in America and France) by notions of reviving and adapting ancient forms of government and citizenship.

The English Civil Wars

The English Civil Wars of the mid-seventeenth century were a conflict for supremacy between king and Parliament, although complicated and exacerbated by religious differences. Parliament won, but the victory had to be consolidated a generation later by the Glorious Revolution of 1688. However, behind the struggle between ancient institutions and ancient claims to rights and privileges were new ideas: liberal ideas of freedom, rationality and individuality that would come to challenge the authority of tradition as such. The traditional medieval outlook tended to see people in terms of their social position and the community they belonged to. Claims to freedom and toleration challenged the traditional authority of the king who knew what was best for his subjects, and the Church who told them what to think. Liberalism developed as a rejection of tradition in the name of reason.

The English Civil Wars were as much wars of words as of killing and destruction. The nature of society and how it should be organized and run was at the heart of the conflict and it was accompanied by a flood of pamphlets about how these things ought to be accomplished. They ranged from those advocating absolute power by anyone who could maintain it, to various kinds of theocracy (rule by the Church), to a variety of democratic solutions; even forgetting about politics altogether to prepare for the Second Coming.

Among the more cogent proposals were those of the Levellers, a group in Cromwell's army who advocated limited democracy, demanding the vote for all men who were not servants, and claiming freedom and equality (what contemporaries called 'social levelling', hence their name) for all. However, with the restoration of the monarchy in 1660 came the restoration of the old social order and such ideas soon appeared remote and obscure. Nevertheless, Civil War divisions to some extent remained, especially since the king still harboured ambitions of absolute royal power. Opinion divided between royal supporters (Tories) and those who upheld parliamentary authority (Whigs). The upshot was the driving out of King James II in 1688 in the 'Glorious Revolution' and the consolidation of parliamentary supremacy. The Whig writer whose work provided the justification for the Revolution was John Locke.

John Locke

Locke's ideas owed a certain amount to the Civil War radicals, but in his two *Treatises on Government* (1690) he created a more coherent and less iconoclastic theory, that went roughly thus. All individuals are endowed by God with reason, by means of which man could discern what is right and wrong and how he should live. This was the old medieval theory of 'natural law' which stressed everyone's social obligations. What was new was Locke's individualist interpretation of it. His central idea was that God endowed every man with certain natural rights, most importantly the rights to life and liberty and property. Locke also maintained that, even without God, natural law and natural rights would still be true (although it could be argued that the idea of 'natural law' does not make much sense unless there is a God to lay down the law).

Initially, Locke argued, men lived a perfectly adequate social life without any government in a 'state of nature', guided only by their reason. However, this presented certain difficulties in dealing with criminals, serious disputes and other problems. To overcome these difficulties men agree to a 'social contract' to create government as a trust, for the sole purpose of protecting their pre-existing rights. Government must, therefore, be based upon the consent of the governed, expressed in representative institutions. If government does not fulfil its trust, by, for example, attacking property (such as confiscation or taxing without consent), the people are free to remove the government and replace it with one that will do its job. In a separate work, *A Letter Concerning Toleration* (1689), Locke supplemented these ideas by advocating religious toleration (although this was somewhat limited by our standards).

Locke is generally regarded as the first major liberal thinker. He expounded most of the main themes of subsequent theorists: human rights, individual liberty, minimal government, constitutional government, the executive subject to the people's representatives, sanctity of property, civil liberties and toleration. On the other hand, he was no democrat. What he wanted above all was to have the king's government permanently subject to the control of Parliament. He thought that the franchise should be confined to those of substantial property. He had no desire to change existing society in any way. Locke represents the Whig wing of liberalism, while the Levellers and related groups, who did want social change, represent the radical democratic wing.

During the late seventeenth and most of the eighteenth centuries, the Whigs were the dominant force in British politics. The system Locke defended became progressively more corrupt, with the landed aristocracy controlling the Commons more and more. The Whig party was dominated by a number of great aristocratic families who regarded their own rights and freedoms as the bulwark of the rights and freedoms of all Englishmen. Locke himself was somewhat ignored. His thought had more impact in America and France.

The American Revolution

In the course of the eighteenth century, Britain's thirteen

American colonies became embroiled in a fierce conflict with the mother country. When it came to a final break, the Americans turned to Locke to justify their rebellion. *The Declaration of Independence* (1776) reads:

We hold these truths to be self-evident: that all men are created equal; that they are endowed by their Creator with certain inalienable rights; that among these are life, liberty and the pursuit of happiness; that to secure these rights governments are instituted among men, deriving their just powers from the consent of the governed; that whenever any form of government becomes destructive of these ends it is the right of the people to alter or abolish it.

This is pure Locke, with one exception. 'Property' was left out (it was taken for granted as being part of liberty anyway) and replaced by 'the pursuit of happiness', a fashionable notion of the French Enlightenment.

As to the American Constitution of 1787, it is not in fact the pure democratic document it is often assumed to be. It is remarkably Whiggish. Its framers did not want a democracy but a republic, as advocated by many authors of antiquity, particularly Cicero and Polybius, who attributed Rome's early greatness to her republican constitution and the civic virtue (public spiritedness) that went with it. They made a clear distinction, as we tend not to do today, between liberty and democracy, and a republic was thought the best way to secure liberty.

By a republic was meant a mixed constitution like that of ancient Rome, with its combination of rule of the one, the few and the many; with each limiting and balancing the others so that no one class or group or individual would dominate, and the common good would prevail. Britain, with its king, Lords and Commons, was a republic in this sense – that is, with a monarchic element, an aristocratic element and a democratic element – and the Americans accepted it as such (Alexander Hamilton, one of the American revolutionary leaders, called the British system of government 'the best in the world'). The republican idea also implied the absence of hereditary office, but it was not this or any other aspect of Britain's government that the Americans initially objected to, but to the fact that Britain had treated them badly according to Britain's own principles of government.

Of the American leaders, the most sympathetic to democracy was Thomas Jefferson (1743–1826), who had drafted the *Declaration of Independence*, and who was influenced by French radical ideas as well as by Locke. He had an optimistic view of human nature, and had a profound faith in the decency and wisdom of ordinary people, whom he believed to be the best guardians of their own liberties. But he was not a great lover of the city, and his ideal of democracy was of a rural world of independent, educated citizen-farmers. He did not think democracy was suitable to a society of large cities and advanced manufacture, and did not want America to move in this direction.

However, when the US Constitution was being drawn up at the Constitutional Convention in Philadelphia in 1787, Jefferson was in Paris representing his country as ambassador to France, and the Convention's proceedings were dominated by those with a more conservative outlook, who were largely responsible for the elaborate system of checks and balances which characterise the constitution – the separation of powers, the federal system, the president, Senate and House of Representatives voted for in different ways and for different periods, and so on – and which were meant to fragment and frustrate the majority. Different interests would cancel each other out and no group could dominate. The ideal was a balanced constitution, combining the best elements of different forms.

Under the new Constitution the monarchic element (in the strict sense of the rule of the one) was provided by a president, who was not to be directly elected by the people, but by a group of important citizens elected in each state who would come together to choose the best man. This body still exists and is called the 'Electoral College', although it has never worked in the way the framers intended. The aristocratic element (in the old sense of 'rule of the best') was to be provided by the Senate, which again was not to be directly elected by the people, and was, of course, named after the Senate of ancient Rome. Senators were to be nominated by the representative assemblies of the states. Only the

last element, the House of Representatives, was to be democratically elected, although not by all citizens, since there were
property qualifications attached to the right to vote.

Thus the Constitution was republican in the sense of all society
being represented, but it was not, and was not meant to be, fully
democratic. Democracy only came later. On the other hand, great
store was set by the rights of all citizens. These are laid down in
the first ten amendments, or Bill of Rights, which came into force
with the rest of the Constitution in 1791.

Montesquieu

The Whiggish feature of the US Constitution that did not come
mainly from British thought and practice, is the principle of the
separation of powers. This came from the French Enlightenment
thinker, the Baron de Montesquieu. If the essence of Whiggism is
the protection of liberty through constitutionalism without trying
to change society, then Montesquieu is the French Whig. He
argued that tyranny consisted in all the branches of government,
the executive, legislative and judicial, being concentrated in the
same hands. This was true of royal government in his native
France and in continental Europe generally, where kings had
done away with medieval parliaments and made all decisions and
laws themselves, backed up by the theory of the divine right of
kings.

It had been resistance to this development in England that had
led to the civil wars. However, the thinkers of the Enlightenment
changed this perception. Britain was seen by them as ahead of its
time in reducing the authority of priest and king and giving more
liberty to the people.

Montesquieu, rather oddly and mistakenly, believed that the
British constitution was based on the principle of the branches of
government being all in separate hands (in fact then, as now, it is
only the judiciary which is largely separate). Nevertheless, for
Montesquieu liberty demanded they be in different hands, and
the Americans accepted his view and designed their Constitution
accordingly. This is why, for example, neither the American

president nor members of his administration can be members of Congress.

Radicals and revolutionaries

While Whig liberalism prevailed in the Anglo-Saxon world, continental Europe developed its own tradition of liberal thought, especially in France. Locke was also the key figure here, but because there was no tradition of individual liberty or of parliamentary representation, his ideas were much more radical and liberalism developed more as a revolutionary doctrine that was concerned to change society.

The Enlightenment

The Enlightenment was the major intellectual movement of the eighteenth century. The idea of the Enlightenment was to improve the condition of mankind by the light of reason. It involved a conscious rejection of tradition: that is, traditional authority in religion, government, science, the arts, and all forms of human understanding. The starting point was that human beings are essentially rational, and as such are capable of pursuing their own interests and running their own affairs, and therefore should be free to do so.

Such a view of human nature conflicted with the traditional religious conception of man as tainted with original sin and therefore in need of guidance, discipline and firm rule. The theory of original sin was used to explain the crime and violence and misery in the world, and since Enlightenment thinkers dispensed with this view they had to account for these things in a different way. They argued that these things existed not because man was naturally bad, but because man had been kept in the darkness of ignorance and superstition and not allowed to develop his reason; the main responsibility for this lay with the kings and priests who had a vested interest in keeping the population in ignorance. Mankind would only make progress if it learnt to use its reason (above all in philosophy and science) and apply it to its circumstances. That is, the ills of mankind could be cured and people could be happy and fulfilled if they lived rational lives and society was reorganised along rational lines, based upon a genuine science of man.

The main centre of Enlightenment thinking was France, although it was to Britain that the French thinkers looked for inspiration. In particular they regarded the two greatest contributors to human reason as Isaac Newton and John Locke. They took Locke's ideas to provide the basis of the rational society, once the centuries of prejudice and superstition that clouded people's minds had been removed. Only then would there be a new age of reason and unlimited human progress. The idea of progress was in fact an invention of the Enlightenment.

These ideas were extremely radical in authoritarian France, although not by standards elsewhere. Only one of the Enlightenment thinkers was a democrat. Rousseau was the least typical and most original of them, and he demanded a form of democracy that no modern thinker has advocated before or since.

Rousseau

Jean-Jacques Rousseau (1712–78) was Swiss, although he spent most of his adult life in France. His writings gained an enormous following all over Europe. In his main political work, *The Social Contract*, Rousseau argued that all men had an absolute right to be free. His argument was that what distinguishes the human from the animal was not that humans have reason, but the fact that human beings are capable of moral choice, and therefore, man must be free in order to exercise that choice. If people are not free, or if their freedom is restricted, then their humanity is being denied and they are being treated as sub-human, as slaves or animals.

Rousseau then went on to insist that if people had to live according to laws they did not make themselves then they are not free, they are slaves. It made little difference if a law-making body had been elected by the people, since it was still other people making the laws; those subject to them were still denied the freedom which was their natural right as human beings. On Rousseau's theory, the vast majority of us living in today's liberal democracies are denied their rightful freedom and are therefore 'slaves'.

The problem Rousseau's theory led him to was this: how was it possible for people to live in society and yet still be free? It was only possible, he said, if people lived by only those laws they had made themselves, and not by anyone on their behalf. And this in turn was only possible if the entire citizen body gathered in one place and voted spontaneously upon proposals for new laws (he did not want political parties or any discussion). If everyone voted according to what they knew was the common good, and not their own interests, then the laws passed would be valid and binding; in obeying them everyone would be free because they would be obeying themselves. These laws would be, as he put it, an expression of the 'general will'.

Rousseau's idea of the general will may sound straightforward enough but in fact it bristles with difficulties. Only laws based on the general will are valid and binding. But it is never entirely clear which laws are and which are not, for when people vote some, or even all of them, may be voting out of selfish interests, which does not count. It is possible that in fact only one person voting represents the general will. But Rousseau never gives us a sure way of telling. He only insists that the general will is always right and that 'the voice of the people is the voice of God'. But apart from these theoretical difficulties, Rousseau's notion of an assembly of all citizens is clearly not possible in modern states.

His ideal was the city states of ancient Greece (notably the austere and puritanical Sparta). Like ancient city states he wanted a civic religion to which all citizens must conform and which would inculcate patriotism and other civic virtues. But unlike the city states, he wanted a citizenry of equals. His ideal seems to have been a community of artisans and small farmers, each with just sufficient property to be independent. Such a society could hardly exist in his day, let alone ours; and what the practical implications of his ideas for the modern world of nation states might be,

Rousseau does not tell us.

Rousseau is the most exasperating of political thinkers. He is the first modern democratic theorist, and yet he believed in an unattainable form of direct democracy; he did not believe in parties or pressure groups, and believed that people are only bound by laws unanimously consented to, even if they did not vote for them (although apparently they would have done had they been thinking unselfishly). He is insistent on popular sovereignty and the necessary equality of all citizens, yet some writers on Rousseau have attributed to him the intellectual parenthood of modern totalitarianism (most notably J. L. Talmon in *The Origins of Totalitarian Democracy*, 1952). Robespierre claimed to be representing the general will when he inaugurated the Terror, although some think it grossly unfair to saddle Rousseau with responsibility for later regimes that at best only used his ideas selectively. But either way, Rousseau is an important if difficult, thinker. In some ways he is as controversial now as he ever was.

If Rousseau belongs in the liberal tradition, and there are some who insist he does not, he is a very different kind of liberal from John Locke. He certainly did not advocate the kind of liberal democracy we know today, and repudiates many aspects of modern democracy that we take for granted. The main reason why some dispute his liberal credentials is that his ideal appears to be social unity and uniformity; there seems to be no room for the individual who wishes to be different. On the other hand, he believed in freedom, equality, the rights of citizens and popular sovereignty against the claims of traditional authority, all beliefs characteristic of the liberal outlook.

The French Revolution

What happened in France began as a civilized affair. The authority of the monarchy collapsed and the king called the Estates General (the ancient parliament that had not met for several hundred years) to sort out the mess. This led to a conflict where the section representing the common people declared itself the National Assembly, committed itself to human rights in its

Declaration of the Rights of Man, and demanded a government that would protect them. What they had in mind was a constitutional monarchy subject to an assembly elected by a limited franchise, which was the basis of the Constitution of 1791.

However, the tide of events grew faster and favoured the more radical Jacobins, who brushed the moderates aside and introduced the Terror to strengthen popular support for the Revolution in the face of possible invasion and collapse. The king and a large part of the aristocracy were guillotined. The bloodshed and anarchy were horrific, and even when it ceased government remained a shambles. However, the Jacobins did not hold different beliefs from the first wave of revolutionaries, so much as pushed those beliefs to their logical conclusion.

Neither John Locke and the men of the Glorious Revolution of 1688, nor the American revolutionaries of 1776, had any idea of changing society. Indeed, they thought of themselves as preserving their society from alien imposition. Their ideas of constitutionalism and individual rights were meant to defend the social order they knew; any egalitarian or democratic implications their ideas might have had were ignored.

The French Revolution was different. Notions of egalitarianism and democracy were there from the start. They are there in the revolutionary cry for 'Liberty, Equality and Fraternity', and in the *Declaration of the Rights of Man*. Individual rights were important, but the real foundation was the sovereignty and authority of the people, as against their usurpation by king and nobility. The French Revolution was inevitably, therefore, a social revolution. Liberty, equality and fraternity implies that the citizen body is a brotherhood of equals, bound together by a civic virtue that gives priority to the common good.

The Jacobins merely made the egalitarian and democratic content of the revolutionary thinking explicit and acted upon it. As Robespierre put it in a speech to the convention:

Democracy is the only form of state which all the individuals composing it can truly call their country . . . the French are the first people in the world to establish a true democracy, by calling all men to enjoy equality and fullness of civil rights . . .

Now what is the principle of popular or democratic rule, I mean the fundamental motive which sustains and impels it? It is virtue. I refer to the public Virtue which accomplished so many marvellous things in Greece and Rome, and which should create even more wondrous things in our Republican France – that Virtue which is nothing more than love of the Nation and its laws

Civic virtue was promoted by the new religion of the Supreme Being (following Rousseau's belief in the need for a civic religion) to replace Christianity.

The idea of the sovereignty of the people came principally from Rousseau, but it was the Jacobins who took his radical democratic ideas seriously. Their constitution of 1793 guaranteed universal manhood suffrage, annual parliaments, referenda, the 'sacred right' of the people to revolt if government was violating their rights, work for each individual or else support by the state, education for all, and other measures, all in the name of the happiness of the people.

When the Jacobins were overthrown and executed, a more moderate constitution was restored, but instability continued. In fact despite interludes of strong government, the French did not achieve a fully stable system during the next century. There were a series of revolutions and new constitutions as France struggled to come to terms with its own revolutionary legacy.

Contemporary influence of the French Revolution

In Germany, the most important influence of the early Revolution was upon the great philosopher, Immanuel Kant. He was inspired by the ideals of the Revolution, while being horrified by the course of events. As an admirer of Rousseau, he believed that the essence of freedom lay in moral autonomy, in people's capacity to live according to rules they have made themselves. To be genuinely free, therefore, was not to simply pursue one's self-interest, but to act according to one's self-defined moral duty in spite of one's self-interest.

Kant believed that this capacity alone gave human beings a moral stature that entitled all individuals to be as free as was consistent with maximum freedom for all. The good society therefore was one that was consistent with this principle. And that, in Kant's view, meant a constitutional monarchy answerable to a representative assembly elected on a property franchise and guaranteeing civil rights for all. (He did not follow Rousseau in dismissing representative government as a sham.) However, it was a long time before Kant's ideas became influential in Europe, and even longer in Germany. In the meantime, liberalism was divided between its more radical and Whiggish proponents.

The leading radical in Britain during the 1790s was Tom Paine, who also played a significant role in both the American and French Revolutions. His major work, *The Rights of Man* (1791), advocated radical democracy, the abolition of the monarchy and all social privilege. Like the radicals of Paris he was also concerned with equality and advocated what we would call welfare state measures. He could not, however, be called a socialist. Like almost all radicals of the time his main concern was with the rights of man, and he followed Locke in insisting that among the most fundamental of such rights was the right to property.

The British Establishment was badly shaken by the French Revolution and repressed all agitation for reform, banned trade unions and ignored appeals to deal with the appalling social problems caused by the industrial revolution. When political and social reform began, with the Great Reform Act of 1832, the outcome was decidedly Whiggish and far removed from any radicalism. However, by this time a new dimension of liberalism had developed, and was making an impact on the thinking and actions of governments. This was economic liberalism.

Classical liberalism

Liberal ideas were behind both of the great political revolutions of the late eighteenth century, and were principally concerned with the issues of civil rights and constitutions. The other great revolution of the age, which was even more central to the creation of the modern world than those of America and France, was the industrial revolution; liberal ideas were important here as well.

The breakup of the medieval world, with its feudal system and guilds, allowed people more economic freedom and made possible the early growth of capitalism. Nevertheless, the government still had a great deal of control over economic activity in manufacturing and trade. When the case for economic liberalism began to be argued in the eighteenth century, the startling claim was made that if everyone was simply left to their own economic devices, then the result would not be chaos but a harmonious society of ever growing prosperity. The fusion of this economic liberalism with political liberalism produced a powerful doctrine that has influenced governments ever since.

Adam Smith

The Enlightenment aspiration to create a rational science of man did not have much success, except in the field of economics. In 1776, the Scottish philosopher Adam Smith (1723–90) published his great work, *The Wealth of Nations*, which laid the foundations of modern economic theory. Above all, it revealed the wonders of the free market and demonstrated the overall benefits of the unrestricted movement of goods, capital and labour. It argued that the market, free of all government interference, would produce maximum prosperity for the whole nation. Everyone pursuing their own self-interest would in fact result in the maximum benefit of all.

The government policy of non-intervention, or *laissez faire*, that Smith was advocating was at odds with the economic practice of most governments of his day, who sought to control economic activity in great detail. They protected home industry with high import duties, granted legal monopolies and allowed a multitude of internal barriers to trade between regions. It took time, therefore, for his ideas to influence government. But such influence was inevitable in the long run, since his ideas so well reflected the wishes of the new class of industrialists who were creating Britain's industrial revolution. To a great degree, it was the adherence of this group to liberal ideas that gave a more radical liberalism (though not of the revolutionary kind) a certain respectability in the early nineteenth century.

It was the coming together of the ideas of Adam Smith and his followers (now known as the 'classical economists') with the ideas of Locke, and other advocates of civil rights and limited government, that created what we now call 'classical liberalism'. It produced a picture of a free society of self-reliant, responsible, productive individuals, possessed of equal rights, creating a prosperous society with the minimum of government involvement. Such a government would be representative of, and responsible to, the people, according to a constitution.

Although the term 'liberalism' has been used freely up to now, it was not until the early nineteenth century that the word began to be used to denote a political doctrine. The name came to be adopted by some of the more progressive members of the Whig Party, and by the followers of Jeremy Bentham (1748–1832).

Utilitarianism

Bentham founded a system of ideas known as utilitarianism. This was based on the idea that all human psychology could be reduced to the pursuit of pleasure and the avoidance of pain, from which it followed, according to Bentham, that all good was essentially pleasure and all bad was pain. From which it was further supposed to follow that the ultimate good for which we can strive is the greatest happiness of the greatest number. Bentham appeared to think that we all go about our lives making little calculations that set so many units of pleasure against so many of pain in deciding all that we do. People only behave badly, he thought, because they made bad calculations: they thought in the short instead of the long term.

The importance of all this for government, Bentham believed, was that it provided a means of evaluating good and bad laws, and good and bad institutions. The good government, armed with this knowledge, could make calculations of the amount of pleasure or pain caused according to what Bentham called the 'felicific calculus' (from 'felicity', meaning 'happiness'), and could then pass laws and create institutions that could shape and mould human behaviour for the common good. He believed that all existing laws, institutions and practices could be assessed according to his principles and, if found wanting, could immediately be replaced by better ones. The good society could therefore be set up very easily using his ideas.

To begin with, Bentham's ideal form of government was benevolent autocracy, simply on the grounds of greater efficiency. But when governments ignored his ideas he changed his mind. Influenced by his friend James Mill, Bentham became converted to popular government virtually overnight.

Each individual, Bentham and Mill insisted, was the best judge of their own happiness. They should be as free as possible to pursue their own interests, which meant minimal government and minimal legislation (Bentham believed that fewer laws automatically meant greater freedom). This included economic freedom, for they were devoted to Adam Smith's free-market economics. People should vote on a wide, though not quite universal, franchise for their representatives, who would then be mandated delegates: there to express the people's wishes. There would be no monarchy or House of Lords. Many working men would have the vote, although Mill believed that they would vote for middle-class representatives, the professional and business middle classes being the most intelligent and competent section of society.

Bentham and James Mill, therefore, developed a distinct version of liberalism that was radical and democratic (although not in the French sense of deliberately changing society in order to make it more equal). It also differed from previous versions of liberalism in dismissing the idea of natural rights, which Bentham thought was not only nonsense, but 'nonsense on stilts'.

The ideas of Bentham and Mill were disseminated by a body of disciples, including several influential MPs, who called themselves 'philosophical radicals'. But liberal ideas in general were also influencing the main parties, especially the Whigs who eventually became the Liberal Party. However, its leadership was still dominated by Whig aristocrats who were suspicious of democracy, even though it was widely believed that Britain, and indeed the rest of Europe, would eventually go the way of America and introduce a full democratic system.

American democracy

For most of the nineteenth century America was regarded by Europeans with intense fascination. It was the presidency of Andrew Jackson (1767–1845), from 1828 to 1836, that saw the final democratisation of the franchise, and the end of the monopoly of old East Coast families on American government. It was the land not only of free government but also of free enterprise, without any prompting from the classical economists. It was far easier there to start a business and prosper than it was in Europe. In a very real sense, America began as a liberal paradise and has remained so ever since. Neither socialism nor any other ideology has had much impact there, only different varieties of liberalism.

The European fascination led to a number of writers travelling to America and reporting on the new democratic civilization they found there. Much the most thorough and perceptive writing was that of the French aristocrat Alexis de Tocqueville (1805–59). His *Democracy in America* (1835–40) suggested, among many other things, that in a society in which everyone had maximum freedom to do as they please, there was in fact a very strong tendency to conform, reinforced by the strong social pressure of public opinion. This was one of the conclusions that most influenced John Stuart Mill, the son of James Mill and the most distinguished liberal philosopher of the nineteenth century. To understand the importance of de Tocqueville for J. S. Mill, we need to see how he was influenced by the Romantic movement and the continental Liberals who belonged to it.

Romantic liberalism

Liberal movements developed in most of continental Europe in the nineteenth century, although with rather mixed success. While liberalism flourished unchecked in America and infused itself into all the national parties in Britain, continental liberalism tended to confine itself to specific parties and have specific enemies.

European liberalism has a number of distinctive features that distinguish it from the liberalisms of Britain and America, such as anti-clericalism. But Europe has also contributed a number of features to the broad tradition of liberal thinking. Apart from Kant, there had been two major theoretical developments. There is the liberal nationalism of such as Joseph Mazzini (which will be dealt with later in Chapter 4 on nationalism) and there is the development of the concept of individuality that came from the Romantic movement.

Romanticism was a Europe-wide intellectual movement that was a direct reaction to Enlightenment rationalism. Where the Enlightenment stressed reason and universality, Romantics emphasised feeling and particularity. Each individual and each nation was unique.

The Romantic movement influenced all the major ideologies of the time, especially nationalism and conservatism. But liberalism also felt the impact, although for the most part the influence was slow to develop. One thinker who sensed the political implications of an enhanced concept of individualism was the Prussian aristocrat and educational reformer, Karl Wilhelm von Humboldt. As a young man, fired with enthusiasm both for the French Revolution and the new Romantic ideas, he wrote an essay entitled *The Limits of State Action* in 1792. Humboldt stressed the uniqueness of the human individual that must be allowed to develop naturally from inner promptings. The more the state interfered in and directed society the less this was possible. He wrote (in a passage later used by J. S. Mill as the epigraph for his own most famous essay *On Liberty*):

The grand, leading principle, towards which every argument unfolded in these pages directly converges, is the absolute and essential importance of human development in its richest variety.

Thus, minimal constitutional government was essential for human development and happiness.

It should be clear that this conception of human nature is very far from the conceptions prevailing in the versions of Liberalism already discussed. They are all universalistic notions that emphasize how all men are the same: that they are rational; that they are all possessed of natural rights; that they all have a capacity for moral self-direction; that they all seek their self-interest; or that they are all pleasure-pain machines. The Romantic view stresses their uniqueness, and the preciousness of that uniqueness, and advocates the limitation of government in the name of that uniqueness. Freedom is demanded not only so that individuals may pursue their own selfish interests, but primarily so that each individual may develop to their full potential and thereby contribute to the development of mankind.

However, Humboldt's essay was not properly published until 1850, long after his death. Like the works of Kant, and the general Romantic notion of individuality, it did not have much influence until the second half of the nineteenth century. It was part of the intellectual background to social liberalism.

Liberalism and progress

The idea of progress essentially goes back to the eighteenth century Enlightenment. The development of reason in general and science in particular, together with the replacement of superstition and ignorance and the overcoming of the tyrannies of priest and king, were combining, it was thought, to lead mankind towards ever greater perfection. The French Enlightenment thinker, the Marquis de Condorcet (1743–94), was the great exponent of this view. In his book *Sketch for a Historical Picture of the Progress of the Human Mind* (1795) he argued that:

. . . nature has set no term to the perfection of human faculties; that the perfectibility of man is truly indefinite; and that the progress of this perfectibility, from now onwards independent of any power that might wish to halt it, has no other limit than the duration of the globe upon which nature has cast us.

It shows an extraordinary optimism, especially as the author was living in the shadow of the guillotine, which shortly after claimed him.

The idea of progress developed among Enlightenment thinkers during the eighteenth century, but during the nineteenth century it became a commonplace. In the Victorian period everyone believed in progress, although different versions of the concept emerged, such as those of the philosophers Herbert Spencer (1820–1903) and John Stuart Mill (1806–73). However, the horrors of the twentieth century have undermined liberal confidence.

Herbert Spencer

Spencer linked Liberalism to the theory of evolution as developed by Charles Darwin in his *The Origin of Species* (1859). That theory suggested that species evolved in circumstances of competition among individuals, and different kinds of animals, for food and other necessaries of existence. Those individuals and types best adapted to their environment would tend to survive and increase at the expense of the less well-adapted. It did not follow from this that the 'best adapted' were necessarily the strongest or were 'superior' to the less well adapted. But these were precisely the conclusions that Spencer drew, and which he applied to society.

The ideal society was one characterized by maximum competition and the 'survival of the fittest' (Spencer's phrase, not Darwin's), which meant the strongest and the best. The result was progress, which Spencer saw in terms of ever greater social complexity and integration, and an ever diminishing role for the state. These ideas are set out in his voluminous writings on biology, sociology and psychology; their implications for government policy were exceptionally harsh, as seen in his *The Man versus the State* (1884). He systematically opposed any extension of government activity, and particularly any policies to deal with social problems such as poverty or the exploitation of women and children in factories and mines. That the weak should go to the wall was part of the natural evolutionary process, and so helping the poor and exploited merely interfered with the proper order of things and held back progress.

Spencer was influential in late Victorian Britain, although his views became increasingly out of step with the trend of liberal thinking. He was a man of delicate constitution and claimed that he never read views contrary to his own because that made him physically ill. He died in 1903 not having changed his ideas for half a century. In the same period, he was much more popular and influential in the United States among those who wished to justify American business. It was the age when giant business empires were being built and there were complaints of ruthlessness and exploitation and the corruption of the political system. Spencer's work appeared to justify this 'age of the robber barons' as natural and right and essential to human progress.

John Stuart Mill

J. S. Mill was Spencer's contemporary. He was the son of James Mill and had been groomed by his father from an early age to be the philosopher of the philosophical radicals. However, his narrowly academic education (reminiscent of Dickens' Mr Gradgrind) seems to have induced some kind of mental breakdown during Mill's early twenties. As a result, he came to the conclusion that utilitarianism had thus far neglected the spiritual, aesthetic and emotional side of the human being. He was influenced by Romantic notions of individuality, which saw each human being as a complex whole, and each precious in their uniqueness.

In working out the political implications of this new sense of individuality, Mill was influenced from two sources. The first was von Humboldt's belief that the state was intrinsically inimical to the flourishing of individuality. This view lies behind Mill's difficult distinction between 'self-regarding' and 'other-regarding' actions. He argued that '. . . the only purpose for which power can be rightfully exercised over any member of a civilised community against his will is to prevent harm to others' (*On Liberty*, 1859).

Only where an individual's actions affect the lives of others – that is, other-regarding actions – can there be a case for state regulation in order to prevent harm. Where an individual's actions are self-regarding, that is, affecting no one but themselves, then the state has no right to interfere.

Mill went on to defend more specific freedoms of speech and thought, all on the grounds that they are conducive to progress. In open competition, he believed, truth will always drive out falsity. But he was particularly interested in differing beliefs and ways of living, which must be allowed to flourish since they were the source of creativity and therefore also conducive to progress.

The other influence on Mill was de Tocqueville's analysis of American democracy. Its tendency to elevate public opinion as some kind of authority, and the consequent social pressure to conform, horrified him. This created something of a dilemma in Mill's attitude to democratic government. He thought in general that the coming of democracy was inevitable and right, and yet he feared what he called the 'tyranny of the majority' (a view that would have been incomprehensible to Bentham or his father, who saw nothing wrong with social pressure or conformity). Liberals had long fought against the tyranny of priest and king, but none had anticipated further problems once everyone was free of these.

J. S. Mill was, in consequence, a somewhat reluctant democrat. He believed in representative democracy as an educative force, since participation would, he believed, make for responsible citizenship and therefore was progressive. On the other hand, his Whiggish fear of democracy led him to all kinds of devices to prevent government expressing the direct will of the majority. Thus he argued that while every adult should vote, those with education should have more votes. Again, while Parliament should represent all the people and have a final say on legislation, it should be drawn up by a legislative commission of intellectuals. In these ways, Mill sought to protect the individualistic, creative intellectuals he so much admired and upon whom future progress, he believed, ultimately depended.

However, while passionate in his belief in individualism, Mill was among the first liberal thinkers to advocate state intervention in areas such as education, the industrial workplace, and so forth. In this we can see the beginnings of a new version of liberalism, social liberalism, which will be considered later in this chapter. In the meanwhile we need to look at a modern phenomenon that is the very epitome of all that Mill hated and feared.

Totalitarianism

The nineteenth century confidence in progress was rudely shattered by the events of the twentieth century. In Europe, seen as the very heart of Western civilization and progress, a single generation witnessed two of the most appalling wars in human history, which sucked in much of the rest of the world, along with totalitarian regimes that perpetrated crimes against humanity on a colossal scale. People could not believe, until the evidence appeared at the end of the war, the evil of the Nazi extermination camps, and other atrocities which occurred in what was supposed to be one of the civilised and cultured European countries (see Chapter Nine). Finally, the Cold War and the threat of nuclear annihilation seemed again to reach the very depths of irrationality and perversity.

Most of these events have resulted from a new form of government called totalitarianism. The term 'totalitarian' was coined in the 1920s to characterize Mussolini's regime, and it was meant to imply a total control of every aspect of Italian life. This in fact exaggerated Mussolini's power, although it was what he aspired to, and he embraced the word with enthusiasm. While authoritarian regimes in the past had merely sought a monopoly of power over people's actions, the totalitarian regimes of Mussolini, Hitler and Stalin sought complete power over people's minds. A one-party state, with everyone believing in the party's ideology, was the ideal, with terror used to enforce conformity.

Totalitarianism is the very antithesis of everything that the liberal values. Under totalitarian regimes the individual is merged into the mass, is denied basic freedoms, denied the right of dissent, the government knows no restraint, and in its doctrine claims a monopoly of truth from which dissent is banished. Totalitarianism is now seen as the greatest threat to Liberal values. While totalitarian regimes are less common in the late twentieth century, China and other communist states, Iraq, Syria and, some would add, the Iran of the Islamic fundamentalists can be seen as totalitarian states.

With the collapse of the belief in progress under the impact of totalitarianism, liberals have looked to institutional and legal means to prevent future wars and atrocities, but this time on an international scale. This has resulted in the creation of organizations like the United Nations, and the development of the theory of human rights.

Human rights

The concept of human rights is that people have basic rights by virtue of being human, irrespective of what the laws of their particular state may say. The idea is in fact a modern version of the natural rights theories of John Locke and the American Declaration of Independence, or, as the French revolutionaries called them, the rights of man.

The idea of natural rights had gone out of fashion in the nineteenth century, partly because of its unfortunate association with the French Revolution and partly because of its association with the theory of natural law. This was the theory that claimed that God had given all creatures the laws that governed their appropriate behaviour, but whereas plants and animals behaved properly because of instinct, human beings had been given reason with which to work out the right way for them to behave, and the result of this reasoning was natural law. The theory had come in for very powerful criticism during the eighteenth and nineteenth centuries, and leading liberal thinkers, such as Bentham, Spencer and J. S. Mill had rejected the idea altogether. However, with the world wars and the atrocities of twentieth-century totalitarian regimes, the need was felt for a modern version of such a theory, without the old metaphysics.

When the Nazi leaders were tried at Nuremberg (1945–46), they were accused of 'crimes against humanity', a charge that had been virtually invented for the occasion and embodied in international law. The UN's founding charter of 1946 pledges all members to achieve: '. . . universal respect for, and observance of, human rights and fundamental freedoms for all without distinction as to race, sex, language or religion.'

Subsequently, in 1948, the UN issued the Universal Declaration of Human Rights setting out these rights in great detail, and there are now many international organisations with the purpose of protecting human rights. Unfortunately, we live in a world where there is still much war, suffering and oppression. Nevertheless, there are some who see the end of the Cold War as a turning point, after which we can look to the future with optimism. Theories of progress, inevitably more tentative than in the past, are beginning to reappear, and some of these ideas are discussed in the final chapter. In the meanwhile, we need to discuss the new form of liberalism that developed in the late nineteenth century and came to dominate most of the twentieth, namely social liberalism.

Social liberalism and European politics

As the nineteenth century progressed, it became increasingly apparent that giving free rein to the unregulated market was not producing the society of independent, free, self-reliant individuals which the theory had promised. Instead, the few were mightily rich while many suffered poverty, ignorance, exploitation and deprivation. Clearly something had gone wrong. Furthermore, the doctrine of minimal government, the 'night watchman state', was being ignored by governments, Liberal as well as others, in order to cope with the social problems thrown up by industrialisation and urbanisation, problems so dire that they had to be dealt with no matter what the theory said. Consequently, there was legislation in the fields of public health and sanitation, factory conditions, education, child and female employment and other matters. In other words there was state intervention instead of leaving everything to the free market.

A new concept of liberty

Eventually theory began to catch up with practice. The mainstream of liberal thinking began to shift in the direction of abandoning the minimal state in favour of justifying state intervention. A series of liberal thinkers, including J. S. Mill (who combined elements of the old liberalism and the new), T. H. Green in his *Lectures on the Principles of Polotical Obligation* (1879–80, Leonard Hobhouse in *The Labour Movement* (1893), *Liberalism* (1911) and other writings, and J. A. Hobson in *The Crisis of Liberalism* (1909) and other works, all argued for increased state intervention with collectivist social policies to make up for the deficiencies of the capitalist system. Some, especially Hobhouse and Hobson, came close to some of the forms of socialism that were developing at the time. For example, Hobhouse was opposed to capitalism as such, believing that a society based on competition ought to be replaced by one based on co-operation. What kept such thinkers within the liberal fold was their central commitment to individual liberty.

The argument was essentially this. A person may have a whole array of civil liberties, but if they are uneducated, live in squalor and are overworked for starvation wages, in what real sense can they really be said to be free? People can only truly be said to be free when they have a genuine opportunity to participate fully in the life of their society. Therefore, collectivist intervention is justified in liberal terms if it enables people to so participate; or, to put it another way, if it removes obstacles to people's freedom to fully develop their individuality. It is here that we see the influence of Romantic notions of individualism. In practical terms, the argument points towards a programme of welfare legislation, providing such things as education, decent housing and a system of social security. And this indeed is what it led to.

It was a Liberal government that laid the foundations of the welfare state in Britain in the years before the First World War.

The comprehensive welfare state we have had since the Second World War, although created by the Labour Party, was in fact largely designed by two Liberals, John Maynard Keynes (1883–1946), who laid the economic foundations, and William Beveridge (1879–1963), who designed the welfare system itself.

The Keynesian Revolution

Keynes was the economist who challenged the orthodoxy of classical economics which had dominated the economic thinking and policies of Britain and the other major powers for more than a hundred years. That orthodoxy assumed that the free market always solved its own problems so long as it was not interfered with by government. Thus, when Europe suffered a decade of economic recession after the First World War, governments did nothing, and when the American economy collapsed after the Wall Street Crash of 1929 and recession turned into a massive slump, the orthodox policy was still to do nothing. But Keynes in his great work *The General Theory of Employment, Interest and Money* (1936) demonstrated that it is not in fact the case that the free-market economy is always a self-righting mechanism and that in certain conditions (such as those prevailing) it was quite possible for slump to go on indefinitely.

The answer, Keynes argued, was not to get into a slump in the first place. Governments could break out of the pattern of boom and slump by actively managing the economy. This could be done by the management of demand (the amount people have to spend), by such means as taxation, government spending and credit control. If the economy is growing too fast, then the total amount of people's spending can be reduced by higher taxes, cutting public spending and making it harder to borrow money, thereby slowing the boom down. If there is recession, with goods unsold, factories closing and people losing their jobs, then the answer is to cut taxes, increase government spending (by borrowing the money if necessary) and make acquiring credit easier. This will increase demand for goods, needing more factories and workers to make them.

By these means, it was argued, it would be possible to break out of the cycle of boom and slump and replace it with steady economic growth and permanent full employment. In putting forward his theory, Keynes was undoubtedly seeking to save capitalism from itself. For him it meant preserving the free market by civilising it and making it more humane.

The modern welfare state

Keynes's formula appeared to solve one of the most central and intractable of social problems, unemployment, which was a key to poverty, and its attendant social problems. However, it was another Liberal, William Beveridge, who was to make this the basis of a comprehensive welfare state, set out in his report *Social Insurance and Allied Services* (1942). Taking full employment as a basic assumption, Beveridge designed a system of social security that would protect every citizen 'from the cradle to the grave'. His vision was of a civilised society in which none would be denied the necessities of education, health care, work, or decent housing because of poverty. That a society without fear in which all had the opportunity to develop to their full potential.

It was only after the Second World War that these ideas were put into practice, although not by the Liberal Party, which had gone into terminal decline after the First World War. The post-war Labour government of 1945–51 introduced the welfare state, which fitted in well with its socialist ideals, and was soon converted to Keynesian economic management. It also nationalised a number of key industries, thereby creating the 'mixed economy'.

These policies became accepted by all parties and this general agreement on policy, known as the 'consensus', dominated British politics until the mid-1970s. It was also known as social democracy, since it was also a kind of mild version of socialism, a compromise between socialism and capitalism, that had been introduced by a socialist government (see Chapter 5). These policies also came to dominate post-war Europe, where, as in Britain, a triumph of liberal ideas was accompanied by a strange failure of liberal parties.

Liberalism in twentieth century Europe

While liberalism had been entirely secured in Britain and America in the nineteenth century, this was not so of continental Europe, where totalitarianism of both left and right during the 1920s and 1930s for a time virtually wiped out liberalism on the European mainland.

Liberalism, however, survived and eventually triumphed in Western Europe, with the rest of Europe following later. Apart from acquiring liberal democratic systems, the post-war governments of Western Europe pursued social liberal policies. However, what is curious, and needs some explaining, is that for all this intellectual success, political parties that are avowedly liberal have hardly benefited. The social liberal policies of the post-war world were not put into effect by governments controlled by liberal parties, despite the major role played by liberal thinkers in devising them. In Britain, Sweden and elsewhere it was social democratic governments that were responsible, while in West Germany, Italy and elsewhere it was Christian Democrats (that is, Conservative in British terms). As in Britain, there were strong liberal parties all over Western Europe in the late nineteenth century, whereas today liberal parties tend to be weak centre parties, such as the Free Democrats in West Germany and the Liberal, Republican and Radical parties of Italy (in Denmark the liberals are rather confusingly called the Left Party).

It seems that the moderate parties of the left and the right have in some way managed to divide the liberal inheritance between them. Why Liberalism as a political movement has declined is not entirely clear. There seem to be a mixture of theoretical reasons, which will be considered later, and also reasons of social change and practical politics.

The failure of liberal politics

For most of the nineteenth century in representative systems like Britain, the main political divide was between two forms of property, with conservative parties representing the aristocracy and landed interest, and liberal parties representing the commercial middle classes. But when, towards the end of the century, the working classes gained greater representation there began a realignment. Politics was re-polarized into a conflict between those with and those without property. As the propertied classes closed ranks they tended to look to the Conservatives to represent them, while the liberals tried to appeal to both sides. The socialists and conservatives absorbed liberal ideas, and from time to time adopted liberal policies, but it was these parties that were able to command large sections of the electorate, which the liberals failed to do.

The adoption of liberal ideas by other parties was easiest in Britain, where both conservative and socialist thought already had strong liberal elements (see chapters Three and Five). Continental conservatives and socialists tended to be more extreme and anti-liberal, so that the absorption took longer. Since 1945, it has been the Christian Democrats and Social Democrats that have been the standard bearers of liberal values, while liberal parties have dwindled. Even the West European Communist parties came to accept the necessity of liberal democracy. In one way or another, therefore, liberal ideas have come to thoroughly infuse European politics today.

Liberal parties in Europe now find their niche at the centre of the political spectrum. Often, as in Britain, they seek a middle way, rejecting the left's dislike of free enterprise and the right's dislike of social provision. The situation in North America is somewhat different.

American liberalism

In North America things are a little different, the most general difference being the absence of socialism as a serious political movement. There is, in consequence, a major Liberal Party in Canada, where the main contest for power there is between Liberal and Conservative parties. The USA itself is different again, since unlike Canada and Europe it does not have a party system firmly based on ideological difference.

Left and right in the USA

The USA has national parties in only a partial sense. Traditionally, the parties that fight presidential elections every four years are coalitions of state parties that come together to fight for the highest office and then revert back to their previous condition. For example, the Democrats of the South have traditionally been right wing, while northern Democrats are traditionally left wing. Similarly the Republicans have their right and left wings, although the Democrats in general tend more to the left and Republicans to the right. There is some national organization in Congress, but these are not the tight disciplined parties of Europe and elsewhere.

Ideologically, all US parties are Liberal and always have been. Essentially they espouse classical liberalism, that is a form of democratized Whig constitutionalism, plus the free market. The point of ideological difference comes with the influence of social liberalism. How far should the free market be left alone; how far should the state regulate or manage, and how far should government at federal or local level provide social security and welfare services?

The American right has nothing to do with maintaining the traditional social order, as in Europe. What it believes in is extreme individualism and *laissez faire*; that is, individuals should be left to sink or swim on their own and big business can do no wrong. Left-wingers are social liberals, believing in greater state intervention in the economy and provision of welfare (although few today would want this on a European scale). In American political parlance, right-wingers are 'conservatives', while left-wingers are rather confusingly called 'liberals'. Thus, to an American conservative 'liberal' is a term of abuse and means virtually the same as 'socialist'.

The American right has tended to towards the extreme version of classical liberalism associated with social Darwinism, which insisted on the virtues of competition and the evil consequences of state interference in economic or social matters. The late nineteenth century in America became known as the age of the 'robber barons' or of the 'anarchy of the millionaires' when big business exploited people and corrupted politics with no apparent accountability. Their attitude was summed up by the railway tycoon, William Vanderbilt. When asked if he ran his railroads to benefit the public, he replied 'The public be damned . . . I don't take any stock of this silly nonsense about working for anybody's good but our own . . .' This kind of attitude was justified by the social Darwinism of Herbert Spencer and his American follower, William Graham Sumner, for whom the strong succeeding at the expense of the weak was natural and healthy and was a sign of progress and civilization.

Populists and progressives

The rapacity of big business and corruption of politics resulted in a considerable degree of disillusionment with *laissez faire* towards the end of the nineteenth century. It first found expression in the Populist movement which flared up in the South and Midwest in the late 1880s. It was essentially a movement of farmers exploited and threatened by big business, financiers and transport companies, to whose dealings the politicians turned a blind eye. They demanded financial relief and graduated income tax, and even nationalisation of transport and communications. But greatest faith was placed in increased democracy, hence demands for the direct election of Senators, local 'primaries' (popular election of party candidates instead of nomination by party 'bosses'), 'recall' (popular removal of elected representatives who do not do their job), initiative referenda and other measures. However, despite becoming a major political force, with the failure of the Populist bid for the presidency, the two main parties reasserted themselves.

However, Populism's democratic demands were taken up by the Progressive movement of the next two decades. This was a more middle class, intellectual movement that embraced all parties and most parts of the country. Whereas the Populists were suspicious of government in general, Progressives were influenced by social liberal ideas and saw the state as potentially a positive instrument for social justice. Presidents Theodore Roosevelt and Woodrow Wilson were Progressives and the movement's successes included direct elections for the Senate after 1913, votes for women, and the introduction of referenda and primaries in many states. This was in addition to a good deal of welfare legislation in individual states, as well as state and federal 'anti-trust' laws and other measures to curb the abuse of power by big business.

John Dewey and social liberalism

Despite these developments disillusionment with unbridled free enterprise was still strong in the 1920s, and it rose sharply following the Wall Street Crash of 1929 and the mass unemployment and social distress that followed for a decade.

The most forceful theoretical expression of this disillusionment with American capitalism came in the writings of John Dewey (1859–1952), in such works as *Individualism Old and New* (1930) and *Liberalism and Social Action* (1935). Dewey is better known as a philosopher and educationist than a political theorist, but his ideas on all three fit together. As a philosopher he was a pragmatist, which meant that he thought that what was true was what was useful to us and not what corresponded to some alleged world of objective facts. We best found out what was useful by experiment and discussion, a process that produced science and progress and should be the basis of education. It was also both essentially democratic and collectivist, relying on people working together to find common solutions. This was what democracy was really about: a way of life rather than merely a system of government, and ordinary people participating and working together in all aspects of social activity.

Dewey proclaimed a 'new individualism' that was collective and co-operative and progressive, and which would enable all to grow and fully develop their potential. This would replace the old,

selfish, *laissez faire* individualism that was anti-social and ultimately destructive. He called for extensive state intervention in
the economy and society in order to provide all individuals with
the security and the opportunity to participate in society and fully
develop themselves. This involved planning and social engi-
neering based on the fullest social research and consultation,
together with severe curtailment of corporate capitalism. However, Dewey was less concerned with legal or institutional
arrangements, since the key to progress was a properly educated
citizenry committed to democracy as a way of life.

The New Deal and after

Dewey's influence was largely confined to education. It was events
that dictated the extension of a degree of social liberalism. The
Great Crash of 1929 and the subsequent depression were a
serious blow to the 'American way'. For several years American
government did nothing, believing in the accepted wisdom of
classical economics which said that the free market was a self-
righting vessel and the more government left it alone, the more
quickly it would right itself and recover. Eventually America lost
patience and President F. D. Roosevelt launched the 'New Deal',
which meant extensive intervention by government in the
economy to create work, combined with welfare measures. The
New Deal did not end the Depression (the Second World War did
that) but it did alleviate it, and began an era of 'big government'
that culminated in the 'New Frontier' and 'Great Society' programmes of Presidents Kennedy and Johnson in the 1960s.

There was a great deal of hostility from the right to the social
liberalism of the New Deal and the Kennedy/Johnson programmes, but they were too popular for there to be any impact.
However, the 1970s were a period of economic difficulty and
retrenchment, which led to a reaction in the 1980s with the era of
Reagan and the New Right.

Rawls and social justice

The New Deal and the programmes of the 1960s represent the high point of social liberalism in practice in America. Apart from John Dewey, a leading social liberal theorist was John Rawls, whose *A Theory of Justice* was published in 1971. In this he attempted to determine the basic principles of social justice. To do this he made use of an old device of political theorists (such as Locke and Rousseau), the social contract, where people are imagined to come to some sort of agreement to set up a good society in which they are going to live.

Rawls imagines a group of people charged with drawing up a social contract that laid down the rules of how society should run in such a way as to ensure that all their interests would be protected. The unusual feature is that the people concerned do not know what their interests are, because they are not allowed to know their identities. They are behind a 'veil of ignorance' which does not allow them to know whether in society they will be male or female, young or old, from rich backgrounds or poor, disabled or not, talented or not, and so on. This may seem rather far-fetched, but the point is to ensure that the society to be decided upon does not disadvantage any group, because the participants may find themselves belonging to that group.

Rawls believes that such a group would inevitably settle on two principles of justice upon which their society would be based. The first principle is an equality of freedom. That is, that everyone should have as much freedom as possible provided everyone can have the same amount. The second principle is equality of opportunity. This implies, Rawls argues, an equal distribution of power and wealth; unless, that is, some unequal distribution benefits everybody, and particularly the worst off. If, therefore, an equal distribution gives everyone an income of, say, ten dollars per week, then an unequal distribution (to give, for example, more incentives to the most gifted) must give the worst off at least a little more than ten dollars per week, otherwise it cannot be justified.

Against the objection that the more talented and energetic deserve to earn more, Rawls argues that such talents and endowments are gifts of nature or upbringing which are not earned and therefore do not inevitably justify extra reward. In general in our society those with the highest ability and special knowledge tend to receive higher rewards: doctors are paid more than shop assistants. This is not, Rawls thinks, a matter of who deserves what, but of what is of most benefit to society, including the worst off. If it is right to pay doctors more than shop assistants it is because this ensures better medical care for society as a whole, including the worst off.

It follows that if the wealth and power of those at the top of society does not truly work for the benefit of those at the bottom, then that distribution ought to be changed: wealth and power must be re-distributed. Neither genuine liberty nor genuine equality of opportunity are possible, Rawls believes, if society is characterised by great and unjustified inequalities of wealth.

Nozick and the minimal state

Rawls' book was soon followed by a rejoinder from the conservative wing of American liberalism. Robert Nozick's *Anarchy, State and Utopia* appeared three years later in 1974. Where Rawls was concerned with the claims of society, Nozick asserts a pure individualism. In many ways he goes back to John Locke and insists that individuals have certain natural rights: most importantly, Locke's 'life, liberty and property'. Consequently, when considering how someone exercising their abilities should be rewarded, while Rawls asks 'How does this benefit society?', Nozick asks 'by what right does society deprive them of whatever they can earn in the market place?'. Nozick is only prepared to concede that government can tax in order to provide for the protection of the individual's rights, but nothing more. To tax for roads, street lighting, social services or anything else, Nozick insists, is a violation of the individual's rights.

Nozick's book represents the 'conservative' side of American Liberalism, which was reviving itself in the 1970s with the new right-wing thinking and political support that culminated in the presidency of Ronald Reagan. This was a political and intellectual movement known as the New Right, to which Chapter Ten is devoted.

Problems of liberalism and democracy

Liberal democracy is taken for granted in the West and looks to be ultimately triumphant in most of the rest of the world in the foreseeable future. This goes along with liberal ideals such as freedom, equality and tolerance. Yet none of these concepts is unproblematic. There are inherent difficulties and there are charges made by opponents that are sometimes difficult to answer satisfactorily; some of these problems are discussed below.

Freedom and equality

There is arguably a fundamental conflict at the heart of liberal theory. Individual freedom is the great liberal value, and yet equality in some form is inherent in all liberal thinking. For the American revolutionaries the very first thing they believed to be self-evident was that 'all men are created equal'. And for all liberals it seems that equality should at least mean that people should be equally free; that every individual is of equal worth; that every individual equally has the capacity to reason and make moral choices; that everyone should have an equal opportunity to develop their talents, and that everyone should be equal before the law. Yet, for all this, freedom and equality do not seem to fit together very well.

Crudely put, if you let people be completely free, especially economically free, they will end up being unequal. But if you keep people equal, especially economically equal, you will end up denying their freedom. And you can get quite different versions of liberalism according to which value is stressed. In consequence, right from the very beginning of liberalism there have been different movements stressing the different sides: Whigs and Radicals, Spencerians and social liberals, and so on. Today this is expressed in European politics in parties of left and right: Labour and Conservative, Christian Democrat and Social Democrat, while in American politics it is expressed as 'conservative' and 'liberal'.

One could say, then, that the liberal inheritance has been divided between left and right, with both claiming that liberalism alone is an inadequate vehicle for its own ideals. In British terms, the Conservative Party has always had a liberal dimension to its doctrine (distinguishing it from continental versions of conservatism), while for British conservatives and their continental equivalents (such as the Christian Democrats) the defence of property is central to the defence of liberty and Christian values. Yet, at the same time, the mainstream of British socialism (and post-war social democracy elsewhere) has always maintained that only socialism could genuinely fulfil the ideals of liberalism, and that if liberal ideals are pursued consistently, liberal society will inevitably evolve into socialist society.

In recent years much of these arguments within liberalism, and with other democratic ideologies, has centred around the concept of citizenship. What does being a citizen in a modern democracy entail in terms of rights and duties? All liberals would agree on basic civil liberties, but should these be supplemented by welfare rights? Some would put greater stress on economic rights, the right to start a business and make a profit, the right to hire and fire as one pleases, the right to pass on one's property intact to one's heirs. Another contentious argument is that citizenship of an individual state is no longer enough, that we ought to have duties and loyalties and rights in terms of 'world citizenship'.

The moral weakness of liberalism

A quite different set of charges against liberalism allege that it is morally vacuous. If freedom and toleration rule, then what moral values should people have beyond not interfering with others? The answer is that this is a private matter. People can believe in what they like, or in nothing at all. At least ancient republicanism demanded civic virtue and attention to the public good. But modern liberal democracy demands nothing beyond conformity to the law. Human nature is rational and individuals pursue their own interests, and no one is justified in stopping anyone doing just what they like, so long as they stay within legal bounds.

On these grounds some argue that liberal democracy is materialistic, self-indulgent and decadent and breeds a meaning-less, mindless, alienated individualism; a brute selfishness that is devoid of higher values, or any sense of community, or any need to consider one's fellow human beings. People turn to all kinds of strange beliefs to give some degree of emotional and spiritual satisfaction to fill the spiritual emptiness that modern free-market consumer society leaves.

Defining democracy

Despite these criticisms, there are few in today's world who would challenge the legitimacy of democracy as the appropriate form of government for the modern world. But just because it is so universally approved virtually every form of government and every modern ideology lays claim to it. Considerable ingenuity is shown providing justifications for the most unlikely regimes on demo-cratic lines, while the modern world has shown the relative ease with which popular enthusiasm for a regime can be manufactured.

This tends to muddy the discussion of what democracy actually is. After the Second World War, the United Nations agency UNESCO, seeking to clarify the ideals of democracy, set a body of scholars the task of reaching a definition upon which all could agree. In their report, *Democracy in a World of Tensions* (UNESCO, Paris, 1951), they had to admit failure. There were so many conflicting definitions and theories that it was impossible to reach agreement.

The word and the concept go back to ancient Greece, and it is worth reflecting on the fact that what we understand as democracy today would not have been recognized as such by an ancient Greek. The democracy of fifth-century Athens, for example, meant all citizens participating in the law-making process, and also having an equal chance of participating in the day-to-day government through a system of election by lot. Thus by ancient Greek standards our modern representative democracy is not a democracy at all, because the ordinary citizens do not participate but elect people to go away and decide things on their behalf; indeed, some modern thinkers, most notably Rousseau, have agreed with them.

It has long been argued that the 'direct democracy' of the Greeks is not possible in the modern world, and clearly it would hardly be possible to cram all the citizens of the United Kingdom into Trafalgar Square every time a law needed to be passed. On the other hand, it is now technically possible for all households to be 'cabled up' so that all television sets could have a 'voting button', so that a decision by the nation could be called for and instantly given. In principle all government decisions could be based on such votes. This would surely be more democratic than our present representative system. But whether we would necessarily want it as our form of government is another matter.

However, even if we take representative democracy to be authentic democracy and the only possible kind for the modern world, there are still problems. In the first place, democracy is supposed to be based on the sovereignty of the people and therefore government should be an expression of the people's will. The French revolutionaries claimed to represent the true will of the French people, and since that will must be a single will, then those who disagreed with them must at least be putting their selfish interests above those of the people, and at worst must in some way be enemies of the people. However that may be, divining the will of the people is no easy business, since people appear to have genuine disagreements as to what the good of the community really is. The usual way around this is to say: the will of the people is the will of the majority. The question then is, just how much authority does the will of the majority have? Does it mean that fifty per cent plus one has an absolute right to do what it wants? Does it have the right to ignore dissent, or to force the minority to conform? Does it have the right to persecute a minority, especially if that minority is permanent?

Modern liberal democracies insist on the protection of minority rights, but is this a diminution of democracy or an essential part of it? Pluralism is certainly an essential part of liberal democracy, but some would say that it is more liberal than it is democratic. It could be said to represent an endorsement of self-interestedness as against public spiritedness and care for the common good. Again, the radical might argue that the pluralism the liberal sets so much store by really masks the way that the system protects the interests of the privileged classes. The logical conclusion of this is the socialist case against liberalism, which is that genuine liberty is impossible without genuine equality. That is, that true liberty and true democracy are only possible in a society where no one is markedly better off than anyone else. We are then back to the counter-argument that a society where equality has to be enforced cannot be a free one.

The mechanics of democracy

If we take modern pluralist liberal democracy to be in principle the most desirable form of democracy, there are still problems. For example, there is the issue of different voting systems: is the British 'first-past-the post' system more or less democratic than the Israeli 'list' system, which is perfectly proportional? Many would say that the British system is less democratic because it undoubtedly favours the big parties disproportionately, but others might argue that the Israeli system favours smaller parties disproportionately. What voting system is the most efficient and democratic is a tangled and difficult question.

Then there are awkward questions concerning representation, such as whether representatives need to be *socially* representative; whether they ought to be mandated delegates or free to use their own judgement; whether hereditary elements, such as the British House of Lords are compatible with democracy, and so on.

Finally, there is the question of participation. It was fashionable among political scientists in the 1950s, especially in America, to argue that mass participation in politics was only characteristic of totalitarian regimes, and that a good deal of apathy was in fact necessary for the good working of democracy. Others have argued that the more ordinary people participate the better, which leads ultimately to the question as to whether democracy is just a form of government or a whole way of life.

3

Conservatism and the right

Many of the ideas, attitudes and arguments that we associate with conservatism go back many centuries, if not millennia. And yet conservatism, as a coherent political doctrine, is really a modern phenomenon that developed in response to the French Revolution. This curious disparity between antiquity of outlook and modernity of articulation exists because central values of conservatism, such as tradition, established authority, customary practice and time-honoured hierarchy, were long sanctified by religion and taken for granted by most people, for whom their value went without saying. For the greater part of human history the life of the majority was precarious in a way that today we find difficult to conceive of, and these values were deemed essential to the order, stability and security upon which civilised life depended. They hardly needed defending, for longevity alone guaranteed worth.

In the eighteenth century, when educated people were aware of these values being questioned, the debate was still peripheral to most of the population. The French Revolution changed all this. Unlike previous upheavals (such as religious wars in France and Germany and the English civil wars), the French Revolution was pursued in the name of the people. That is, all of the people, and just about every person in France was caught up in it. More importantly, it was a revolution against tradition, against the *ancien régime*, the established order. Tradition, prejudice, established authority, customary ceremony, and all similar fixed points of society, were all despised and reviled. It was this radical challenge to people's habitual ways of thinking and believing that called forth attempts to turn what had hitherto been instinctively accepted into a reasoned doctrine designed to have wide appeal. Those with wealth and privilege and position believed that they had these things as of right, a right that had to be defended against those with untried ideas and with interests to satisfy and axes to grind.

However, defence of the *status quo* inevitably took different forms according to the different traditions and societies being defended. Thus, we have different versions of conservatism developed in different countries either experiencing the Revolution or threatened by it, especially in France, Germany and Britain.

French reactionary conservatism

The French Revolution divided French society much more deeply than the English civil wars divided Britain. In consequence, French politics in the nineteenth and much of the twentieth century has been more polarised, and more bitter and uncompromising than in Britain. The same ideas did not infuse different parties as they did in Britain, and parties tended to take up more rigid positions. French opposition to the Revolution, especially among emigré aristocrats, took the form of a reactionary demand for a return to the pre-revolutionary world. The restored Bourbon monarchy of 1815 was a constitutional monarchy and not the absolute monarchy that preceded it. On the face of it, this seemed a fair compromise, but it satisfied nobody.

De Maistre and de Bonald

The right wanted a full restoration of Bourbon absolutism. This seemed implausible after France had changed so much in a quarter of a century, and it needed a theory to justify it. The chief theorists of the reactionary outlook were Joseph de Maistre and

Louis de Bonald. They wished to portray the Revolution and all it stood for as a disaster for France and the world. This necessitated the complete rejection of Enlightenment thinking, which they blamed for causing the Revolution in the first place.

They argued for a unified Christendom under the absolute rule of church and state: that is, the rule of kings and the pope. Society should reflect the God-given order, with everyone assigned their place. De Maistre insisted that contrary to Enlightenment thinking, human reason could create nothing of any worth. The social order of the old regime had been created, like the family, from the instincts which God had implanted in man. Those same instincts led men towards obedience to their church and their social superiors, and only when men fully returned to their true natural obedience would God's harmony be restored. De Maistre and Bonald looked to a return to a pre-Revolution unified Christendom that in fact did not exist, and had never really existed.

Everything was attributed to God, including the Revolution, which was the expression of divine wrath. The so-called Enlightenment had set human reason above God's wisdom and the Revolution was both the punishment for, and the demonstration of, the anarchic consequences of denying God's work.

Democracy, however limited, was an abomination. For democracy institutionalised a society permanently divided in its beliefs and values, which allowed a legitimate place for error and evil at the expense of morality and truth. And because an ideologically divided society could not survive, its ultimate consequence was anarchy, as the Jacobin Terror demonstrated. People had to accept the authority of church and state which God had placed over them. Politics were subordinate to religion: kings were the servants of the pope, who embodied the will of God on earth.

Today these seem rather obscure points, but royalism, including the idea of restoring the pre-revolutionary monarchy, recognising the authority of the Catholic Church and blaming all France's troubles on the French Revolution, was a significant political outlook right up to the 1940s. This points to a more general fact about French politics throughout the period since the

Revolution, which has been the chronic problem of legitimacy. Essentially it was a conflict between the sovereignty of the king, sanctified by time and the church, versus the sovereignty of the people based upon theory. France has never quite solved the question to the satisfaction of all the French. Since 1789 France has had two monarchies, two Napoleonic empires and five republics; in all there has been fifteen constitutions.

Not all of the French right were dedicated to reaction. There developed a more pragmatic conservatism. But the most common form of this is perhaps best described as conservative liberalism, a kind of cautious, pragmatic, elitist liberalism that distanced itself from the Revolution and from egalitarianism. It was concerned with property rights and the maintenance of order. Although recognising the inevitability of democratisation, liberal conservatives wanted it to come slowly; they did not look forward to it, and they did not count its advent as in any sense progressive. Holders of this view included Benjamin Constant and Alexis de Tocqueville. Liberal conservatism is much closer to British conservatism.

Reaction elsewhere

Other countries in post-revolutionary Europe tended to reaction, although for the most part this required no theorising but merely a continuation of the *status quo* and a determination to stamp out any manifestations of liberalism. This was true of Spain, Austria and Russia. In the case of Austria and Russia, a major consideration was the association of liberalism with nationalism. A growth of nationalist movements with a French-style emphasis on popular sovereignty would threaten to disrupt and destroy their multinational empires. A further consideration that needs to be borne in mind is the hostility of the papacy to liberalism throughout the nineteenth century, though this had no significance in much of northern Europe. Germany was in some ways a special case in the sense that its traditionalism took on a distinctly German form, one not based on popular sovereignty or a unified state. It developed its own form of conservatism, which although reactionary had distinctive features, based on its connection with Romanticism.

German Romantic conservatism

At the time of the French Revolution, a profound intellectual revolution was taking place in various parts of Europe, which influenced the work of thinkers and especially artists of all kinds. This was the Romantic movement, which was to have an important impact on political thinking in Britain and to a lesser extent, in France; however, the greatest impact was in Germany. Here the influence of Romanticism was felt in liberal and socialist thinking, but was most significant in relation to conservatism and nationalism, in the writings of Johann Fichte (1742–1814), Novalis (1772–1801) and Adam Muller (1779–1829). In Germany nationalism and conservatism were closely connected, in contrast to France where nationalism was associated with liberalism and the Revolution.

Romanticism

Romanticism in general is best understood, at least initially, as a reaction against the Enlightenment. The Enlightenment stood for universalism, particularly in the interconnected forms of reason and science and human rights, as against tradition, emotion, prejudice, particularity, individual and regional differences, established authority, habitual attitudes and customary practices. Reason was the standard of knowledge and truth, tradition the source of ignorance and error. Romantic thinking put all this into reverse. The uniqueness of the particular, whether it be an individual or an experience or a nation, was what was emphasised and celebrated. What was common and what was the subject of science was a poor and narrow version of anything and no guide to its true nature. The reason glorified by the Enlightenment was a shallow and therefore misleading guide to reality. Man was an emotional and spiritual being whose true essence was revealed in art far more than in science. Individuals as well as societies had to be understood as concrete wholes, not as a collection of universally shared attributes.

The shallowness of the enlightenment

In political terms these ideas had a number of implications, some of which the German Romantic conservatives shared with conservative thinkers elsewhere (notably Edmund Burke in Britain), while others were particular to themselves. The French Revolution was regarded as an outcome of Enlightenment thinking and a demonstration of its inadequacy. Universal rights of man, freedom and equality, all ignored the diversity and wholeness of people and peoples. It was a shallow freedom and meaningless equality. Defining people in terms of their common human rights denied their individuality, their so-called liberty and equality were a fraud.

All that the liberty and equality demanded by the liberals amounted to was the freedom of individuals to be selfish, to pursue their own interests at the expense of their neighbours and the community in general. The community, the family and all personal obligations were sacrificed for the sake of the pursuit of wealth in a war of all against all. Shorn of their social connections individuals become isolated and rootless and vulnerable to exploitation. Traditional society, with its nobility, clergy, guildsmen, merchants and peasants, was one in which everyone knew their place and their duties, but within which all had security and protection within a community, itself part of a wider community, the greater family, of which the monarch was the head. Liberal freedom would destroy all this for the sake of a freedom that meant no more than a selfish freedom for the few at the expense of the many.

The Romantic state

The German Romantics insisted that genuine liberty was only possible when human nature was fully expressed in all its variety, and no individual could achieve this alone. Only a state could do this because only the state could stand for the whole. No other body or class could, and certainly not individuals. This would be like saying that an arm could represent the whole person, when only the mind could do this, and the state was the mind's equivalent for society. The state was therefore morally superior to any of its parts or to the individuals that made up its population. The individual could achieve his greatest degree of fulfilment and freedom only through the greater whole. By means of this kind of reasoning the Romantics came to the rather chilling conclusion that the state was more real than the individuals of which it was composed (a view which contrasts with an English waryness of the state).

However, the kind of state the Romantics had in mind was not the modern legal state, but rather the medieval feudal state of the distant past. It was a society based on personal arrangements between each individual and his lord, not on universal laws, constituted an organic unity. Thus Romantic nationalism was not about creating a modern united Germany, but more about pre-serving a politically fragmented feudal Germany. As admirers of feudalism, the Romantics looked to the social leadership of an idealized, enlightened aristocracy devoted to the arts and sciences, rather than the ill-educated aristocracy of the time (or indeed the past). Moreover, they believed that political leadership should be in the hands of poets and scholars who had the neces-sary insight and understanding to rule their ideal society wisely.

At the time the Romantics were writing, Germany was a patchwork (although simplified by Napoleon) of independent feudal territories, mostly characterised by reactionary absolutism. As Germany was still an economically backward part of Europe, there was a relatively small middle class, from which most of the Romantic thinkers were drawn. The middle class had very little political influence and the fuling aristocracy had little interest in ideas of rule by poets and scholars. Liberalism, which was largely confined to the same small and weak middle class, had even less political influence, and was suppressed in most areas. The liberals stood for constitutionalism, individual rights, German unification and a national economy, all of which the aristocracy saw as a direct threat to their position. The Romantics wanted to preserve the set of feudal states of old Germany that embodied their values of organic society. Their nationalism was essentially cultural.

After the liberals had been defeated in the series of revolutions across Europe in 1848, the policy of German unification was taken up by the German right, who interpreted it in their own terms. It was part of the new or radical conservatism that developed in Europe in the second half of the century.

Radical conservatism

Early nineteenth-century continental conservatism, in its various forms, was largely nostalgic and backward-looking, hankering after a past world that had been idealised to the point of fiction. But in the second-half of the nineteenth century a new kind of conservative thinking developed in which old right traditionalism came to be supplemented by new ideas and attitudes. This 'new', or 'radical', conservatism sought to come to terms with the modern world. It can be seen as a reaction to the growing influence of liberalism in Europe from mid-century, when simple nostalgia for lost age no longer seemed adequate.

New conservative themes

The new conservatism had all the authoritarianism of the old, but was more stridently nationalistic. It was more militaristic and imperialistic, glorifying war to such an extent that populations went to war with enthusiasm in 1914. It was racist in general and anti-Semitic in particular. Modern scientific and technological developments were embraced, especially for military purposes; the importance of economic strength was recognised; and to some extent it came to terms with representation. It remained firmly anti-democratic, although aware that right-wing causes could be popular.

Several factors contributed to this change of mood. One of these was realism, in that politicians recognised that governments and peoples could not live in the past and that a new world was being created by industrialisation and urbanisation. In other words, change was coming anyway and it was better to understand and control it than ignore it and eventually be swept away by it.

Ideas like nationalism were too popular to be ignored. Hitherto nationalism had been associated with liberalism and such concepts as popular sovereignty, but the right discovered that nationalism could appeal to the masses in a more aggressive and xenophobic form. National self-assertion could excite popular enthusiasm at least as much as representative government. Military power was the obvious expression of this, especially in terms of territorial expansion and the acquisition of colonies abroad. This was in turn associated with the conviction that a strong state must be economically independent and self-sufficient (in contrast to the liberal emphasis on free trade and a more integrated world). The Prussians were by no means alone in glorifying war, but it was they above all who realised the importance of industrial might for success and power in the world. Finally, a major influence on the new conservative thinking was social Darwinism.

Social Darwinism

Darwin's theory of evolution was the intellectual sensation of the age. It appeared to undermine religious truths people had for centuries taken for granted as the very foundation of European civilization, and it constituted a great blow to traditional conservative thinking). On the other hand, it appeared to offer a new foundation for truth. As a consequence, across the ideological spectrum theorists looked to evolutionary theory to provide a foundation for their own political values. Herbert Spencer's liberalism was one example and Prince Peter Kropotkin's anarchism another. Right-wing thinking was influenced considerably by Darwinian theory.

The right-wing interpretation of Darwin was far from subtle. It portrayed life as a struggle for dominance among individuals, nations and races in which the strongest (and therefore 'superior') came to dominate the weak and inferior. This seemed to justify

the ruling elites in society, wars of national expansion and the
seizing of colonies as both natural and right. Social Darwinism
was an important development in the new conservative thinking
which developed in many countries, but especially in Germany
and France.

German conservative nationalism

German conservatives were first to grasp the possibilities of
nationalism. German liberalism had continued to grow in the
second half of the century, despite the failure of 1848, partly due
to its popular policy of German unification. However, it was not
liberals who brought about German unification in 1871 (as was
the case in Italy) but, in Bismarck's phrase, the 'blood and iron' of
Prussian force of arms. Bismarck, the Prussian Chancellor, in
effect stole the policy and made German unity and greatness (and
imperialism) a conservative cause which even the liberals supported.

Bismarck thus developed a new conservatism which united
authoritarian, hierarchic, aristocratic absolutism, with a tamed
parliament and even some paternalistic, welfare state policies to
head off the growing support for the socialists. Although
authoritarian, it was not reactionary and backward-looking, but
embraced industrialisation as a means to national greatness. It was
modernisation from above (as also happened in Japan).

Austria, by contrast, resisted any social or political change and
sank ever deeper into reactionary traditionalism, becoming a fossil
of pre-revolutionary Europe. It had opposed German unification, but could not resist the Prussian war machine.

The German Romantics had not been admirers of such
bellicosity. Their glorification of the nation was not a glorification
of brute power. This dimension of German conservatism
developed during the second half of the nineteenth century, and
the works of the historian Heinrich von Treitschke (1834–96)
were significant in this respect. He insisted that politics was about
power and that states were not bound by ordinary morality (a
concept known as *Realpolitik*). Proudly calling himself a 'radical

reactionary', he glorified Prussian militarism and believed everything should be subordinated to German unity and expansion
under Prussian leadership.

Treitschke believed that Germany had a divine mission to
civilise the world, and he resented the power and dominance of
the British Empire. He despised the British preoccupation with
individual rights and minimal government, and the idea that the
state only gained its power at the expense of its citizens. But then,
the British could afford these delusions, being an island people
and ruling over a distant empire of uncivilized natives. Germany
understood the true necessity of power and of subordinating
individuals to the greater good of the state. Civilized life was not
possible without the protection of the state, in defence of which
individuals must be prepared to die if necessary, despite any
so-called rights to life, liberty and the pursuit of happiness.

Treitschke was contemptous of democracy and believed that
socialism should be suppressed by force. He also wanted
sociology suppressed as an academic subject, considering its class
analysis to be divisive, subversive and dangerous. The explanation
of history and society lay in the unfolding of God's will, of which
Prussian institutions were the highest expression. Any concessions to mass opinion would lead to a decline of discipline and
the traditional moral standards upon which Prussian greatness
depended.

War was exalted because it purified the nation of corrupting
individualism and self-indulgence. Treitschke saw history in
terms of a struggle between the races, of which the Germanic
peoples were superior because they were born warriors and state-
builders, and state-building was the highest function of man, the
condition of civilization (see Chapter Nine). The German people
therefore had a world-historical destiny. Treitschke was fiercely
anti-Semitic. He thought that the world would eventually be
dominated by German and Anglo-Saxon peoples, and if necessary by Germans alone.

Treitschke was an extremely influential teacher and his ideas of
Realpolitik were to dominate German political thinking until the
defeat of 1918. Thereafter, Germany had a liberal democracy

thrust upon her by the victorious allies. It was a failure for many reasons, unable to cope with the problems, especially economic problems, that faced it. Its collapse signalled the rise of Hitler's fascists, who were able to draw on the traditions of state-worship and authoritarianism of past German history. The Nazis made Treitschke required reading.

Roman Catholicism and the new conservatism

Some radical conservative ideas found favour in Austria. Authoritarian and racist doctrines suited an imperial power trying to hold down a multi-national and multi-ethnic empire. The right in Austria, as well as in France and elsewhere, gained considerable support from the ultramontane movement that was coming to dominate the Catholic Church in the nineteenth century.

Ultramontanism was the doctrine of papal supremacy, as against the authority of the national churches. 'Ultramontane' literally means 'beyond the mountains' and implies churches north of the Alps looking to Rome for authority and guidance. That authority was at a particularly low ebb in the eighteenth century, but attacks on the church during the French Revolution – when many priests were executed, churches closed and Notre Dame Cathedral 'dechristianised' and turned into a 'Temple of Reason' – led to a revival of ultramontainism in France and the rest of Catholic Europe. The movement's greatest triumph was the adoption by the Vatican Council of 1870 of the doctrine of papal infallibility in faith and morals.

Morals were here deemed to include politics, and ultramontanism tended to accompany extreme traditionalism in the political sphere. In the past the church had always tended to favour pragmatism in its dealings with states, but in 1864 the Pope declared liberalism, nationalism and socialism to be 'false doctrines of our most unhappy age' and 'incompatible with Catholic truth'.

Later a series of papal encyclicals spelt out the position in more detail. While not condemning any system of government if properly subject to Church guidance, unrestrained capitalism, individualism, popular sovereignty, free speech and toleration were all specifically condemned, together with socialist ideas in toto. The ideal was a Christian commonwealth under church guidance, with estates and corporations and other social bodies, each with its proper sphere of authority, all joined together in an organic harmony. It is essentially a medieval picture, in which government was deemed to be an expression of the whole social organism, underpinned by the church. Short of this ideal, the Catholic Church generally tended to support the right in Catholic countries up to the 1940s. It signed agreements with both Hitler and Mussolini, both of whom suppressed moderate Catholic parties without there being any serious protest from the church hierarchy.

The radical right in France

French conservatism in the late nineteenth century was also influenced by the ideas of the radical right, especially after the humiliating defeat by Prussia in the Franco–Prussian war of 1870–71. After being the most powerful nation in the world a century earlier, France, it was argued, had sunk into decadence. The reason for this was obviously the Revolution and its consequences. Nationalism became the most important right-wing cause, together with a glorification of militarism. Military strength and unity of purpose were essential for a revival of French supremacy. This is the period of the cult of Joan of Arc, with the erection of countless statues and festivals held in her honour, as the symbol of French valour and resistance to foreign aggression.

Nevertheless, despite similarities with the radical right of Germany and elsewhere, French radical conservatives remained distinctive. For one thing it retained much of the traditionalism and veneration for the Catholic Church of earlier writers such as de Bonald and de Maistre. But whereas they had looked to a return to a unified medieval Christendom that in fact had never really existed, the radicals of the late nineteenth and early twentieth centuries sought other sources of inspiration to justify their elitism, rejection of democracy and insistence on uniformity of values. Radical conservative thinkers such as the novelist and MP, Maurice Barres (1862–1923), and the journalist and political organiser Charles Maurras (1868–1952), were much more narrowly nationalistic. What mattered for them was French civilisation and French greatness. Catholicism happened to be a part of this, while the shallow rationalism of the Enlightenment and the Revolution was not. The true Frenchman, they believed, thought with his instincts, which told him what was good for France, whatever his reason dictated.

Charles Maurras

Maurras was the leader of the Action Française, movement from 1899 until 1944, which although not an effective political party was an important influence on French politics during this time. He believed that the 'real' France, pre-revolutionary France, had been the true heir of ancient Greece and Rome and the most perfect expression of European civilization, the model of order and beauty. But France had been ruined by the Revolution and its consequences, and had become corrupt, decadent and weak in relation to inferior peoples like the Germans and the British.

He chiefly blamed ideas for this decline, and in particular those that had flowed from the Enlightenment and inspired the Revolution: that is, liberalism, individualism, liberty, democracy and equality. His particular *bête noire* was Rousseau, with his ideas of popular sovereignty and the authority of the individual conscience. Maurras attacked all of these things with great vehemence in his writings, along with socialism, communism and anarchism. His chief charge was that these political theories were foreign, usually of Germanic or Jewish origin (or, in the case of Rousseau, Swiss). The chief object of his attacks was democracy.

Maurras regarded democracy as a terrible wasting disease from which France was suffering. It had reduced France from being the leading world power in the eighteenth century to its second-rate position in the twentieth. Democracy was, he argued, not a form of government so much as a form of anarchy, involving endless, debilitating discussion and with the pressure of private interests forcing out the national interest. Under democracy nothing was ever certain, nothing was under control, and the state consistently fell victim to the greed of individuals, classes and organisations.

Democratic government was government by windbags, who had to pander to the ignorant masses and base their policies on vacillating and uninformed public opinion. It was rule by the ignorant and unworthy, who want only to satisfy their selfish needs. Democratic government could only react to events without controlling them. It had no memory and was ignorant of tradition. It neglected the state's primary duty of readiness for war and could conduct neither military action nor diplomacy effectively. The foresight, continuity and determination essential to survival in the modern world were necessarily lacking. It was a system of government that encouraged the internal division which weakened the nation in its struggles in the world. It was, therefore, a permanent conspiracy against the public good, and must be destroyed.

Maurras' alternative was the restoration of a strong monarchy. A full restoration of the Bourbon monarchy would alone have the necessary legitimacy and therefore the authority to do what was needed to restore France to greatness. There would be no question of a constitution, for nothing must diminish royal absolutism. All traces of democracy or any other such representation would be abolished. The king alone was able to represent the true France. The monarchy was the living embodiment of French history and stood for order and discipline in society and in art. It represented the permanent interests of the nation against the selfishness of individuals and groups. And of course the King was the very antithesis of hated democracy.

Along with the monarchy, Maurras envisioned a restoration of what was left of the hereditary aristocracy, supplemented by new recruits from the ranks of the French social elite, especially the officer corps. As to the rest of society, there would be a restoration of some kind of system of guilds and corporations to which all would belong according to their work or profession. Each corporation would have its own authority over its members with powers to regulate work, taxation and provide welfare. These would overcome class conflict, competition and the disorder and indiscipline they brought. An assembly of corporations and social classes would replace the National Assembly and would advise the monarch.

Maurras regarded the Catholic Church as essential to the very essence of the 'true France', even though he was not a religious believer. The Catholic Church, he argued, had taken a foreign and alien religion (Judaic Christianity) and Latinised it, making it a society of order and hierarchy to mediate between God and man, and in the process turning it into something precise and beautiful. The German Reformation had been an attempt to return the Church to its primitive, and therefore Jewish, beginnings. Protestantism was therefore alien and must be resisted.

Maurras was happy to have the Church teach the God-given order where everything had its place with good reason, but this was not in fact his own view. He appeared to regard the universe as a hostile and anarchic place, although the conditions capable of creating order and beauty were occasionally thrown up. But when it happened, as it pre-eminently had in France, the result was fragile and easily lost and immense efforts were needed to preserve it.

Action Française was not a political party in the usual sense of standing for elections, although it had a substantial membership and its daily paper, *L'Action Française* was widely read. However, Maurras was so violent in his hatreds and in his attacks on politicians and prominent people that he became an embarrassment, and was disowned by both the Pope and the Bourbon Pretender to the throne. He also had violent young followers who beat up opponents, broke up meetings, and threatened any dissenters. Some classify Maurras and Action Française as Fascist, and certainly there are Fascist features that grew stronger as time went on. His ideal monarchy increasingly appeared more as a figurehead in an essentially military state. On the other hand, the movement looked to the past rather than the future and it was not populist. Maurras had only contempt for the masses. There was no call to mobilize the people, as there was among the more obviously Fascist organizations that developed in France in the 1930s.

Vichy France and After

The nearest Maurras came to seeing his ideal government was between 1940 and 1944, when the part of France that the Germans had chosen not to conquer was run from Vichy by an extreme right-wing government under Marshal Pétain. The government shared theoretical sympathies with German Fascism, was a virtual dictatorship and was avowedly authoritarian, paternalistic, anti-Semitic and very admiring of Maurras, who enthusiastically supported it. It was close to Germany in terms of its thinking and collaborationist in practice.

Although he detested the Germans, Maurras nonetheless rejoiced that they had destroyed the French Republic (for whose inadequacies the defeat had been a punishment) and were anti-Semitic. The Pétain government declared an end to the cosmopolitan, masonic, capitalist state, to class war, demagogy and the cult of pleasure, and a return to the principles of religion, patriotism and the family. Trade unions were abolished and replaced by professional corporations, to put an end to strikes and industrial unrest. A corporatist system was envisioned in which the interests of workers, employers and the state would be reconciled. Jews were excluded from government, teaching and a host of other professional jobs and deported.

In 1945 Maurras was imprisoned for collaboration, though when he died in 1952 he was entirely unrepentant. And although his extreme reactionary, authoritarian conservatism continued to have its admirers, its closeness to Fascism and the Vichy experience discredited the far right in France for a long time.

After the war it was de Gaulle who was to unify the French right. Gaullism was moderately right wing and very nationalistic, although de Gaulle came into conflict with the extreme right over his policy of giving up the French empire in North Africa (the famous thriller, *The Day of the Jackal* was loosely based on right-wing plots to assassinate de Gaulle). But since his death in 1970 the French right has split into various factions. The extreme right in France is now represented by Jean-Marie Le Pen's National Front, which is authoritarian, racist and too close to Fascism for respectability, and which has achieved a certain amount of electoral success (see Chapter 9).

British conservatism

Traditional British conservatism (as distinct from the conservatism of the 1980s) has an altogether different character to the various continental conservatisms. If conservatism is about preserving a pre-existing way of life, then what was to be preserved was very different from continental practice. Britain was already deeply permeated with liberal ideas and values before British conservatism crystallized as a political doctrine; a Parliament and a strong tradition of civil liberties were already in existence. The chief exponent of Conservative ideas, Edmund Burke (1729–97), was in fact a Whig and devoted to liberty and representative government; consequently these things were part of the British conservative tradition from the beginning, in marked contrast to the thinking that prevailed in Europe.

Burkian foundations

Burke's conservatism is most fully and eloquently set out in his *Reflections on the Revolution in France* of 1792, in which he fiercely attacked the revolutionaries of Paris for mindless destruction of what they did not understand for the sake of an abstract theory which was for all practical purposes useless and dangerous. In his view, a complex social organism was being obliterated in the name of the idea that human beings had certain natural rights, whose existence nobody could prove. The result could only be bloodshed and chaos (Burke wrote before the deposing of the king and the Terror). These origins are significant. Traditional conservatism is, broadly, a defence of the status quo, of the established order of things, against radical or revolutionary change. It is a sophisticated defence that traditional conservatives today still express in essentially Burkian terms.

Traditional conservatives reject the idea that society is like some sort of machine that can be taken to pieces and reassembled at will. Society, they insist, is much more like a living creature, which cannot just be cut up and rearranged to suit theory. Society is infinitely complex and interconnected, so that changing one part of it affects every other part and may do so in any number of unforeseen ways, probably most of them bad. Sudden or radical change is therefore bound to lead to disaster and chaos because its consequences cannot be controlled. Conservatives are always suspicious of change, while at the same time recognising that changing things is from time to time necessary. Society must always adapt to new circumstances; but the organism must be allowed to evolve at its own pace. The politician can assist this process with reform, though this must always be piecemeal and pragmatic in order to minimize any negative consequences.

For conservatives, stable and well-organized society is the work of centuries. It is built out of institutions, such as the family, church, private property and local communities. It is through these institutions that individuals have rights, and also obligations, while others hold office and have authority. All are bound together in an established pattern of living that embodies long-held values and is sustained by custom and tradition. It is custom and tradition, and even prejudice, that are the best guide to action, since these represent the stored-up wisdom of the past. Relying on theory or 'pure reason' is a very poor guide.

This is a very different picture from the liberal view of the ideal society which is based upon contracts between free individuals, which in principle can be changed at any time. Authority arises from such contracts. Above all there is the social contract, which, in its simplest version, involves an agreement by citizens to obey the law in exchange for the protection of the state. If the government does not do its job, then the contract is broken and the people can change it. For the traditional conservatives, however, society is more than just a collection of individuals making contracts with each other, but a community bound together by a multitude of ties of loyalty and affection. Like other critics of liberalism, traditional conservatives see liberals as having no sense of community, of what it is that binds human beings together.

Every long-established and well-ordered society is a unique achievement, and makes a unique contribution to civilisation. But this achievement is vulnerable to breakdown and destruction if subject to drastic change. Politics is the art of preserving what is best (that is, conservation, hence 'conservatism') and adapting it to new circumstances. This cannot be done by following some blue-print or plan which gives a picture of the ideal society that can be achieved. Conservatives view politics as a matter of experience and judgement, not the application of doctrines, as Jacobins, radicals, communists, fascists, and umpteen varieties of socialist have believed. Conservatives reject abstract theory in politics, which they call 'ideology', and claim to be non-ideological. Conservative principles, they argue, are pragmatic and derived from history and tradition, which is the guarantee of what does and does not work.

The preservation of the established order implies inequality. Conservatives believe all should have the opportunity to better themselves, but the idea that everyone should be equal is anathema. Since people are unequal in talent and energy, society has to reflect this. Besides, without differences of wealth and status there would be no incentive for people to work and strive. The fact that there are different stations in life, and different social classes, is not something to be lamented; it is a functional necessity. Different people need to do different kinds of jobs, and be rewarded according to their contribution. Social class is essentially an integrative feature of society, not a divisive one as the socialists think. As with any living organism, all the parts must work together in harmony if the organism is to be healthy. The task of conservative government is to maintain that harmony.

Conservatives place special value on order and stability, along with the social hierarchy and discipline that are necessary to maintain them. They put little faith in unrestrained human nature and entertain little hope that it can be improved. Human nature has an evil streak in it, which no amount of social tinkering will eliminate. The best that can be done is to have a society that, as far as possible, encourages the good and minimises the bad. Rational schemes to fundamentally improve the human condition (that is, ideas for a better organised society that will solve all social problems) are viewed with suspicion.

Greater faith is placed in established ways of doing things and in traditional values. Patriotism is important, as is respect for authority and law, while good government and strong leadership are admired. Leadership is a key conservative concept; it is a skill which can be fostered and developed, but resides most naturally in the traditional ruling elite who can command authority without engendering hostility.

These attitudes have been characteristic of a traditional conservative outlook since Burke. However, a number of other themes have become part of conservative thinking since then.

Later development of conservatism

Burke's views very much reflected the outlook of the landed aristocracy who ruled Britain, but as the nineteenth century progressed other ideas were added as the Conservative Party sought to widen its appeal.

The Conservative Prime Minister Benjamin Disraeli (1804–81) gave the party a new vision as the party of national unity. This involved care for the interests of the whole of society, including the problems of ordinary people, as well as those of high position who had a duty to rule. The idea was to form an alliance between the old ruling class and the working classes, to some of whom Disraeli extended the franchise in 1867. Conservative reforms to help alleviate social problems would be in sharp contrast to the destructiveness and divisiveness of *laissez-faire* capitalism, which was associated with the Liberals. This was Disraeli's conception of Tory democracy; that is, of one nation instead of the 'two nations' of rich and poor that unbridled free enterprise was creating in his day. On this basis, Disraeli was able to claim that the Conservatives were the party of the national unity which, unlike other parties, represented the whole nation.

One further dimension which Disraeli added to his party's vision was that of empire. Britain was seen to have an imperial mission to bring peace and civilization to distant lands. Burke had

had little concern with the 'condition of the people' and still less with empire, but this proved immensely popular, and the theme of empire, along with Tory democracy and one nation, held appeal for all classes and conditions. It was a conservatism redolent with aristocratic paternalism and the values of the land-owning class (in sharp contrast with liberal *laissez-faire* individualism) and yet designed for a new age of democracy, seeking a mass appeal.

Nevertheless, by the end of the century the Conservatives were increasingly seen as the party of free enterprise. Hitherto, the Liberals had been the pre-eminent party of capitalism and business, and the Conservatives the party of the landed interest, but social and political changes were moving towards a realignment. The increasing number of working-class voters, and the revival of socialism from the 1880s onwards, suggested that the political future lay in a conflict between those representing the propertied and those representing the propertyless. It was the Conservatives who most successfully presented themselves as the defenders of all property, both landed and commercial, while the Liberals made greater efforts to capture the new working-class vote. They were left in the middle, trying to appeal to both sides with a more collectivist social liberalism (once the Labour Party became successfully established the Liberal Party was doomed).

With the recruitment of more middle-class members, especially from the world of business, the Conservatives increasingly adopted and defended classical liberal values and preached the virtues of free enterprise and individualism, and the horrors of state intervention and collectivism. The superiority of a capitalist society over a socialist one became a major theme, although these principles were held within a framework of traditional conservatism.

The Conservative leader in the closing years of the century, Lord Salisbury, was a partisan figure in this new polarisation. He was, in a sense, a class warrior: elitist, anti-democratic, defending property, trying to slow down democracy, and having little Disraelian concern for the 'condition of the people'. In consequence the Conservatives were then much closer to the continental right than they had been previously, or indeed since.

In the twentieth century the Conservative Party returned to being a pragmatic and moderate party of reform. After 1945 it accepted the 'consensus' policies of Keynesian economic management, the mixed economy and the welfare state (see Chapter Two), although it sought to interpret these in terms of traditional Conservative principles that stressed individual enterprise and responsibility. However, the economic difficulties of the 1970s opened the way for the 'Thatcher Revolution', which was in many ways a contradiction of traditional Conservative ideas (discussed more fully in Chapter Ten). The extent to which the Conservative Party has reverted to traditional conservatism following Mrs Thatcher's departure is an arguable point.

The Continental right since 1945

In the post-war period, British conservatism was sufficiently flexible and pragmatic to accommodate the dominant social democratic ideas and the policies that went with them. Continental conservatism also took these ideas on board, but had to make much larger adjustments. The radical right, with its authoritarianism, racism and hostility to democracy had been entirely discredited by the Fascist experience. In many countries the dominant position on the right of liberal democratic politics was taken by Christian democracy.

Catholicism and liberalism

Christian democracy came into its own after 1945, but its origins are much older. The 'Christian' in Christian democracy is largely Catholic Christianity (except for example, to an extent in Germany). Ideas of reconciling Catholic teaching with democracy go back to the French Revolution. However, for most of the nineteenth century, French republicanism and the Catholic Church were deeply hostile. The Revolutionary government had attacked the Church, confiscated its lands, and even attempted to create a new religion of Reason and Supreme Being.

Apart from the attack on the Churt by the French Revolutionaries, there were other reasons for regarding liberalism as a threat to Catholic values. Modern industrialisation and urbanization, the result of capitalist development, were destroying traditional communal and family life, while the policy of *laissez-faire* threatened a war of all against all. Liberal economic theory sanctified selfishness and promoted materialist values. At the same time, the Liberal stress on individualism, tolerance and free expression allowed all kinds of self-indulgence and permissiveness to flourish.

The hostility of the traditionalist Catholic Church was not therefore surprising. Nevertheless, there were some who thought a catholicism reconciled to some degree with liberalism was a possibility, although it was not until the 1830s that it was a significant political position in France. Elsewhere, as in Ireland, Belgium and the USA, the church's experience suggested that in the right circumstances it could at least live with democracy. On the other hand, towards the end of the century democracy became not only associated with liberalism but with socialism, which in continental Europe meant atheistic Marxism. Few thought in terms of a genuine synthesis of liberalism and catholicism. One of the few was the British historian Lord Acton (1834–1902), who said that he rejected everything in catholicism that was incompatible with liberty and everything in politics that was incompatible with catholicism.

From about the 1870s political catholicism, based on the idea that it was to the Church's advantage to participate in the modern political process, became a significant political force in Germany, Switzerland, Belgium and Austria. These movements tended to have similar programmes of opposition to liberal secularism, civil marriage, state control of education, and other policies. They were closely connected with the Church and membership was confined to the faithful. They implied no commitment to democracy, merely making use of the system to the advantage of what they believed to be right. Their ideal was for the church to have a privileged position in the state, able to influence policy, as against the standard view of liberalism that church and state must be clearly separated.

Initially, these Catholic movements tended to oppose capitalism and socialism equally, as both based on materialism and productive of social conflict, preferring the idealised self-sufficient peasants and the guild-organised craftsmen that the Catholic encyclicals (especially *Rerum Novarum* of 1892) advocated. However, many such movements had reconciled themselves to capitalism by 1914 as the prevailing economic system (socialism had come to seem the greater threat), while at the same time helping to organise Catholic peasants and workers to defend their interests within that system.

The Christian democracy movement

Between the wars, political catholicism flourished in Italy and gave rise to Christian democracy as we know it today. The first such party was founded in 1919 by Luigi Sturzo, a priest who believed that catholicism and democracy could be positively reconciled to the advantage of both. His party was independent of the church and advocated social reform, based on Catholic social teaching. Similar parties were established in other parts of Europe and in South America. However, political catholicism generally had little success in stopping Fascism, and even helped it in some cases. In Italy, Sturzo's party was suppressed by the Fascists and he went into exile in France in 1924. In Paris he founded an international movement among whose aims were the establishment of a common market and European integration to prevent wars. Among those active in this group were Alcide De Gasperi, Konrad Adenauer and Robert Schuman, each of whom became leading figures in their respective countries (Italy, West Germany and France) and major contributors to the setting up of the European Community in the 1950s.

Furthermore, until the Second World War Christian Democratic parties were essentially for the faithful and therefore lacked a certain general appeal. When parties were re-founded after the war they had a much wider appeal, and with the discrediting of the far right, had a much clearer field. They were especially strong and electorally successful in former Nazi-dominated areas, and areas were there was a strong Communist Party; that is, where traditional Catholic values had been under threat. This includes most of continental Western Europe, but especially Germany, Italy, Austria and the Benelux countries. There was a French Christian Democratic party after the war, which was absorbed by the Gaulists, while Spain and Portugal have acquired modest parties since the end of their dictatorships in the 1970s. However, post-war Christian democratic parties have not been exclusively Catholic. In West Germany's Christian Democratic Union around 40 per cent of the membership is Protestant, and there is a similarly large Protestant following in the Dutch Party. Scandinavian Christian Democratic parties are mostly Protestant.

Christian democratic ideas

Christian democratic ideas have, however, been largely based on Catholic social teaching. While supporting the rights of property and the traditional social order, society is seen as an organic whole where all the parts must work together. There is a paternalistic concern for the less well-off, expressed in policies of social reform to improve their conditions and protect their rights. This involves a recognition of the role of trade unions, and all the major Christian democratic parties (with the exception of the West German) have strong trade-union wings. Opposed to notions of class-consciousness and class conflict, Christian democratic parties claim to represent all sections of society (although they tend to get proportionally fewer votes among the industrial working class). The Christian Democratic block in the European Community (they call themselves collectively 'The European People's Party') is a strong supporter of the European Community's social programme.

The French Catholic thinker, Jacques Maritain, gave the movement the principle of 'personalism' which claimed to be a third way between liberal individualism and socialist collectivism. 'Personalism' is the idea that the individual can only fully develop through responsibility to other people, especially to the family and the community.

Christian Democrats have always been strong advocates of European economic and political union. The point is to foster co-operation and prevent war. This reflects a certain distrust of the power of the sovereign state that is answerable to no one. Another aspect of this is the advocacy of federalism as a check on centralised national power. They have been strongly anti-Communist.

These social and political principles have not, however, been accompanied by any distinctive economic theory. Christian democratic parties adopted Keynesian economics post-war, which, along with the mixed economy and the welfare state, fitted very well with their outlook. West Germany's Christian Democratic Finance Minister in the 1950s, Ludwig Erhard, introduced a particular version of this known as the 'social market', the idea being of a free market with a social conscience. (This in fact has been the one significant Protestant contribution to Christian democratic theory.) The decline in the authority of Keynesian economics has given Christian Democracy something of a problem concerning their values and economic policies.

Post-war Christian democracy has had a much wider appeal beyond the Catholic faithful than it had previously and as a result of this wider appeal Christian democracy has been, since 1945, Europe's most successful political movement. Christian Democratic parties have had the lion's share of power in Austria, Belgium, Holland, Italy, Luxemburg, West Germany and Switzerland. However, the more general appeal of these parties has tended to dilute their religious doctrine, so that now there are worries that these parties have lost their distinctive identities, and in particular their Christian inspiration, becoming merely centre-right parties representing the interests of the well-off. Such fears have been exacerbated by the advent of New Right neo-liberalism which puts so much stress on the market at the expense of social policy.

There are other moderate Conservative parties and outlooks apart from Christian democracy. One of the best known and most successful has been the Gaullist movement in France.

Gaullism

Charles de Gaulle (1890–1970) was a senior French army officer who came to England when France fell to the Germans in 1940. While the Vichy government collaborated with Germany, de Gaulle raised the standard of resistance. After the Liberation he became progressively disillusioned with post-war politics, and he retired in 1952. However, the Fourth Republic ran into increasing difficulties and de Gaulle was asked to draw up a new constitution, ushering in the Fifth Republic in 1958, which de Gaulle himself dominated as President until his retirement in 1969.

Gaullism advocated strong leadership and centralised republican government, nationalism, traditional (that is, Catholic) values, and a capitalist economy. National security, political stability and economic growth are all emphasised. The Gaullist party survives, although there are many factions. It has been held together since 1974 by the dynamic leadership of Jacques Chirac, and is still the most important party on the French right.

Right-wing dictatorship

In other parts of the world, for example in some South American and Asian states, the right is represented by military dictatorships. In modern states the military is frequently a bastion of right-wing views. As perhaps befits their profession, the military tends to stand for order, discipline and national unity, and is inclined to see itself as the guardian of the nation; whereas democracy may seem to represent chaos and disunity. When disunity and political conflict appear to threaten the national interest the military may intervene, claiming to save the nation. Such *coups d'état* are rare in Europe, although a fairly recent example was in Greece in 1968. They have been much more common in South America, where the justification of saving the nation from left-wing insurgency has been used.

4

Nationalism and internationalism

Among modern ideologies, nationalism is the simplest, the clearest and the least theoretically sophisticated, but it is also the most widespread and the one with the strongest grip on popular feeling. It has successfully demanded of people their highest loyalties and greatest sacrifices, and as a result has been among the most powerful agents of political change in the last two hundred years.

At its simplest, nationalism is the belief that humanity is divided up into nations and that all nations have the right to self-government and to determine their own destiny. Multi-national states and nations divided between states are inherently wrong. It is the nation-state, therefore, that is the one legitimate political unit and the creation and preservation of national identity and national unity are primary objects of political action. Nationalism is a political doctrine, an ideology, because it insists that one particular political form is natural and therefore right.

What is perhaps surprising is just how recent this idea is. Of all modern ideologies nationalism is the most unequivocally a product of the French Revolution. This is despite the fact that a sense of national identity and national loyalty can be found as far back as the ancient world, while nation-states have existed for at least several hundred years. What the French Revolution did was to fuse together these older phenomena with a notion of 'the people' as the ultimate source of legitimacy and authority. This was in contrast with traditional and religiously sanctioned notions of the dynastic claims of princes to sovereign rule over any territories which they inherited, irrespective of the wishes of the people who lived there. For example, in the three centuries prior to the French Revolution what we now call Belgium was successively ruled by the Duke of Burgundy, the King of Spain and the Emperor of Austria and nobody thought this was odd or illegitimate.

In the hands of the Jacobins, nationalism was a revolutionary idea which they sought to export to neighbouring peoples, which in turn called forth other forms of nationalist thought informed by quite different principles. When the dust of the revolutionary period had settled, the revolutionary and counter-revolutionary strands were integrated to produce the nineteenth-century concept of nationalism, which despite its difficulties is still broadly with us today.

Revolutionary and Romantic nationalism

The French revolutionaries invented nationalism almost by accident. It was a by-product of their attempts to put their Enlightenment ideas into effect.

Defining 'The People'

Like the revolutionaries of America, they were inspired by John Locke's ideas of natural rights, government by the consent of the governed, and the right of the people to overthrow a tyranny. They were also more directly inspired by Rousseau's ideas of popular sovereignty and the general will. However, these ideas said little about who exactly 'the governed' or 'the people' who possessed these rights and in whom sovereignty resided were.

Enlightenment theory tended to see society as a collection of individuals with natural rights, bound together by a contract entered into for the protection of those rights. This treated the state like a voluntary association of the like-minded, which ignored those things that bound societies together, such as ties of community and common culture, a sense of common history, purpose or destiny.

When the French revolutionaries attempted to turn the Enlightenment abstractions of popular sovereignty, social contract and the assertion of individual rights into political reality, it was natural for them to assume 'the people' to be the French nation, which for centuries had been one of the most distinct and united peoples of Europe. It was the nation that was sovereign and not the King, and the nation which was the politically significant unit, not the nobility.

The Abbé Siéyès

The most important French theorist of nationalism at this time was the Abbé Siéyès (1748–1836). He was a cleric who identified himself with the ordinary people and was elected to the Third Estate of the Estates General in 1789. He wrote that: 'The nation is prior to everything. Its will is always legal: indeed it is the law itself.' (*What is the Third Estate?*, 1789). The nation is the fundamental unit and it has a will which is the basis of all legitimate authority. The nation has a right to express its will, and consequently has the right to self-determination. Furthermore, by using a somewhat doctored version of Rousseau's general will, Siéyès was able to maintain that the Third Estate expressed the will of France. The other two Estates (the Nobility and the Clergy) represented those who gave nothing to the nation and were parasitic upon it. They could only redeem themselves by identifying with the Third Estate and therefore the nation. The Third Estate turned itself into the National Assembly in 1789 and laid down the basic principles of the Revolution in the *Declaration of the Rights of Man*, Clause III of which declared:

The Nation is essentially the source of all sovereignty; nor can any individual, or any body of men, be entitled to any authority which is not expressly derived from it.

This laid the foundation of nationalist theory.

It became characteristic of all subsequent revolutionary leaders to identify themselves with the will of the French nation. The nation was seen as a single person with a single will and a single common purpose. And those who opposed the will of the people in some sense betrayed the nation and were outside it. The revolutionaries in general wanted to use this new conception of the nation to overcome the provincial and feudal loyalties of the old system, and replace them with the single loyalty to the nation of free and equal citizens, having a common identity and common destiny.

This conception was successfully used to mobilise the French people in defence of the Revolution, especially when France was attacked from outside. When defence eventually turned into attack and French armies under Napoleon began conquering western Europe, these ideas provided the French with a sense of mission, to bring freedom and self-determination to the nations of Europe.

Romantic nationalism

The French revolutionaries' concept of nationalism was an outgrowth of Enlightenment thinking. The rights of man, national self-determination and the sovereignty of the people were the kind of rational and universal ideals that were characteristic of Enlightenment thought. However, there is no reason why national unity should not be developed around quite different principles.

The French revolutionary armies, who saw themselves as liberating Europe, provoked nationalist reaction in Germany, Spain and elsewhere that was more to do with pride in a traditional way of life and cultural uniqueness than notions of popular government or individual rights. These very different principles were connected with the movement of ideas that was a reaction to the Enlightenment: the Romantic movement.

In many ways nationalism had more of a natural affinity with Romantic than with Enlightenment thought. The Romantic outlook (discussed in Chapter 3) insisted on the uniqueness of every nation: its history, language and culture. Romanticism inspired much historical research into national origins, folklore, traditional customs, music and other manifestations of culture that develop a sense of national identity. These ideas developed first and most strongly in Germany, which was at that time a somewhat backward region of Europe and a patchwork of small independent states.

Among the earliest of Romantic thinkers was Johann Gottfried von Herder (1744–1803). He believed that God had divided mankind into different nations so that each, through its distinctive language and culture, could make its unique contribution to civilization. The adoption of other people's cultures was an interference with the plan, and Herder was particularly exercised by the German upper classes adopting French culture and language in a spurious attempt at sophistication, to the detriment of native German thought and art and custom. His belief that a nation's spirit or soul is embodied in its language and cultural life, and needed to be preserved and celebrated, became an important feature of subsequent nationalist thinking, when scholars and artists were important figures in preserving and promoting national culture.

German nationalism

When the French revolutionary armies occupied Germany in the name of German liberation, the Germans reacted against the French and developed their own version of nationalism. It was Johann Fichte (1763–1814) who converted Herder's ideas into a political programme. In his *Addresses to the German Nation* of 1807–08, Fichte exhorted the German people to unify and defeat the occupying French. The German nation should not only rid itself of foreign political influence, but also purify itself of foreign intellectual and cultural influences.

Nineteenth-century nationalism

If we add this Romantic notion of national uniqueness to French ideas of nation and self-determination, as represented by Siéyès, we have the nineteenth-century notion of the national state. The nationalist outlook may be summarised as follows:

a) Humanity is naturally divided into nations.

b) The nation is more than just a political association. It is a community and a social and economic unit.

c) Membership of the nation implies more than pursuing one's own private purposes. It involves not just rights, but a duty to contribute to the good of the whole, and to be a patriot.

d) The nation is a unity because its members have, in some sense, a common will. This implies a common culture and territory, and a common purpose. The nation is an agent with a history and a destiny.

e) If the nation is an agent with a will and destiny then it must be free to exercise that will to pursue that destiny.

f) It is the first duty of political leaders to foster national unity and identity and to lead the nation towards its common goals.

It follows from this conception that every nation must have its own state and not be under the domination of any other state. Multinational states and nations divided between states are wrong on principle. It is precisely these circumstances that have inspired the growth of nationalist sentiment and writing. Two of the most significant nationalist theorists wrote in situations where their nations were fragmented in a patchwork of small states. Fichte in Germany has already been mentioned; the other was the Italian patriot, Joseph Mazzini (1805–72).

Joseph Mazzini

Mazzini perhaps more than anyone else personified the fusion of Enlightenment and Romantic nationalism. He argued that God had divided humanity into natural nations, with natural territories and frontiers. Evil governments, based on barbaric feudal notions of territories as the personal possessions of their ruling families, had subverted this plan and were the cause of oppression and war. Self-determination, where nations could live according to their true identities within their natural boundaries, would enable the people of Europe to co-operate with each other in mutual respect. Proper national governments would provide liberty and care for the welfare of the people and ensure international peace and progress.

Mazzini believed it was Italy's destiny to lead mankind towards a new era of peace and harmony. He took it for granted that all national claims to territory were compatible and that only sincere good will was necessary to solve disputes permanently. These ideas may seem naïve, but they were influential and inspired nationalists across Europe (although it must be said that the unification of Italy was more a matter of power politics than idealism).

Nineteenth-century Europe was littered with nationalist causes and conflicts. As well as Italian unification, there were the causes of the Greeks and other Balkan peoples wanting to escape Turkish rule. The rash of revolutions across Europe in 1848 were mostly inspired by liberal nationalism. They followed Mazzini's belief that personal liberty and national self-determination were inseparable. Such revolutions were seen as a particular threat to the Austro-Hungarian empire, and to the ruling dynasties of fragmented Germany.

Nationalism was seen as a threat to the old order of dynastic states and feudal loyalties, and was associated with liberalism with its implication of the modernisation of society and the economy. In 1848 German unification was seen as very much a liberal cause, but, as we saw in the last chapter, the German aristocracy astutely turned it into a popular right-wing cause.

Right-wing nationalism

The late nineteenth century saw the development of a more aggressive, xenophobic, right-wing nationalism in Germany and elsewhere. It emphasised national self-assertion, and national economic self-sufficiency, expressed in wars for territorial expansion and the development of overseas empires. It became bound up with notions of racial superiority which appeared to find justification in Darwinian theories of evolution, the argument being that the principle of 'survival of the fittest' applied to nations and races (see Chapter 9). The creation of empires and the subjection of 'lesser peoples' was thus a mark of a nation's superiority.

Not all justifications of empire were so crude, and not all who believed in empire did so on grounds of inherent racial superiority. It was taken for granted, however, that European peoples (including their outstations in North America and elsewhere) were more 'advanced' than the non-European world. For some, therefore, it was a moral duty to bring a higher civilisation to non-Europeans who were not already subject to colonial rule by older European empires. Thus the late nineteenth century was characterised by a new round of imperial expansion, where the European states sought to divide up parts of the world not already under European control as colonies or spheres of influence.

It was a combination of the aspirations of European peoples still ruled by foreign states, and the aggressive national rivalry of the major European states that created the conditions for the First World War which exploded in 1914. National self-determination was a major principle of the victorious powers, but it was not the basis of the lasting peace that was hoped for. For one thing, there seemed to be too many peoples to be accommodated as nations; some peoples had to be bound together in artificial fusions, such as Czechoslovakia and Yugoslavia. Secondly, although this principle of self-determination was supposed to be universal, it was only applied to the empires of defeated countries, those of Germany, Austria, Turkey and Russia. It was not applied to the victorious powers (such as Britain in Ireland) or their overseas empires. The settlement left plenty of scope for future conflict over various national questions. These have emerged in the conflicts of the Second World War and since.

Anti-colonial nationalism

In the nineteenth century, nationalism began to develop beyond Europe, initially in the old empires of the European powers, where generations of settlers had created their own way of life and aspired to be free from the tutelage of the 'mother country'. Sometimes this was done by agreement, as with Australia and Canada, but sometimes it involved 'wars of liberation', as with the

Spanish colonies of South and Central America.

Anti-Europeanism

However, the 'right of self-determination' was only considered appropriate for those of European stock. It was not for non-Europeans, no matter how ancient and venerable their civilizations were. Those parts of the world not already under the control of Europeans were to be divided up among the European powers as either new colonies or spheres of influence. Ancient civilizations like China and Japan were humiliated and forced to cede trading rights and in some cases territories (Hong Kong was the last remnant of this). Anti-colonialist nationalism of the twentieth century is, as a consequence, anti-European nationalism.

The first non-European country to develop a nationalism in reaction to, and imitation of, the European model was Japan. It developed a particularly right-wing and aggressive variety as many were to find to their cost in the course of the following century. But Japan was a somewhat unusual case in that it was a united, proud and warlike people affronted by foreign arrogance (this was similar to the German reaction to Napoleonic invasion). It imported Western technology and Western ideas in order to preserve its identity, and in so doing became the first non-Western nation state. This was achieved by the existing feudal aristocracy, which thereby retained its dominance in Japanese society. In China, however, foreign humiliations led to the collapse of the old Chinese empire and its replacement by a new nationalist government in 1911, led by Sun Yat Sen.

However, the more usual pattern of emergent nationalism has been one of reaction to European colonization, where the colonists were a small elite. In the case of much of Africa and the Middle East, the patterns of political boundaries imposed by colonial powers were entirely arbitrary, bearing little relation to the locations of indigenous populations, and often making traditional enemies part of the same political unit. Nigeria, for example, was made up of over 200 linguistic groups, with several religions and other cultural differences. Sometimes the imposition of these boundaries led eventually to civil war, as happened in Sudan, Nigeria and what is now Zaire. What was to unite all the indigenous groups in such situations was resentment of the common European enemy. At the same time, it was the Europeans who were to provide the local nationalists with all the tools for their eventual overthrow.

In the first place, there was the modernisation that could make a post-colonial state viable: a centralised administration, communications, industry, an education system, and so on. Secondly, there were European ideas of nationalism and human rights, as well as theories of imperialism and exploitation that could be turned against the Europeans.

It was in the more developed parts of Asia, such as Japan, India and China that nationalist movements developed first. India was different from Japan or China, in that it had a more mixed population and was under direct British rule. Nationalism grew up, not amongst the traditional ruling class, still less the ordinary people, but among the Europeanised middle class that had grown up under European rule and had benefited most from it.

Indian nationalism

Indian nationalism saw its early development in the late nineteenth century, but developed into a significant political movement in the years following the First World War. One of its most striking features was its pacifism. Traditional pacifistic influences included Buddhism and Jainism, as well as the example of the great Emperor Ashoka of the third century BC, who abjured war and violence as instruments of policy. This strand of Indian tradition was brought out by the movement's remarkable leader Mohandas Gandhi (1869–1948) (although he was also influenced by Western pacifists like Thoreau and Tolstoy). Gandhi was often known as 'the Mahatma' ('man of great soul') because of his saintliness. He refused to countenance the terrorist methods some nationalists urged upon him. Non-violent civil disobedience was his preferred method, emphasising the moral strength of the cause in contrast to those who opposed it (which influenced later leaders like Martin Luther King).

In nationalism in general there is often a conflict between tradition and modernisation. Gandhi was predominantly a traditionalist. He did not want India to industrialise, but wanted an India based on the traditional village with its agriculture and craft industries. On the other hand, he also believed that independence must be linked with social reform to overcome inter-communal conflict and the problem of the 'untouchables' (that is, the despised outcasts of the caste system). Jawaharlal Nehru (1889–1964), who became India's first prime minister and founder of a ruling dynasty (his daughter was Indira Gandhi), was a moderniser and a socialist who wanted industrialisation and a planned economy.

Indian nationalists did not exploit Britain's weakened position during the war, but when it was over nationalism had become a force that could no longer be controlled. Independence came in 1947, but the new India could not hold together. It split amidst horrifying communal violence, of which Gandhi himself was a victim. The main conflict was between Hindus and Muslims, resulting in the setting up of the states of India (predominantly Hindu but with substantial Muslim and other minorities), and the Muslim state of Pakistan.

African nationalism

The new European colonial empires of the late nineteenth century in Africa experienced their first stirrings of nationalist feeling around the beginning of the century in the west and south (what became the African National Congress or ANC, for example, was founded in South Africa in 1912). Initially nationalist movements were often concerned with greater democracy and better living conditions for indigenous peoples under the colonial regimes. Later, mostly after the First World War, they became dedicated to the cause of national independence. During these years pan-Africanism (see p.96 below) was influential, and the notion of 'negritude', an early version of Black Consciousness, was developed (see Chapter 9).

It was only after the Second World War that nationalism became a major force in most of these countries. It was then that new nationalist parties were founded or re-founded. They were usually led by Western-educated elites, who often had little commitment to traditional cultures. They were bent on modernisation and were often influenced by socialist ideas, which they sought to adapt to African conditions. Mainly in the 1960s, Britain, France, Holland, Belgium, and eventually Portugal, all gave independence to millions of square miles of colonial territory, with greater or lesser degrees of agreement or violence.

Anti-imperialism

Often these liberation struggles, both in Africa and Asia, were caught up in the wider conflicts of the Cold War and many of the new regimes were Communist, although wedded to nationalist aspirations and modernisation rather than to the world proletarian cause.

Communists promoted the view that formal independence did not mean genuine freedom or self-determination. Imperialism, it was argued, was more subtle and operated through trade agreements and aid, which exploited the former colonial world just as effectively as under direct rule. This theory drew on Lenin's analysis of imperialism as a global extension of the capitalist system (see Chapter 7), which sees the problems of new nations as rooted in capitalist exploitation and the determination of Western capitalism to keep the rest of the world in thrall. Whatever the merits and demerits of this theory, many of these new states are now poverty-stricken and hopelessly dependent on the West.

Most of the successful independence movements aspired to create new states on the European model, with all the symbols of national status: flags and anthems, a modern administration, modern armed services, a national airline and a seat at the United Nations, and so on. However, in some cases modernisation has created a Westernised middle class and a large urban population that is dependent on imports of both consumer goods and food supplies, with old tribal loyalties and ways of life broken up and unable to sustain the country in food. This was true of many former colonial territories in black Africa and the Arab north. This situation was sustainable as long as aid flowed in and international trade was buoyant. But economic problems in the West during the 1970s and early 1980s left such countries stranded in a no man's land between traditional cultures that were no longer viable and an equally unviable modern state.

Such countries were encouraged to borrow from the West, but huge rises in interest rates during the series of economic recession since the 1970s left many of these countries with mountainous debts that they cannot possibly repay. India was more fortunate. After an initial drive to industrialisation which, like many newly independent states attempting to follow the Western path to prosperity, failed to come up to expectations, India switched resources into improving agriculture in the late 1950s. This has helped to make India self-sufficient and relatively prosperous (at least until the late 1980s), while many countries are beset with insoluble economic problems. The burden of debt to the West is one of the reasons for the rise of anti-Western religious fundamentalism in some Third World countries.

Many people see solutions to these problems in a growing internationalism, the growth of a self-conscious world community where such problems are seen as world problems. However, first we will consider pan-nationalism.

Pan-nationalism

The idea of pan-nationalism is that nation-states may participate in or even be subsumed under, a higher unity based upon ethnic, religious, geographical or other common features. Pan-nationalism today is very much part of anti-colonial nationalist ideas. However, the first pan-nationalist movements grew within the context of nineteenth century European nationalism. These were the pan-Slavonic, pan-Germanic and Scandinavian movements.

Pan movements in Europe

Pan-Slavism was the earliest of these movements, developing among various Slav nations within the Austro-Hungarian and Turkish empires during the 1830s and 1840s. Among its theorists was a Slovak Protestant minister, Jan Koller (1793–1852), who saw the Slavs fundamentally as a single people with a common cultural heritage. He thought, therefore, that Slavs should strive to end their fragmentation and seek spiritual and political unity, which was the key to the Slavs achieving their potential greatness.

The first All-Slav Congress was held in 1848. However, the movement was soon taken over by Russians, becoming an expression of Russian imperialist ambitions to extend their empire to Constantinople and the Balkans, in the name of Slav freedom. The movement died out towards the end of the century, although much later the USSR revived ideas of this kind to help the Communists justify their empire in Eastern Europe.

Pan-German thought was similar; in the late nineteenth century German unification was seen as merely a step in the creation of a greater Germany, to include the Austrians and all other German speakers. However, in the pan-Germanic case there was much more an element of dominating neighbouring peoples among whom ethnic Germans had settled, and pan-Germanicism drew on the aggressive nationalist and racist ideas of the late nineteenth century (see Chapter 9). Pan-German ideas have been discredited by German expansionism in two world wars.

'Scandinavianism' was initially a cultural movement inspired by Romantic ideas in the early nineteenth century, but the military defeat of Denmark by Prussia and Austria in 1864 led to calls for a political union of Norway, Sweden and Denmark. Although this did not happen, various Scandinavian organisations of economic and political co-operation have developed during the twentieth century.

In 1923 a pan-European Union was founded in Vienna by private initiative. The idea was that Europe had been fragmented after the First World War and that it needed unity in the face of the Bolshevic threat. The movement aimed to bring together the states of Europe in greater economic and political co-operation with the ultimate aim of creating a United States of Europe. The movement faded away in the 1930s, but was clearly a precursor of the post-war European movement.

Pan-African and Arab movements

Just as the Slav and Germanic versions of pan-nationalism grew out of the nationalism of their time and place, so Arab and African pan-nationalism grew out of anti-colonial nationalism after the Second World War. A growing nationalism in Africa and in the Arab North were both accompanied by the feeling that the territories into which such nationalisms were channelled, and which formed the basis of the new states, were entirely artificial and alien impositions by colonial powers, which in fact hampered the development of the peoples which such boundaries divided. It was felt that the populations of the whole of Africa or of the whole of the Arab world had more in common than the populations within particular states. The hope was that increasing co-operation among African or among Arab states would eventually lead to a dissolving of colonial boundaries to create a new and stronger unity.

Ideas of pan-Africanism were first put forward by former slaves in America and the Caribbean at the end of the nineteenth century. The movement held its first congress in 1900 in London. However, these ideas were more important in their areas of origin than in Africa itself until after the Second World War. The idea was that all the indigenous peoples, including the Arabs in the North, had a common heritage and therefore a common political identity and destiny. It was taken up by nationalist politicians seeking independence for their colonies, who saw opportunities to forge common links and mutual support among groups otherwise divided by race, religion or by the culture of the different colonial powers (that is, there was a certain commonality among English-speaking or French-speaking colonies, and so on).

In 1963 the Organisation of African Unity (OAU) was founded in Addis Ababa. However, despite the efforts of some enthusiasts its role and aims were modest. It was and remains a forum for discussion and co-operation among African states (excluding racist states such as South Africa). The impulse to create a genuine pan-African integration diminished as more and more states became independent.

Pan-Arabism had better chances of succeeding in creating significant political structures than pan-Africanism, if only because the Arab people had a greater homogeneity and sense of common heritage. The movement had an organisation, the Arab League and also a cause in the destruction of Israel and restoration of the Palestinian homeland. The Arab League was founded in 1945 and imposed upon its members the duty of integrating foreign policy and settling disputes between members by reference to the League.

Furthermore, the movement for some time had a charismatic leader in Gamal Abdel Nasser, President of Egypt, victor of Suez and symbol of Arab unity from Morocco to the Persian Gulf. Since Egypt had a stronger sense of national identity than most Arab states, Nasser was inclined to see the future of the Arabs as a series of independent socialist states working closely together under Egyptian leadership. The alternative vision, of a single socialist state embracing all Arabs, was put forward by the Ba'ath parties found in most of the other Middle Eastern states.

Islamic fundamentalism always offered an alternative to pan-Arabism and was often in conflict with it. Islamic fundamentalism tends to be traditionalist, while the pan-nationalists tended to be modernising, westernising and secular (see Chapter 11). In the 1950s and 1960s the centre of Islam was Saudi Arabia and in 1962 its religious leaders proclaimed socialism to be incompatible with Islam. This condemned both Nasser and the Ba'ath parties, who in turn condemned the conservative Saudi regime as corrupt and reactionary.

Ba'athism

One of the most dynamic expressions of Pan-Arabism has been the Ba'ath movement, founded after the Second World War when most of the Arab lands (except for Saudi Arabia) were either European colonies or under some other form of European tutelage. 'Ba'ath' in Arabic means 'renaissance', and the movement sought a re-birth of the Arabs as a single modern nation. Ba'athism essentially combined Pan-Arabism and a socialism that borrowed and adapted a number of theoretical and organisational elements from Communism.

The Ba'ath slogan is 'Unity, Freedom and Socialism'. Unity is conceived in terms of uniformity of outlook and purpose, the melding of all individuality into a single united mass with a single national will. That will is represented by the party, which thereby has the right to control everything: government, the economy, education, the media and all other aspects of national life. This is the socialist element of Ba'athism, although the Ba'ath Party represents no particular social class, in the sense of proletarian or peasant, although the ordinary masses are seen to be nearer the heart of the Arab nation because of their experience of oppression and suffering. It is their interests that the Ba'ath can alone represent.

The Ba'ath movement rejects the Western sense of the term 'freedom' as being connected with capitalist selfishness and exploitation. The individual finds fulfilment and self-realisation, and therefore true freedom, by identifying with the mass. The mass finds self-realisation and true freedom in the self-determination of the nation. To achieve this the masses, led by the Ba'ath Party, must overthrow the enemies of the nation – imperialism, Zionism, and reaction among traditional Arab ruling elites – and overcome the divisions of the Arab nation which they have imposed or perpetuated. Ba'athism grew in the 1950s and early 1960s and had parties in the various countries of the Middle East. Today there are only two countries with significant Ba'ath parties, Syria and Iraq, and in both cases they are the instruments of totalitarian tyrannies of great ruthlessness. That Ba'athism has lost its initial idealism is clear from the fact that Presidents Assad of Syria and Saddam Hussein of Iraq are long-time enemies (Assad joined the coalition against Iraq in the 1991 Gulf War). Insofar as Ba'athism still has a connection with pan-Arabism it is in providing the ideological underpinnings to Assad and Hussein's imperial ambitions. Assad wishes to control Lebanon, and perhaps Jordan, destroy Israel, become the dominant power in the Middle East and the recognised leader of the Arab world. Hussein wanted as much and more. His invasion of Kuwait in 1990 would seem to have been part of a wider strategy to become a world power. Controlling the oil fields of Kuwait and possibly Saudi Arabia, and possessed of a nuclear arsenal, he would have been in a position to destroy Israel and become the ruler, and not merely leader of the Arabs. The Gulf War of 1991 put a stop to the ambitions, although he remained in power in Iraq.

The Ba'ath movement is perhaps still the main representative of pan-Arabism today, although the likelihood of it succeeding in bringing about the merging of states seems remote. On a more pragmatic level, the Arab League is still a major vehicle of Arab unity and co-operation, much more so than the Organisation of African Unity. But, like the OAU, the Arab League is more an instrument of regional co-operation, and comes under the category of 'internationalism', than a serious repository of supra-national aspiration and identity. In the 1980s and early 1990s pan-Arabism became less significant in the Arab world than Islamic fundamentalism.

The coherence and autonomy of nationalism

Nationalism is the simplest and most powerful of ideologies, but intellectually the weakest. This is because the central concept upon which the ideology is based is quite remarkably vague and difficult to pin down.

What is a nation?

The French revolutionaries had little trouble in identifying the French nation, since France had been probably the most unified and homogenous people in Europe for many hundreds of years. But in much of Europe, and most of the rest of the world, national identity has had to be created. This has involved much symbolism of flags and anthems and parades and national teams, the creation of a national history and culture, with national heroes and myths of national birth and struggle, and so forth. These things are very familiar to us in the modern world. Yet however familiar they may be, they do not tell us much about what nationality is and by what means we can recognise it.

The question is, what exactly constitutes a nation? By what criteria can we unambiguously identify a candidate for nation-statehood? It might be thought that a certain ethnic homogeneity would be a necessary condition. After all we think of the Chinese and Poles and Egyptians as definite ethnic entities that form 'natural' states. But then, many nations are ethnically mixed. Indeed, the USA, which on some reckonings is the most successful of modern nation-states, has the most mongrel of populations and has seen this as a source of strength.

Another significant criterion is a shared language. But again, there are many counter-examples. The case usually cited is Switzerland, where the Swiss most definitely regard themselves as a distinct nation of long standing, and yet they speak four separate languages: French, German, Italian and Romanche. Several hundred languages are spoken in India, yet most Indians see themselves as one people.

What, then, makes a nation? The answer would seem to be that a people sees itself, or feels itself, to be a nation, because of a shared history and language, and whatever other reasons. Theoretically this is not very precise or satisfactory. It cannot, for example, decide questions where it is a matter of dispute as to who does or does not belong to the nation, or (as with Northern Irish Protestants) one part of the nation refuses to identify with another part. Nevertheless, the highly subjective criteria of what a body of people perceive themselves to be is about the best defining characteristic of nationhood we have.

The viability of states

However, even if we were able to identify unambiguously 'natural' national units, there is no guarantee that they would be suitable for states. A state needs a national economy sufficiently autonomous that it is not dependent on others. But if a people or its territory are too small for a state to be viable, what then?

At the other end of the scale, the phenomenon of pan-nationalism illustrates some of the theoretical problems arising from nationalism as such. For example, are the existing Slav states the appropriate political units for these peoples, or should the smaller ethnic groups, such as Slovaks and Slovenes and many more, each have their own state? Or should the whole of the Slav-speaking peoples be the natural political unit? The Soviet Union, as was, may yet shatter into literally hundreds of national fragments.

The autonomy of nationalism

A further problem of nationalism is illustrated by the Arabs. Pan-Arab nationalism was seen as a secular modernising force by most of its proponents, who wanted to see the Arabs as a major force in the modern world. But there were also those who saw modernity in terms of an alien Westernisation that was destroying the essence of Arab culture and identity. The often acute conflict between tradition and modernisation has been a common feature of nationalist movements since the nineteenth century.

The question is, of course, bound up with the kind of society nationalists in any given situation want their nation to have. This in turn leads to questions concerning the relationship between nationalism and other systems of belief which are more concerned with these matters. At various times and places nationalism has been associated with liberalism, conservatism, various forms of socialism, and even Marxism, which on the face of it is an antinationalist doctrine. The reason for this is that the core ideas of nationalism as such say nothing about how society ought to be organised. That is, it fails to answer the questions that we normally expect an ideology to answer. It needs, therefore, to be supplemented by other ideologies that do answer those questions of social organisation.

Is, therefore, nationalism a complete and autonomous ideology? It is not clear that this question can be answered conclusively. On the one hand, we might say that ideologies are about priorities in respect of values, and that for the nationalist, as long as the nation is united and independent, questions of what kind of social system or government the nation has are secondary. (Something similar might be said of other ideologies, for example, feminism.) On the other hand, virtually all expressions of nationalism are normally associated with some other ideological doctrine, which becomes essential once independence has been achieved. On balance the second seems the stronger argument, suggesting a category of 'partial ideologies'.

But for all its inadequacies as a doctrine, nationalism is still an immensely powerful force is the world. Many have seen it as an irrational and destructive force that needs to be countered within a wider vision and organization.

Internationalism, federalism and conflict

The twentieth century has been an extraordinarily violent one, with world wars and a multitude of lesser conflicts, terrorism and the threat of nuclear annihilation, all involving total populations in a way unknown in the past. The greatest single cause of this violence has been nationalism in various forms. It is not surprising, therefore, if some have come to see nationalism as a curse of mankind, and have sought to develop an antidote to it in various forms of internationalism. The first priority of the advocates of internationalism is the prevention of war. There is wide agreement as to the need for some international body that can ensure this, although the practical difficulties are immense. The much larger issue of the possibility of a world government is a very different matter, which many regard as a mere fantasy.

International organisations

The First World War was called 'the war to end all war', and in its aftermath it was hoped that institutions would be set up to prevent future wars through international agreement, co-operation and mediation. The peace conference at Versailles duly created the League of Nations, but this was a failure.

After the Second World War there was initially more hope. The United Nations (UN) was established in 1945, but the hopes and ideals which attended its creation were defeated by the coming of the Cold War. It became a battleground for super-power rivalry, and could do little unless both were in accord. Consequently, it failed to stop major conflicts like the Korean and Vietnam wars. However, it has proved a useful forum for debate, a sometimes powerful instrument of international co-operation in areas like health, and an extremely useful neutral broker and arbitrator on lesser disputes.

What is interesting is the possible development of the UN, given the collapse of European Communism and the end of the Cold War. The Gulf War of 1991 was an extraordinary display of international co-operation to reverse the conquest of a tiny nation. President Bush of the US spoke of a 'new world order', of world peace and co-operation, and this would certainly enhance the role of the UN. However, whether this would amount to a move towards world government is another matter. There are certainly many who would wish such a move.

Liberals in particular have always set great store by the idea. Nineteenth-century liberals believed passionately that free trade would bring people together and be a great force for peace. However, that hope proved a false one, and the prospect of world government still looks distinctly unlikely.

The problem lies in the enforcement of international law. At present there are world courts, such as the International Court of Justice at The Hague, which make judgements against states, but if a state chooses to ignore this, then there is not much anyone can do about it. Any world government would have to have some kind of police and armed forces to enforce its decrees, and existing states would have to submit to them or suffer the consequences. There seems little likelihood of that. For one thing, the notion of the state and its sovereignty, bound up as it is with notions of national independence, is an extremely powerful one that will only be given up with the greatest reluctance.

Regional integration

On the other hand, these factors seems less powerful than they were even a few years ago. The collapse of European Communism and the ending of the Cold War has ended a seemingly permanent rigidity in international affairs, the consequences of which may take some time to work themselves out. Even so, if there are moves towards world government it seems highly unlikely that they will come directly. It is much more likely to come from groups of countries working together and building up links and networks of co-operation out of which the need for supra-national government will grow. There are various co-operative groupings in different regions of the world, but by far the most important development in this direction is the European Community.

Our present world of independent nation-states, jealously guarding their sovereignty and answerable to no one, is very much a product of European thought and political development. There is, therefore, a certain appropriateness in Europe leading the way in exploring the possibilities of transcending the modern state. Two world wars, while they dragged in much of the rest of the world, were essentially European wars and were a culmination of centuries of warfare between nation-states. The escalating horror and destructiveness of modern warfare has made possibile bringing together the states of Europe in a union strong enough to prevent war, a persistent dream of statesmen and thinkers for two hundred years or more. After the Second World War Europe had to be rebuilt, old hatreds buried and an integrated Western

Europe established as a defence against the threat from the East. Because the community was an economic success, the original six countries who signed the Treaty of Rome in 1956 attracted new members. They now stand at twelve, but with a queue of potential members at the door.

Although long known as the European Common Market, the ambitions of its founders and advocates have never been confined to creating a free trade area and this is clear from the institutions of Commission, Parliament and Council of Ministers. There have always been those whose ideal has been a United States of Europe with a federal government. During the 1960s and 1970s new members were absorbed into the established system, while the 1980s have been characterised by a fresh impetus towards greater integration, hence the significance of '1992' and the proposal for a common currency leading to a common economic policy. The latter is seen as a major step towards political integration and a federal government.

Such a step has its sceptics and the debate over a common currency has sharply divided federalists from those who wanted essentially just a free trade area and greater co-operation between members of a club of forever-sovereign states (most notable among the latter in the UK are Lady Thatcher and some of her colleagues). The future development of the EC is therefore very much bound up with nationalism. There are British objections to closer political union on the one hand, but on the other, some see EC federalism as a counter to a future resurgence of German nationalism. However, recent evidence of federalism being an effective check on upon nationalism is not encouraging.

Federalism

Federalism is a form of government where a great deal of power, including legislative power, is devolved to federated units in a way that is guaranteed by the constitution. Legal sovereignty is divided so that neither the centre or the units can unilaterally change the relationship. This is in contrast to, say, local government in Britain (or even proposed schemes of devolution to Scotland and

Wales), where Parliament can change powers and structure at any time. The powers of the federated units may be set out in detail (for example, the right to control education), but in cases such as the USA the powers of the federal government are specified and the states have rights in every other area.

Federal systems have been introduced to limit the power of the centre (the USA and Germany) and to deal with great distances (Australia), but federalism has also been seen as a way of overcoming problems of nationality within states. We tend to think of the nation state as the norm, and certainly the overwhelming majority of nationalities, however small, want and feel entitled to run their own affairs. However, for a multiplicity of historical and other reasons a great many states contain one or more minority nationalities. A great many of these states would disintegrate if all nationalities had their own state, many of which would simply not be viable. Besides, some territories may be disputed between one or more nationalities, and there may be differences between members of the same nationality.

Federalism can be seen as a partial answer to some of these problems. A national minority may be accorded a degree of independence within a federal system that may satisfy national aspirations and give greater security. Or a group of nationalities may each be too small to be the basis of a viable nation-state and may join together in a federal system that does constitute a viable state, while at the same time respecting the individuality of the constituent nations.

However, federal states that give autonomy to national groups have not been notably successful. Least successful have been the Communist federal systems. Most striking in recent years has been the almost tidal wave of nationalism generated by the collapse of European Communism. Not only has there been the reassertion of national independence of Eastern European states, but the Soviet Union itself has disintegrated and may fragment further into a host of mini- and micro-nationalisms. The result may be bloodshed, as in Yugoslavia where an appalling civil war has been the dreadful consequence of the collapse of the Communist regime. Nationalism in Eastern European countries had been suppressed by the totalitarian Communist regimes, but with the weakening of that iron grip, nationalism has re-emerged, with all the ethnic rivalries, hatreds and conflicts that go with it.

Federal systems involving national differences have not been entirely successful in the West either. The largest example is India. Here there is a multitude of nationalities, and India has been a relatively successful state. But there are now great strains. The Sikhs are only one of several nationalities who want their own independent state, and there is growing violence. Even Canada, one of the most peaceful and prosperous states of the modern world, is in imminent danger of breaking up because of the demands of the French Canadians for their own state, despite a considerable degree of autonomy under the present federal system.

It would seem that federalism can be successful as a device for limiting central government, although in many cases power has gravitated towards the centre over time (for example in the USA and Australia, although not in Canada or Switzerland). It would appear to be rather less successful in coping with nationalism.

Nationalism and conflict

This has a bearing on the European Community beyond the present issue of governmental integration. Even while the European Community was developing in the 1960s, there was a resurgence of nationalism in the settled states of Western Europe. From 1968 we saw the violent emergence of minority communities in several countries determined upon independence or unification: Basques in Spain, the Republicans in Northern Ireland, the Corsicans in France. Other nationalities began to assert themselves by more conventional and constitutional means: including the Scots and Welsh in the UK, Bretons in France, and Catalans in Spain. The existence of an EC framework has encouraged such national minorities to seek independence within the EC. It could be that if the EC strengthened its centre, the nation-state would weaken.

Nationalism has an almost endless capacity to generate conflict and violence, as is apparent from any survey of the world's violent trouble spots. The present and former Communist world apart, we might consider the Middle East, the Punjab and Sri Lanka, Northern Ireland, Iraq and Northern Spain, among other areas, to see nationalism creating conflict. It is nationalism (whether combined with religion or other political ideologies or not) that is the most potent source of terrorism in the modern world.

There are hopeful signs that internationalism and regional integration will lessen the prospect of wars, but nobody can say that these will not be undermined by the power of nationalism.

5

Varieties of socialism

Of all ideologies socialism is perhaps the most difficult to pin down. Debates among socialists about what constitutes 'true socialism' are notoriously indecisive, long-lasting and bitter. We are well advised to take the view that there is no such essential socialism and that we must accept all varieties short of the plainly outlandish, although this position can also have its problems as we shall see.

Trying to classify the different types of socialism is a difficult exercise and what follows does involve some groupings and labels not usually made, but none should be taken entirely seriously. For clarity's sake Marxist theory is dealt with separately in a later chapter, as are various versions of socialistic anarchism.

Primitive and classical socialisms

It will be useful, first of all, to distinguish between socialism as a modern, fully-developed ideology and what might be called 'primitive socialisms'.

From time to time in human thought – usually in periods of upheaval and social distress – there have been those who have offered the view that mankind's problems could be solved if only wealth and poverty were eliminated and the goods of the world more fairly shared amongst all. Ideas of this kind appeared, for instance, during the period of the Reformation, the English Civil

War and the French Revolution.

Babeuvism

It was entirely appropriate that socialism should make an appearance on the stage of the French Revolution, along with all the other ideologies that were to dominate the nineteenth century, even though its contribution to the ideas of the time was brief and insubstantial. It made its appearance shortly after the Jacobins had fallen from power and their radical democratic constitution replaced by one that gave power to the better-off who dominated the new government. François-Emile 'Gracchus' Babeuf was a Jacobin sympathiser who had escaped the purge that followed their fall. He came to the conclusion that the radical Jacobin programme to make all Frenchmen free and equal could be accomplished by an abolition of property.

To this end, Babeuf planned a seizure of power by himself and his followers, who called themselves the 'Conspiracy of the Equals'. They would then set up a dictatorship for the purpose of seizing all wealth and redistributing it on an equal basis. It would be a policy enforced by a reign of terror even more ferocious than that of Robespierre.

However, Babeuf revealed little as to how his ideal society would be organised, or how long the revolutionary dictatorship might be necessary, or what freedom individuals would have. The influential aspect of Babeuf's thinking was his notion of how to seize power and then use it. He had very modern ideas as to how to stage a coup in a planned and professional way, much copied up to our own time, while his idea of a revolutionary dictatorship influenced Marx, Lenin and many other revolutionaries. But as a theorist of socialism, Babeuf really belongs among the primitives. He had no developed theory of the nature and necessity of a socialist society. Modern socialism, as a fully developed ideology is better understood as a product of that other great revolution of the age, the industrial revolution.

Classical socialism

Modern socialism developed in the early nineteenth century as a response to the social impact of industrialisation. The factories destroyed many people's livelihoods, forced them to work immensely long hours for starvation wages and live in the vilest conditions in the new industrial towns. At the same time, the attempts of working people to organise in order to improve their conditions were made illegal and brutally suppressed. In Britain particularly, where industrial development was far ahead of the rest of the world, there were strikes and industrial unrest, as well as much nostalgia for a disappearing world. Working-class discontent was used to press for parliamentary reform, widely offered by radicals as the solution to all ills.

The authentic socialist note was struck by those who argued that what people were really suffering from was not the greed of individual employers, nor a conspiracy of the ruling class, but the nature of the capitalist system itself. It was, they argued, a system that had exploitation built into it, and a system which could be replaced by a better one in which the evils of capitalism would be ended for good and a new system of co-operation, harmony and justice put in its place.

The evils of capitalism

There are many varieties of this kind of socialist thinking, often claiming to be the 'true' socialism compared with rivals. The easiest and clearest way to give an initial characterisation of socialism as such, that can embrace different varieties, is to say what socialism is, and consequently what, in broad terms, a socialist society would be without. What links all socialists is the belief that capitalism is bad, and that unrestrained capitalism necessarily produces certain evil social consequences, including the following:

- Capitalism necessarily produces the class system, which is socially divisive and sets class against class. Inequality means unnecessary and unjust differences between rich and poor, which involve differences of wealth, power and opportunity. A situation is created in which some people have power over the lives of others. It is a system that is based on exploitation, in which the workers who create the wealth are denied their fair share of it. And inequality is perpetuated from one generation to the next through inheritance.

- It is also a system that is profoundly inefficient. People suffer poverty, unemployment and squalor because of the blind workings of a system over which they have no control (such as with the 'trade cycle'). Production is for profit instead of for use. For example, the consumer society produces useless but profitable products, while people's needs are not met where it is not profitable to do so.
- Finally, the capitalist system has a deleterious effect on human nature, bringing out the worst in people and suppressing the best. It tends to make people competitive, greedy, selfish and ruthless. Important human values, such as co-operation and compassion, are suppressed or distorted by greed. Everyone is out for themselves and that sense of community, which human beings need, is undermined.

It should be noted that these criticisms of capitalism are a combination of the ethical and the practical. Capitalism is bad because it is unjust: people are robbed of the proper reward for their work because it is appropriated as profit. The few, therefore, appropriate the wealth that others produce and live in luxury, while the many live poor and diminished lives. The system is simply unfair. And if it is argued that it is perfectly fair that success and its rewards should properly go to those with energy and talent, it rapidly becomes unfair once the first generation pass on their wealth and privileges to their heirs.

The moral case against capitalism continues with a different set of arguments to do with the impact of capitalism upon human nature. Capitalism is powered by a selfish individualism. It is the law of the jungle; a war of all against all. This makes people greedy, selfish, grasping and cruel. It brings out the worst in people and suppresses the best. One might even say that because it is so at odds with human nature, capitalism is 'unnatural' and therefore wrong.

Thirdly, capitalism is wrong on practical grounds. It is wasteful and inefficient: it cannot effectively do what an economy properly exists to do. The waste of capitalism is most strikingly seen in the periodic slumps to which the free market is subject. Goods go unsold, people are out of work, factories and machinery lie idle. Nobody wants any of this and yet it is apparently unavoidable. The trouble is that goods are only produced for profit, instead of in a properly planned manner to cater for people's real needs.

In modern society we are encouraged to spend money on an endless array of objects that we do not really want and certainly do not need. At the same time many people's genuine needs (for better housing, clothing and so forth) are ignored because supplying them cheaply cannot be done profitably. A perfect example of the capitalist outlook and its alternative arose during the 1984–85 miner's strike. The National Coal Board's position was roughly thus. There are a certain number of pits in operation, some of which are profitable, some break even and some lose money. The loss-making pits put up the average price of coal, which makes it harder to sell and harder for the industry to be successful. By closing unprofitable pits the industry will be more competitive, efficient and successful and will be able to offer its miners a secure future. Arthur Scargill's argument was that there was a need for coal. Every winter old-age pensioners suffer from hypothermia because they cannot pay their heating bills. If they cannot afford the coal then it should be given to them. We had in this instance two diametrically opposed arguments, one characteristically capitalist, the other characteristically socialist.

The socialist alternative

The only real alternative to a capitalist society is a fully socialist one, which would have the following features:

- There would be common ownership of the economy, with little or no private property. There would therefore be no class system and no one would have the means to exploit anyone else.

- There would be equality of wealth, and therefore of power and opportunity.
- Production would be for use and not for profit, while competition would be replaced by co-operation. The competitive free-for-all would be replaced by planning.
- Everyone would work for the community and contribute to the common good; society would be based on the principle, in Marx's words, of 'from each according to his ability, to each according to his need'.
- Human nature would flourish, no longer distorted by poverty or greed, and a society would develop in which the goods of the world were freely shared and where everyone cared for each other.

It should be noted that this picture rests on certain assumptions that are not always made explicit and may be difficult to accept. It assumes that human character is essentially good and that the evils of the world – such as poverty, crime, cruelty, ignorance and war – are not due to any evil inherent in human nature, but to the workings of the system in which human beings find themselves. Change the system in the right way and human nature as we know it will improve. There is the further assumption that famine and scarcity are also the result of the 'system' and not in the nature of things. If only the economy were properly organised and planned there would be abundance for all.

These complimentary accounts of capitalism and socialism are of course only skeletal and can be filled out in an infinity of ways, many of which may contradict. This criticism of capitalism, and this vision of the ideal society which would follow its elimination, was shared by all varieties of socialists until at least the 1940s (although for some of them it was a very long term ideal). It will be convenient to label it 'classical socialism' to distinguish it not only from primitive socialism, but also from those more recent versions of socialism that ceased to see the elimination of capitalism and its replacement by a fully socialist society as essential to their programme.

These later versions of socialism developed after the Second World War. Needless to say, believers in classical socialism are inclined to view their exponents as not true socialists at all. This is an issue we will return to; in the meantime we need to examine the development and the variety of classical socialism.

Utopian socialists

Once Europe had settled down following the Revolutionary and Napoleonic Wars, pressure for political change came principally from liberals and nationalists. Socialism began to develop where industrialisation was creating a new working class. This was true of Britain more than anywhere else, but it was also true of France, which had its own tradition of working-class revolutionary participation in the sans-culotte support for the Jacobins. However, this was largely confined to Paris.

Early socialism in Britain

It was different in Britain where the industrial revolution was gathering momentum and its social impact was far greater and apparent to all. Here was the greatest exploitation, the worst working conditions, the greatest misery, and also the most developed working-class movement. There was a good deal of working-class activity accompanied by a good deal of socialist agitation in the form of speeches, pamphlets and so on condemning the capitalist system and demanding redistribution of wealth in various forms. The crucial message to be put across to people suffering exploitation was that their troubles were not the result so much of greedy and rapacious employers, as the nature of the system they represented, and that capitalism was an evil that could be replaced by something better. Sometimes this took the form of schemes suggesting alternative possibilities, such as producer or consumer co-operatives that would prove more efficient and humane and therefore ultimately replace capitalism.

One group of writers came to be called the Ricardian socialists, who took their name from their adaptation of the 'labour theory of value' of the classical economist David Ricardo. The theory says that the real value of an object is a function of the amount of labour that has gone into producing it. Ricardo drew no social, political or moral conclusions from his labour theory, being an ardent *laissez-faire* liberal himself. However, his labour theory could be interpreted differently from the way he chose. The Ricardian socialists argued that since the workers provided the value, that is the wealth, it was clearly unjust that they should gain so little while the capitalist claimed the lion's share.

The most notable Ricardian Socialist was Thomas Hodgskin (1787–1869). In his book, *Labour Defended Against the Claims of Capital* (1825), Hodgskin argued that there should be a radical redistribution of wealth in favour of those who create the wealth. The chief instrument for effecting this transformation, he thought, should be the trade unions. He though the working class should be independent and self-reliant; he had little faith in political action, and none at all in alliances with middle-class radicals, who were supported by most labour leaders at that time. However, it should be noted that he sought for a radical redistribution within the existing system. Capitalists, rather than capitalism, were the enemy. What he objected to was the capitalist who did nothing but put up money and take profit without actually contributing any work, which he regarded as a kind of usury. He had less objection to those that actually ran their factories.

Hodgskin's writings only had a limited impact, yet his ideas are important. He was not a classical socialist in the sense that he did not wish to replace capitalist society with a socialist one. But he did articulate an extremely important outlook in the working-class movement that remains strong to this day. It is sometimes termed 'labourism', that is, redistribution within the capitalist system in order to make that system more fair. It is essentially the politics of trade unionism.

Theory of a more comprehensive and systematic kind, with a view to a complete transformation of society, was more rare.

Modern socialist theory really begins with a group of individual, and very individualistic, thinkers who are generally regarded as more notable for their imagination than their practicality. Karl Marx dismissed them patronisingly as 'Utopian socialists' and the label has stuck. They were in some respects rather naive, yet they were not insignificant.

Saint-Simon and his followers

The first of these thinkers to develop his ideas was Henri de Saint-Simon (1760–1825). He had been born into a poorer branch of one of the most distinguished aristocratic families in France. He had fought in the American War of Independence and supported the French Revolution. But unlike many in the same position, he did not become a reactionary. He tended neither to the left nor to the right, but worked out his own unique conception of an ideal future. His ideas might be described as 'socialistic' (that is, having socialist features) rather than purely socialist, but he had a number of able followers who pursued his ideas in that direction.

Saint-Simon's imagination had been caught by the potential of industrialisation, and the possibilities this held out of a new civilisation based on harmony and abundance. He conceived of human history in terms of alternating periods of integration and change. The first he called 'organic periods' in which society and technology were matched and there was social peace. In between were revolutionary periods of technical change when change is resisted by the old order and society becomes unbalanced and prone to conflict. The French Revolution was a manifestation, not a cause of such a period of change. Saint-Simon looked forward to a time when present developments would result in a new society based on industry and science, and a more united and better organised society in a new organic period.

He thought that working out how this new society was to be achieved and sustained was a matter for intellectuals, who should work together in Academies of Science and Social Science and Arts, and advise governments on how to re-structure society on rational scientific lines. These intellectual elites would have the permanent duty of working for the good of society as a whole, so that their advice would be to the physical, intellectual and moral benefit of everyone, especially the poorest and most numerous classes. The elite would also control the compulsory educational system which would inculcate the principles of a scientific indus-trial civilisation upon the nation. Governments would have the duty of finding work for all inhabitants, who, in their turn, all had the duty of working for the common good.

There is not much that is democratic or egalitarian in all this. It is highly elitist and paternalistic. And while there would no longer be genuine poverty, there would certainly still be wealth. People would be rewarded according to their contribution to society. Everyone could make some contribution, though some people would contribute much more.

There is a sense in which Saint-Simon wanted to do away with politics and replace it with administration. Government would be conducted through an assembly of three chambers. The first would consist of engineers, artists and other creative people who would propose schemes for improvement, a second chamber of scientists would evaluate it, while a third, consisting of financiers and industrialists (there would still be capitalists, though not, it would seem, a free market) would supervise its implementation.

Saint-Simon's socialism was, therefore, limited. He thought people should have wealth and privilege if it was the proper reward for hard work and service to the community. He did not in fact object to individuals creating great wealth for themselves so long as all were properly cared for and equal opportunity was not impaired. It had to be recognized that wealth had social obliga-tions attached. He also foresaw a time when the economy would be taken out of politics and run by experts in a rational manner. He wanted to replace orthodox Christianity with a new religion of universal brotherhood. He was the first to insist that it was the duty of the state to care for the welfare of all its citizens.

Although Saint-Simon was only as it were a semi-socialist, his followers went further. They advocated state ownership of land and factories to ensure that Saint-Simon's ideals were fulfilled.

Charles Fourier

Charles Fourier (1772–1837) also had visions of a better ordered, harmonious and abundant society, the organisation of which he worked out in sometimes bizarre detail. He was a self-taught man who worked much of his life as a clerk. It was in his spare time that he allowed his vivid imagination (and his fantasies) full rein. He wrote much and had many followers.

He insisted that life and work had to be made pleasurable and happy. To achieve this, people should set up communities based on co-operation. Competition produced only waste and parasitism. In his co-operative communities, which he called phalanxes, means must be found for everyone to work in a productive, lucrative and fulfilling way. This did not mean that all such communities would be the same, nor the individuals who composed them. They could create wealth, so long as it was co-operatively done, and a decent standard of life was guaranteed for everyone.

For all the strangeness of some of Fourier's ideas, there is a very modern concern with the conditions of individual self-fulfilment. (The young Marx was similarly concerned with alienation around this time.) He believed that God's plan for mankind had clearly gone wrong if God was loving and caring and yet so much of mankind lived in misery. The key to human satisfaction was to do work that was satisfying and meaningful, that is, work in which individuals could be creative and express themselves. It should be various, social, involve the making of useful and/or beautiful things, require skill and craftsmanship, and be specially suited to each individual. Ideally people should live in the countryside, or at least in small towns. Either way, communities had to be small enough for everyone to know each other, yet large enough to be self-sufficient.

It was the business of the community to organise suitable, fulfilling work for everyone. The community also had the task of organising other aspects of human existence necessary to individual fulfilment. This included the individual's sexual life. Fourier was among the first to see liberation from repressive convention as an aspect of human liberation generally. In his ideal communities, therefore, sexual fulfilment went along with fulfilment through work.

Fourier's ideal communities, or phalanxes, would have a population of around 1,600 with around 5,000 acres of land. The phalansteres, or communal living units, would have common facilities, leisure areas and restaurants, although there would be no imposed use or other uniformity beyond the pressures of community opinion. People would have their own apartments and furniture, and could buy better ones. Better work would be rewarded and all would be able to invest savings in the businesses of the community and share in their profits. Such communities would be so attractive to live in, and their enterprises would be so much more efficient than capitalist ones, that more and more would develop as an alternative to capitalist society. Federations of communities would replace governments, possibly on a world scale. Thus would socialism emerge gently and democratically from below, with no revolution, no bloodshed and no conflict.

Fourier abominated the new industrialism, with its factories, its division of labour and its new industrial towns. It destroyed the pleasure of work, along with human individuality and natural sociability. Like Proudhon after him, essentially he wanted a more humane version of an older world of peasants and craftsmen, but without the oppression of the upper classes. He shunned the new world of science and industry that Saint-Simon embraced with enthusiasm.

Robert Owen

Robert Owen (1771–1858) was a third utopian socialist. He was far more practical than the other two, having come from humble origins he had become rich and successful in the cotton industry. He was part of the industrial revolution that was far more advanced, and developing much faster, in Britain than elsewhere. It was here that the working-class movement was growing and where the moral indictment of industrial capitalism was most fierce and alternatives most discussed. Owen was merely the most comprehensive and effective of the British socialist thinkers.

Owen came to prominence for his creation of the community at New Lanark, which he built up after taking control of the cotton mill in 1800, with its good quality housing, education and other facilities for the workers. Visitors came from all over to see the results, which flew in the face of the current wisdom that minimal wages were essential for maximum profit. However, New Lanark had less to do with socialism than with that enlightened paternalism that was later associated with the model communities of Victorian industrialists like Sir Titus Salt. Owen's ideas were set out in his writings such as *New View of Society* (1813) and *Address to the Inhabitants of New Lanark* (1816), in which he attacked the new factory system as practised by his fellow industrialists as selfish, stupid, inhuman and degrading of human character.

However, Owen moved progressively to the left in his thinking. He thought more and more in terms of working people creating their own solutions to problems. His success at New Lanark made it possible for Owen to be heard with respect in quarters no other socialist could reach, including Parliament. He advocated the setting up by government of 'Villages of Co-operation' as a solution to poverty. People should have a right to work, and the necessities of co-operation would be educative and morally improving.

But what was initially a solution to specific social ills, Owen developed into an alternative to present society. He advocated universal non-religious education and the gradual replacement of an industry based on competition to one based on co-operative principles, principles that could then be applied to the whole of society. As he began to advocate the building of a new secular society, the establishment lost interest in him, although he sent his schemes to the rulers of Europe. When that failed, he went to America to found his own co-operative community, New Harmony. It was not a success and he returned to England.

As with Fourier, Owen thought in terms of communities opting out of the new industrial system and creating industrial and agrarian villages based on principles of co-operation. Working men coming together to organise themselves was his ideal. He was behind various attempts to establish co-operative communities both in Britain and in America, as well as various attempts to create producer co-operatives; he was aslo deeply involved in the beginnings of the trade-union movement. He published books and newspapers (the word 'socialism' made its first appearance in an Owenite paper in 1827) and had many followers.

The importance of the utopian socialists

Owen's attempt to found a 'Grand National Moral Union of the Productive Classes', designed to lead working people away from the capitalist system by not co-operating with it, and towards a new society based on producer co-operation, ended in failure. Many of Owen's followers joined the Chartist movement to campaign for universal male suffrage and parliamentary reform. But when the Chartist movement collapsed after 1848 the link between working-class movements and socialism was broken for a generation. The only exception was a small group of Christian Socialists, which included F. D. Maurice and the novelist Charles Kingsley, who for a few years attempted to campaign in favour of a Christian version of Owenite co-operation. But this came to nothing and their campaign was effectively over by 1856. Henceforth there were developments in working-class organisations, such as trade unions, co-operative societies, friendly societies and other forms of mutual aid, but there was little new socialist thinking. The working-class organisations were more concerned with bread-and-butter issues such as wages and cheap food.

The year 1848 was one of revolutions across Europe. It saw the publication of perhaps the most important socialist document of the century, the *Communist Manifesto* of Karl Marx and Friedrich Engels. It was not their first work, but it was the first in which Marxism really crystallised as a complete doctrine. It was also the work in which Marx so airily dismissed Saint-Simon, Fourier and Owen as 'utopian socialists'. What Marx meant by this was that their theories were not 'scientific' like his own, that they had no understanding of the dynamics of society and history and could not demonstrate that socialism was both necessary and inevitable, and for that reason their ideas were little better than fantasies. Given Marx's beliefs it is possible to see his point of view. But from a more objective standpoint the term 'utopian', used pejoratively, was not entirely fair.

Saint-Simon was an extremely learned and very shrewd social analyst in his own right, and his ideal of a better society was far from outlandish. Fourier was somewhat more unusual. He had neither the education of Saint-Simon, nor the practical experience of Owen, yet was capable of psychological insights that many contemporary thinkers (like Bentham and James Mill) entirely lacked. Robert Owen's socialism grew out of a more direct experience of industry and the working-class movement than Marx had had in 1848 or after. Where there was perhaps naivety was in their notion of the means of bringing their versions of socialism about. All three believed in the power of intellectual persuasion. But then why not? That had been the vehicle of all political thinkers from Plato to Bentham. They were, however, prone to the belief that the ruling class would read their works and immediately become fired with enthusiasm for implementing their ideas.

Furthermore, they were convinced of the power of example. Both Fourier and Owen put money and energy into setting up model communities. They all failed, and their efforts today do look naive. But the establishment of new communities on better lines had been a commonplace of European thinking as far back as the seventeenth century, when the main impetus was religious (the Pilgrim Fathers, for example). The utopian socialists can hardly be blamed for not anticipating a form of working-class politics yet to be created.

More interestingly, there has been a revival of interest in recent years in the utopian socialists, and later writers such as William Morris (of whom more below). This is partly due to the general disillusionment with centralised state socialism, and partly owing to the growth of Green ideas (see Chapter 10). Leading Green theorists, such as Rudolf Bahro and Jonathan Porritt, have acknowledged their influence and importance.

International socialism

The year 1848 was a year of revolutions across Europe. They were liberal inspired, although they were supported by working-class organisations where these existed. The result was virtually universal failure, setting back the liberal cause, and the socialist cause even more so. Large numbers of socialists ended up in prison or exile, and many came to London, including Karl Marx and Friedrich Engels.

Marx and the International Workers Movement

There followed a long lean period in the organisation of the socialist movement, although it was a time when Marx and Engels were developing their theory (discussed in Chapter Seven) and extending their influence. Things began to move again in the early 1860s. In 1864 the International Workingmen's Association (now known as the First International) was established with headquarters in London in order to promote international solidatiry and co-operation among workers. It was a loose gathering of representatives from trade unions and other worker's organisations across Europe. There were socialists of various kinds, as well as followers of the French anarchist, Proudhon, together with a few radical democrats and republicans. The movement adopted a parliamentary socialism that was sufficiently moderate and practical for all delegations to accept.

As to the British, it seemed that the working class had lost all interest in socialism, or at least its theory, since the collapse of Chartism in 1848. The British representatives were only interested in concrete issues, such as preventing British employers bringing in cheap foreign labour. Marx became secretary of the Association, and he had a considerable influence on the policies and workings of the organisation as it helped to foster working-class organisations and recommend common policies to them. Workers' parties and trade unions grew steadily in various countries, and socialist ideas made important advances.

Marx became the leading socialist thinker in Europe, except in

Britain, with only anarchists as a rival in some areas. Many European countries were industrialising and working-class movements were springing up in need of their own philosophy, which is just what Marxism provided. In many ways the greatest success was the German Social Democratic Party (SPD), formed in the mid-1860s by Marx's German followers, which became the largest working class party in the world. (At this time most Marxist parties called themselves 'Social Democratic'.)

The French socialist movement was more fragmented, but with the help of the Second International eventually came together in 1906 as the Section Française de l'International Ouvriere (SFIO), with Marxism the dominant theoretical influence. Other European parties were formed, including in Russia, where the Russian Social Democratic Party was illegal and its leaders had to live in exile.

These various parties and other organisations were brought together in the Second International, founded in 1889, five years after Marx's death. It met in various congresses and in 1900 created a permanent secretariat. Marxist socialism was easily the dominant form of socialism and was truly international.

However, all this impressive show of unity did not disguise deep divisions. The trouble was that things had not turned out as Marx had predicted. Society had not become more polarised or the working class more miserable and desperate. He had not foreseen growing general prosperity, the growth of democracy and the increasing recognition of workers' rights. As a consequence, Marxist parties tended to divide internally between those who wanted to work for a revolution and those who wanted to extend and make use of the new democratic opportunities.

The German SPD, the Marxist flagship one might say, became riven with internal conflict, known as the 'Revisionist Debates' (discussed in Chapter Seven). They came to a head when Edward Bernstein (one-time editor of the party's newspaper) wrote a series of articles culminating in a book, *Evolutionary Socialism* (1899), which advocated the revision of the party's official Marxist revolutionary doctrine in favour of parliamentary socialism. Bernstein's attempts to have the party's official doctrine changed failed. But although he lost the battle, there is a sense in which he won the war, for while revolutionary Marxism remained party orthodoxy, the party in fact behaved increasingly like the reformist party Bernstein wanted, with the kind of policies that he had wanted to see.

Other European socialist parties suffered internal conflicts, though usually less publicly. The formation of a united socialist party, the SFIO, in France disguised strong differences. One party that did actually split was the Russian Social Democratic Party. The majority view of the party was that Russia was nowhere ready for revolution, having only a tiny and undeveloped capitalist economyu and a small industrial proletariat. Lenin disagreed and formed his own Bolshevic Party to work for revolution as soon as possible.

Communism and social democracy

It was Lenin and his Bolshevics who seized power in 1917 and turned Russia into the first communist state (see Chapter 7). Lenin then condemned the Marxist social democratic parties of Europe for abandoning revolution and betraying the working class with false promises of progress through democratic means. Far from representing the interests of the working class, the social democrats were its enemies. There could be no common ground with such people, who had no intention of ending capitalism, whatever they said in theory. And indeed, social democracy became synonymous with reformist parliamentary socialism, even though such continental parties continued to pay lip service to the ultimate revolution following capitalism's inevitable collapse. Only the Communists (as the Bolshevics now called themselves) could truly represent the workers.

In 1919 Lenin set up the Third International (often referred to as the Communist International or Comintern) in which only parties which generally supported Bolshevic aims were allowed to join. In most western European countries there were rival communist and social democratic parties, whose rivalry was often more bitter than that with non-socialist parties. In Germany, for example, the hostility between communists and social democrats during the 1920s prevented them working together to prevent the rise of Hitler and the Nazis, which a united effort might well have prevented. Far from being an instrument of world revolution, the Third International was no more than an instrument of Soviet foreign policy. Co-operation was eventually achieved in the fight against Fascism, but hostility resumed once the Second World War was over.

British socialism

After a period of fallow lasting more than thirty years when there was little or no native socialist theory or activity, there was a revival in the 1880s that set British socialism on a new and distinctive path. The last two decades of the century saw the development of anglicised versions of Marxism, with the Social Democratic Federation and the Socialist League; the more successful development of Fabian socialism; the founding of the Independent Labour Party with its distinctive (though eclectic) ethical socialism, all culminating in the creation of the Labour Party in 1900.

However, before looking at these developments in more detail, it must be remembered that the numbers of people involved in these movements was very small. Only when the Labour Party really became established did this change. Most trade unions, which were the main working class organizations, were indifferent. Insofar as they were interested in political ideas, radical liberalism was far more important.

The Social Democratic Federation

The first significant figure in the socialist revival of the 1880s was H. M. Hyndman (1841–1921). He was a rich banker, but devoted most of his adult life to propagating a heavily anglicised and idiosyncratic version of Marxism. Hyndman set out his initial views in his book, *The Text Book of Democracy: England for All*

(1881). It consists of an analysis of Britain's development from a Marxist point of view. However, despite his use of the Marxist concepts of surplus value, necessary historical stages, and so forth, it was a rather crude version of Marxism. (Marx himself, whom Hyndman knew, was angry about the distortions but furious about the fact that Hyndman made no acknowledgment of the source of his ideas.) Furthermore, Hyndman added some of his own ideas that were distinctly un-Marxist. He combined a fierce nationalism, support for imperialism and a paternalistic concern for the lower orders with a distinctly elitist disdain for ordinary people's capacity to do anything without firm leadership from above, and some socialists were inclined to dismiss Hyndman as a Tory.

Hyndman believed that capitalism was not only unjust but disastrously inefficient. As the greatest nation and the leading industrial power, it was up to Britain to lead the world in moving to the far more productive and morally superior system of socialism. He wanted the ruling class to be so convinced of the inevitability of bloody revolution that they would begin to abdicate their power rather than face these inevitable horrors. The socialist transformation, together with the subsequent socialist society, would need to be guided by an intellectual elite with the necessary theoretical understanding. Hyndman had little sympathy with spontaneous working-class movements such as the trade unions, which he dismissed as reactionary, and he refused to support the Bolshevic Revolution on the grounds that it weakened the war effort and cast doubt upon his dream of Britain leading the world towards socialism.

Hyndman founded the Social Democratic Federation (SDF) in 1881 and dominated it until it broke up in 1918. It was the first Marxist party in Britain. However, its membership was never large, nor its influence great.

William Morris

Hyndman was a somewhat domineering and dogmatic figure who managed to alienate some of the early members of the SDF, including Eleanor Marx (Karl's daughter) and William Morris, who broke away to form the Socialist League (1884–90). This body was chiefly distinguished for the theoretical writings of William Morris (1834–96), who was a painter, poet and novelist, but above all a great designer. He produced another anglicised version of Marxism; this time even more diluted (unlike Hyndman he had no interest in Marxist economics, which he claimed he did not understand and did not care to) with a more creative, consistent and attractive blending of other elements.

Morris believed in the necessity of revolution, in the sense that ordinary people would need to seize power and use it to transform society, but he cared little about how this might be done or in organising to achieve it. What did interest him was demonstrating the injustice and cruelty of the current division of society into rich and poor, and the nature of life in the kind of society that could replace it. His hatred of modern industrial capitalism was as much aesthetic as moral (though he would not have separated the two so clearly). Like the art critic John Ruskin and others, he condemned the ugliness and squalor of industrialism, its destruction of craftsmanship and of the workers' pride in their work. He blamed industrialisation for an unnatural divorce of art and life, which was also reflected in contemporary notions of 'high art', that needed education and sensitivity to appreciate it. The ideal society would dispense with machinery, restore craftsmanship, and with it the joy of work, and bring about a full and genuine integration of art and life.

This ideal society would not, however, be the centralised bureaucratic state envisaged by many fellow socialists (whose elitism Morris detested), but a collection of self-governing communities. In this Morris was close to the anarchists, although he insisted he was not one of them. His vision of the ideal society is set out in his novel, *News from Nowhere* (1890), which describes an idyllic way of life in which politics as we normally understand it does not exist.

ILP socialism

The Independent Labour Party was founded at a conference in
Bradford in 1893 under the leadership of Keir Hardie, who had
been elected as an independent MP the year before. The new
party was created through a coming together of various working-
class socialist groups and local parties, especially in the north of
England. What was important about the new party was that it was
working class in both its leaders and membership. This was in
contrast to the SDF, Socialist League and the Fabian Society
(discussed below), which were all middle class-inspired and led.
The new party was committed to collective ownership of the
economy and to converting the workers to a simple, direct and
moral socialism.

ILP socialism relied a good deal on emotional appeal against
the cruelty and injustice of capitalism, rather than on theory. G.
D. H. Cole, the historian of socialism, said it was 'socialism almost
without doctrines . . . so undefined as to make recruits readily
among persons of quite different types'. Nevertheless, there was a
basic belief in the socialist implications of the 'labour theory of
value', that the workers were being systematically deprived of the
wealth they created and were therefore entitled to. Capitalists,
because they owned the factories and machines, were able to grab
the lion's share of the wealth created while the poor exploited
workers received only a miserable fraction. It followed for
socialists that the working classes should take control of the means
of production to secure for themselves the whole value of what
they produced.

However, the ILP did not reject liberalism, but rather saw
socialism as the only means of making possible the fulfilment of
the liberal ideals of liberty and democracy. The ILP also drew
inspiration from the Bible, which, it is often said, created more
socialists in Britain than Karl Marx. As with the Christian
Socialists, the painful consequences of industrialism suggested
that mutual love and brotherhood ought to replace the competitive
antagonisms of the capitalist market-place. The religious element
is also apparent in ideas such as the 'international brotherhood of

man', a somewhat vague internationalism which characterised Labour's foreign policy up to the coming of the Cold War.

Socialism was an attempt to abolish the incentive of gain which was the principle motive of capitalism. Robert Blatchford believed it was possible to change people's hearts through changing the economic system. He pointed out in his *Merrie England* (1893) that people already did many things in an unselfish fashion: for voluntary associations, for family and for the community. He believed that this potential for good would be greatly extended if the economic system were changed.

The ILP's main message was a call to people's hearts, and it provided much of the rhetoric for the otherwise rather cautious parliamentary socialism of the Labour Party.

Syndicalism and guild socialism

Syndicalism was a powerful anarchist movement in continental Europe in the years before the First World War (see Chapter 6), and similar ideas seemed to offer a way forward for some British socialists in that period. The movement was based on trade unions ('syndicat' is the French word for trade union) and saw unions, rather than the political party, as the instrument for gaining power and developing socialism.

Tom Mann, one of the trade-union leaders associated with these ideas, insisted that Labour MPs (only a handful at that time) could do little more than make a nuisance of themselves, whereas industrial action could change what was actually important to working people's lives. If the trade unions were to be effective in changing things then small craft unions would not be the means, but big industrial unions. This thinking lay behind some of the amalgamations and moves towards single-industry unions during the period.

Guild socialism drew some of its inspiration from syndicalism, but was essentially an intellectual movement whose leading figure was G. D. H. Cole. He envisaged a socialist economy based on self-governing industrial guilds. They would operate democratically on the basis of workshop committees; there would be competition between factories in respect of quality rather than price; rewards for effort would be in the form of shorter hours instead of more pay. A national 'commune' would be needed to co-ordinate the activities of the guilds and would take the place of the state.

It was the failure of the General Strike of 1926 that fatally undermined the idea of industrial action for political ends, and syndicalism and related ideas tended to fade away in the 1930s.

Fabianism

The Fabian Society was founded in 1884 for the purpose of promoting socialist ideas. Its most prominent early leaders included Sidney and Beatrice Webb, George Bernard Shaw, Graham Wallace and H. G. Wells. It was always a society of intellectuals and had no aspirations to become a political party. Initially it was unsympathetic to the creation of a new working-class party, hoping to disseminate its ideas among the existing Liberal and Conservative Parties. In her account of the period (*Our Partnership*) Beatrice Webb recalled: 'The Fabian aim was, therefore, to make thinkng persons socialistic', rather than 'to organise unthinking persons into Socialist societies'.

The Fabians did not have a fixed doctrine, but rather a general belief that socialism was what liberalism must inevitably evolve into, and that socialism was a far more rational vehicle for liberal ideals than capitalism. They believed that steadily over time, more and more aspects of life would need to be regulated and 'rationally' planned, necessitating increasing municipal and state intervention.

They sought to back up their claims with powerful intellectual arguments and empirical research. The Webbs in particular were extremely diligent researchers and were the inspiration behind the creation of the London School of Economics in 1895 as a centre for social research. They rejected Marxist notions of the class war and the class nature of institutions. If the state was used to maintain capitalism, it could just as well be used to introduce socialism. The classes could and should co-operate when the reasonableness of reform was clear to all. They believed in the 'inevitability of gradualness', that incremental reform would win all the fruits of revolution without its attendant dangers. (The Society had been named after the Roman general, Fabius Maximus, who defeated his opponents by avoiding head-on battles and gradually wearing them down.)

A variety of strands of thought existed within this broad framework. Among the most influential were the ideas of the Webbs. They were elitists, who envisaged the state being run by a group of enlightened and benign administrators who would organise society and the economy in the most rational way that was best for everyone. The future lay in efficient central planning and efficient local administration.

The Fabian Society was one of the founding organisations of the Labour Party and of all British socialist groups has been the most influential. Sidney Webb wrote Labour's socialist constitution in 1918 and at the beginning most of the leading figures of the party were Fabians. However, as the spectrum of belief within the Labour party has broadened, so has the range of belief the Fabian Society has accommodated, including bitter opponents in the left-right battles of the years since 1945.

Socialism and Labour

Strictly speaking the Labour Party did not begin as a socialist party. As it was conceived in 1900, it was to be a party that brought together all organisations devoted to fostering the working-class cause. Thus the Labour Party was seen as a great coalition of bodies, such as trade unions, co-operative societies, intellectual societies and working-class parties. As a matter of fact the intellectual societies (principally the Fabians) and the two political parties (the Independent Labour Party, ILP, was based mainly in Scotland and already had several MPs; and the Social Democratic Federation, a small Marxist Party) were committed to socialism, but this did not necessarily apply to the other working-class bodies, who supplied the bulk of the membership, organisation and funds.

Most working-class MPs thus far had been Liberals, and a number of trade-unionist leaders had stood as Liberal candidates, and even as Conservative candidates (in fact a number of trade-union leaders remained committed Liberals at least up to 1918). The Labour Party in its early years, therefore, devoted itself to furthering the interests of the working class without any wholesale commitment to any political programme.

However, in 1918, when Labour was on the brink of displacing the Liberals as the country's second major party, it wrote itself a new constitution in which socialism was firmly entrenched as the party's official doctrine. Socialism was embodied in the Constitution in the famous Clause IV, which reads:

To secure for the worker by hand or by brain the full fruits of their industry and the most equitable distribution thereof that may be possible upon the basis of the common ownership of the means of production, distribution and exchange, and the best obtainable system of popular administration and control of each industry or service.

This does not actually mention socialism, but it is there none the less. It is implicit in the phrase 'common ownership', but also in the phrase 'the full fruits of their labour'. This is because behind the clause is the labour theory of value, which insists that all the value of a product comes from the amount of labour that has gone into its production. If the workers did indeed receive the full fruit of their industry, then there would be no profit; without profit there would be no capitalism, no class system, no exploitation, and none of the ills that flow from these.

The new constitution of 1918 allowed individuals to join the party directly for the first time, instead of through an affiliated organization. It also confirmed the basic structure of the party which vested sovereignty in the annual conference. Unlike the other two parties, Labour was created outside Parliament. Its conference was seen as a kind of parliament of the working class, attended by representatives of trade unions, co-operative societies, socialist societies and other organisations.

The party organisation was run by a National Executive Committee (NEC), mostly elected by conference and responsible to it.

It was conference alone which had the right to make policy, and the Parliamentary Labour Party (PLP) was there to do its bidding, with only a residual right to establish priorities between policies. This was in striking contrast to the Conservatives and Liberals, which had already existed as parties in Parliament long before creating national organisations, a fact reflected in the right of their parliamentary parties to make policy.

However, although in principle the PLP has always been subordinate to conference, the party has always tended to be dominated by its parliamentary leadership (elected by the MPs alone until 1981). Their policies have tended to prevail against those of the normally more left-wing constituency representatives because the leadership could usually rely on the massive block votes of the trade unions who could outvote everyone else at conference. Later, from the 1950s, when the party was more radically split between left and right, the issue of who ran the party, conference or the PLP, became a bitterly contested one.

It was not until 1945 that Labour came to power and backed by a large majority in Parliament, that it was in a position to put its socialist beliefs into practice. This involved the creation of the welfare state, to which all parties were committed following the Beveridge Report of 1942, but it also meant socialist planning and nationalisation as first major steps to the creation of a socialist economy and therefore a socialist society. It was a government of extraordinary energy in the very difficult circumstances of the aftermath of war. Creating the National Health Service alone would have been enough for most governments, as would the social security system, or the nationalisation programme. The post-war Labour government did all these things and more, including creating the Arts Council, a comprehensive planning system, the green belt and new towns policies and the national parks.

Major steps had been taken towards socialism. Nevertheless, before that government had left office in 1951 there had been a marked shift of opinion within the party. Some on the right of the party had begun to question both the necessity and the desirability of pursuing the ultimate aim of the elimination of capitalism and its replacement by a fully socialist society. Their view came to be called 'social democracy'.

Social democracy in Britain

All the forms of socialism discussed so far can be accommodated within the framework of 'classical socialism', which anticipates the ultimate elimination of capitalism and its replacement by some form of socialist society. The great divide within the socialist tradition was between those who thought this could only be achieved by revolutionary means (principally the Marxists) and those who believed that it could be done, and must be done, democratically (democratic socialists). However, following the Second World War there developed a new variety of socialism, which departed from the classical framework because it did not regard it as essential that capitalism be abolished. It became known as 'social democracy' and established itself as the leading form of socialism in the West.

The social democratic analysis

The emergence of social democracy was partly a result of the Cold War. People argued that if the Stalinist Soviet empire was an example of socialism, where the state controlled everything, then it was not worth having. Democratic socialists insisted that a socialist society achieved by and based on democracy would be nothing like Eastern Europe, but there was nevertheless a good deal of disillusionment. The other important factor was the availability of an alternative. The consensus policies of a mixed and managed economy and the welfare state (much of which could also be described as 'social liberalism', as discussed in Chapter 2) seemed to provide a basis for a viable socialism that would combine prosperity and freedom with social justice and the possibility of a full life for everyone.

In Britain the right wing of the Labour Party adopted this programme as the basis of its ideal, while for the left (that is, the democratic socialists) these policies were regarded as merely a stepping stone to full socialism. The chief theorist of the social democratic view was Anthony Crosland, which was set out in his book, *The Future of Socialism* (1956), in which he argued that the socialist ideal of owning the economy was no longer necessary. The nationalisations of the post-war Labour government plus Keynesian economic management were sufficient to ensure that a socialist government could control the economy to ensure capitalism worked for the people.

As a consequence capitalism was no longer the blindly destructive force it had been in the past and could now be the basis of a fair society. With the wealth that the free enterprise system generated, society could be improved with social services and ever greater equality. It was equality, and not common ownership, that was the great socialist value, and this could be achieved through good education for all, and through the eradication of unemployment, poverty, avoidable ill-health and other obstacles to a decent life for everyone. Common ownership for its own sake had no point if socialist ideals could be achieved more effectively by some other means.

The success and failure of social democracy

These ideas led to severe internal conflict within the Labour Party during the 1950s, when the right wing adopted social democracy and the left rejected it as betrayal of socialism, since it did not involve the replacement of capitalist society by a socialist one, as in genuine democratic socialism. The resulting conflict is sometimes referred to as the 'Revisionist Debates', a reference to a similar period of conflict within the German Social Democratic Party in the 1890s (discussed above). The issues then were different, but they too were about what the party stood for and whether it should 'revise' (in effect abandon) its traditional doctrine.

Despite the conflict, social democracy became the dominant Labour view and largely remains so, although since the advent of the Social Democratic Party in 1981, adherents within the Labour Party have an understandable reluctance to call themselves 'social democrats'. Socialists who remain within the classical tradition, both democratic and revolutionary, have argued that social democracy is not socialism at all. Indeed, some have suggested that since the advent of social democratic ideas the Labour Party has really been two distinct parties occupying the same organisation. Which of them has been dominant at any one time has been a consequence of events rather than the result of debate.

Crosland's vision of a good society depended a good deal on continuing economic growth, which Keynesianism seemed to promise indefinitely. During the 1950s and 1960s social democratic policies, pursued by both Labour and Conservative governments, gave Britain unprecedented prosperity shared by the whole population. It amounted to a revolution in social conditions relative to what had prevailed before the Second World War. It is true that other countries outstripped Britain in economic performance, but they did so on the basis of broadly similar social democratic policies.

However, the economic recession of the 1970s called social democratic policies into question. In particular, Keynesian economic policies could not cope with the critical economic problem of the time, the combination of inflation and growing unemployment. Keynesian remedies no longer appeared to work. Furthermore, an expanding economy was necessary to promote greater equality through social expenditure. Without such expansion the pursuit of equality was not possible without the socially divisive policy of appropriation from the wealthy.

The failure of social democratic policies led both parties to seek new solutions. The Conservatives chose what came to be called 'Thatcherism'(discussed in Chapter 10), while the left of the Labour Party argued that the social democratic compromise had been a mistake all along, and that the party must return to its true roots, working for the end of capitalism and its replacement by a genuinely socialist society. The most forceful advocate of this view in the Labour Party was Tony Benn.

Bennite socialism and the resurgence of the Left

Like Mrs Thatcher, Benn rejected the compromise of the consensus years as having brought the country into crisis, and saw a
clear radicalism as the only solution to the country's problems.
For him, this meant a return to the Labour Party's traditional
Clause IV socialism, but also a return to the earlier roots of
socialism and radical democracy in Britain going back to the
English Civil War. Tony Benn's socialism is distinctive in the
importance he places in combining socialism with radical democracy. For him it is an essential principle that people should be
involved in decisions that affect them. This is not only right and
just, but is also conducive to greater commitment and efficiency.

Benn argued that the advance of democratic power had reached
the point where it was dislocating capitalism. It followed that a
new economic system was necessary. In order to fulfil legitimate
popular demands for better public services, capitalism needed to
be taxed to such a degree that it reduced its capacity to create
wealth. The further development of capitalism could only be at
the cost of reversing social progress. The only alternative was to
move towards a socialist economy which would be able to meet the
demands of the people for such progress.

This could only be done by democratic socialism, involving a
'fundamental and irreversible shift in the balance of power and
wealth in favour of working people and their families'; together
with further nationalization (involving new, more democratic,
forms); policies for full employment; re-equipment of British
industry while protected by import controls; industrial democracy
at all levels; a return to self-government (that is, withdrawal from
the EEC and NATO); unilateral nuclear disarmament; a fairer
society, with reductions of inequalities of income, wealth and
opportunity, and more open government and access to communications. British institutions needed to be made more democratic,
which would include abolishing the Lords and diminishing
the power of the Prime Minister, but would begin with a more
democratic Labour Party to ensure that MPs were accountable to
local activists and the leadership unable to renege on socialist

commitments.

The ideas of Tony Benn and other left-wingers began to influence party policy, and after the party's defeat in the 1979 election there was intense hostility between left and right. Party policy moved sharply to the left (at which point a substantial number of right-wingers left to set up the Social Democratic Party), and the subsequent election manifesto was the most left wing since 1945. The 1983 election was probably the worst election result in the party's history. Since the left was widely blamed for the defeat, its influence henceforth began to decline.

Neil Kinnock was elected leader in the aftermath of the 1983 defeat and began a steady reversal of left-wing policies. After further defeats the Labour Party increasingly accepted Thatcherite policies for the free market: the emphasis on defeating inflation, low taxes, trade union laws, an abandonment of the commitment to full employment, more consumer choice, and so. In brief, the Labour Party has to a considerable degree abandoned Keynesianism and adopted 'supply-side' economics (see Chapter 10 on the ideas of the New Right and its criticisms of socialism). It could be argued that the mainstream of the Labour Party ended up much further to the right than the Social Democrats who left the Party in 1983. Despite this, the Labour Party lost again in the general election of 1992. However, the party substantially improved its parliamentary position, and under the new leadership of John Smith is unlikely to move back to the left in the foreseeable future.

This raises the question of whether Labour has given up socialism altogether. Some certainly believe so. Others argue that Labour is genuinely looking for fresh sources of socialist inspiration, of which 'market socialism' is one possibility.

Market socialism

Market socialist ideas began to develop in the aftermath of the 1983 general election, when the free market and minimal state ideas of the New Right, represented by the Thatcher government, won a crushing victory over the revived traditional socialism of state planning and nationalised industries, represented by the Labour Party. The success of the New Right had been intellectual as much as political, convincing a broad spectrum of people of the general superiority of markets over state intervention.

What theorists such as David Miller, Raymond Plant and others have done is to accept much of the New Right case for markets and against the centrally planned, all-providing state. What they deny, however, is that markets necessarily mean capitalism, or that centralized planning and state ownership are necessarily essential to socialism. Markets, they argue, can be socialist, since they can be made to serve socialist ends.

It is thus possible to envisage a free-market economy so arranged as to eliminate great concentrations of power and wealth, along with the exploitation and inequality they produce. Employee shareholding, co-operatives and other devices could be used to replace large-scale capitalism and prevent the concentration of wealth. There would be competition between co-operatives, and a general absence of state monopolies, state industries and state bureaucracies to interfere with the workings of the market. The state would create the legal framework for a non-exploitative free market and thereafter only intervene to make up for market deficiencies, such as protecting the environment or providing certain social services.

There is also some degree of acceptance by market socialists of the New Right case against the welfare state, with its huge monopolies, lack of choice, domination by professionals, frequent inefficiency and unresponsiveness, and failure to give the greatest assistance to those in greatest need. They are also prepared to countenance Thatcherite remedies to some degree, such as internal markets in education and health and parental choice of schools, believing that these could be weighted to give greater advantage to the poor.

Not surprisingly, followers of the New Right furiously reject the notion that markets and capitalism can be separated, and insist that 'market socialism' is a contradiction in terms, a nonsense. The idea is also attacked from the left, on the grounds that a socialist society must be based on co-operation as opposed to competition and the profit motive. On the other hand, market socialism is arguably more socialist than the prevailing social democracy, which wholeheartedly accepts capitalism and hopes that the exploitation and inequalities of capitalism can be reduced through welfare, education and strong trade unions.

The crucial question is one of feasibility. It may still take some time before the reflections of academic theorists can such as Plant and Miller be translated into a set of serious proposals that would be neither impractical or unpopular. In the meanwhile the Labour Party is still looking for new ideas. One possible source is the socialist parties of continental Europe.

European socialism since 1945

Socialism has been a major force in the politics of most western European countries since the Second World War. Unlike Britain, however, socialist parties were suppressed during the war in much of Europe, and had to make a fresh start after 1945. For many there has been a fresh start theoretically as well as organisationally. Most had Marxist origins which were difficult to reconcile with post-war prosperity, freedom and democracy, and revulsion against totalitarian Communism. This has involved an explicit acceptance of the free market, about which the British Labour Party has remained ambiguous.

Germany

German Social Democrats believed that, since the Nazis had discredited the right, they would dominate post-war German politics. In fact that dominance was achieved by the centre-right Christian Democrats who restored German prosperity and respectability and introduced an extensive welfare state. After losing three elections in a row, the German Social Democrats (SPD) made a decisive break with the past. At a special conference in Bad Godesberg in 1959 they rejected the party's Marxist principles (which too many associated with the Communism of

East Germany) and embraced the free market.

In fact since the last years of the nineteenth century, the SPD had lived a kind of theoretical and practical double life. While official party doctrine was revolutionary Marxist, in practice the party was a moderate parliamentary socialist party. The great 'revisionist controversy' of the 1890s had failed to bring theory into line with practice; but at Bad Godesburg this was recognized as essential to the party's survival.

Accordingly the Bad Godesburg Declaration set out the SPD's revised principles. There was no mention of Marxism. Instead there wa a total commitment to democracy: 'socialism can be realized only through democracy and democracy can only be fulfilled through socialism'. There was also an endorsement of the free market and an abandonment of the objective of comprehensive public ownership: 'Free choice of consumer goods and services, free choice of working place, freedom for employers to exercise their initiative as well as free competition are essential conditions of a Social Democratic economic policy'. It went on: 'Private ownership of the means of production can claim protection by society as long as it does not hinder the establishment of social justice'; what this meant was Keynesian economic management, welfare and a degree of economic planning, that is, an acceptance of capitalism consistent with same kind of controls as in Britain. Beyond this there was a strong emphasis on welfare: 'The social function of the state is to provide social security for its citizens to enable everyone to be responsible for shaping his own life freely'.

This change of course in 1959 gained the SPD a place in government in 1966, and it became the dominant party in German politics until the early 1980s, although it never ruled alone, so that its coalition partner, the Free Democrats, moderated any socialist measures. That dominance ceased when the Christian Democrats returned to office in 1982, where they have remained. The SPD is again concerned to re-define its socialism to take into account new issues, such as feminism and environmentalism. The latter is particularly pressing since during the 1980s the SPD found itself outflanked on the left by a new Green Party gaining

many votes that might otherwise have gone to the Social
Democrats.

The Bolshevic Revolution led to 'social democracy' coming to
mean moderate parliamentary socialism rather than revolutionary
Marxism. The Bad Godesburg revision was instrumental in a
further shift of meaning, whereby social democracy has come to
mean the abandonment of the ideal of replacing capitalism with a
society based on socialism (in the classical sense).

Scandinavia

Social democratic parties have dominated the politics of
Scandinavia since before the Second World War. This has been
true of the Swedish Social Democratic Party and the Norwegian
Labour Party, and to a slightly lesser extent, of the Danish Social
Democratic Party. These have also shown little interest in public
ownership, and have concentrated mainly on Keynesian management of the economy and state investment. The result has been
highly prosperous and successful economies, with high wages and
full employment. But there has also been high taxation to fund, in
Sweden and Norway, the most extensive welfare services and the
highest level of welfare payments in the Western world. The great
emphasis is upon social equality, which includes a non-selective
education system with a large proportion of students entering
higher education.

However, since the late 1980s Swedish prosperity has faltered
and there has been growing resistance to such high levels of
taxation. The Social Democrats are having to rethink some of
their ideas in order remain the major party.

France and Italy

In both France and Italy, socialists have had to share the allegiance
of left-voters with larger Communist parties. This has helped to
keep them out of power until relatively recently. In Italy the issue
of whether to collaborate with the Communists split socialists into
two parties in 1947 (the Socialists and the Social Democrats)

which kept them out of power even longer. It was not until the 1980s under the leadership of Bettino Craxi that they enjoyed power for a while, although it was in coalition with other parties.

In France the long period of moderate right dominance was finally broken in 1981 when the Socialist leader, François Mitterrand, was elected President and worked with the Communists. However, it is widely believed that Mitterrand out-manoeuvred the Communist Party to such an extent that the Socialists flourished while the Communists experienced a serious decline. On the other hand, despite winning two seven year terms as president, Mitterrand has had to abandon many Socialist policies, including a nationalisation programme, and even for a time 'co-habit' with a Gaullist Prime Minister, Jacques Chirac, who implemented a privatisation programme and other right-wing measures. Mitterrand's election as President in 1988 led to a more moderate socialist government which did not reverse Chirac's privatisations, although it has reinstated a more Socialist social policy. However, the Socialists are now much less popular than Mitterrand himself and need to revise their ideas if they are to successfully survive his eventual departure.

Spain, Portugal and Greece

The Spanish, Portuguese and Greek socialists all rose to prominence in the mid-1970s following periods of right-wing dictatorship. As a banned party under Franco, the Spanish Socialist Workers' Party retained its Marxist doctrine. But in trying to cope with the new democratic Spain it needed to change, although it took the resignation of its popular leader, Felipe Gonzalez, in 1979 to persuade it to abandon Marxism. Since then it has enjoyed considerable success under Gonzalez' resumed leadership.

In Portugal the long dictatorship from 1932–68 of Dr Antonio de Salazar was followed by military rule (1974–76), after which the Communist Party attempted a take-over. The newly formed Portuguese Socialist Party led the resistance to this and became the government in 1976–78, led by Mario Soares. It has subsequently been part of later coalition governments.

In Greece, the ending of the 'rule of the colonels' in 1974 led to the creation of the Pan-Hellenic Socialist Union, led by Andreas Papandreou. It has had to contend on the left with no less than two Communist parties, and is the most left wing and aggressively nationalist of the European socialist parties. It is, for example, opposed to Greek membership of Nato, although Greece did not withdraw when it was in power. When in power its government was beset with conflict and scandal.

Social democracy in general

Post-war European social democracy abandoned Marxism, and indeed classical socialism, in order to modernise. In their place they have sought to develop an alternative to totalitarian Communism based upon state intervention in the economy, usually in the form of Keynesian management and planning, an extensive welfare state, individual freedom, a more equal society through welfare, educational provision and progressive taxation and an absolute commitment to democracy as the only way to conduct government and preserve freedom and civilized values. In developing these ideas and policies social democratic parties have sought to transcend their origins as working-class parties and appeal to all classes. This is a growing necessity as there has been a steady decline of labour-intensive industries (coal, steel, shipbuilding, docks and car-making), which used to provide the bedrock of socialist support throughout industrial Europe. The traditional working class is shrinking in size and therefore political importance.

In political terms social democratic ideas have been highly successful, although not all confined to socialist parties. However, the recessions of the 1970s and 80s created a good deal of disenchantment with socialist ideas of all kinds. There has been a mood of disillusionment with the omnicompetent state and a degree of resistance to the high levels of taxation needed to sustain welfare and other social democratic measures. This has been helped by the relative failure of Keynesian economics and the intellectual success of New Right criticisms of state intervention of all kinds (see Chapter 10).

As a consequence, social democratic parties have been forced to re-think their ideas and adapt their ideals to new circumstances and new theoretical developments. These include green socialism, feminism, greater concern for the consumer in welfare as well as economic matters, new and wider notions of citizenship, and various versions of 'market socialism'.It is not possible to predict the extent to which a new socialism might emerge from these developments, or how successful it might be.

6
Anarchism

The word 'anarchy' comes from the ancient Greek and means 'without rule', and in ordinary parlance 'anarchy' means the same as 'chaos'. But there is a long-established body of political theory calling itself 'anarchism' that is based upon the idea that the state, or any other kind of political rule, is not only unnecessary but a positive evil that must be done away with. Such ideas have only occasionally inspired political movements of any size, and the tradition is mainly one of individual thinkers, but they have produced an important body of theory. The first significant anarchist thinker was William Godwin, who developed his ideas around the time of the French Revolution. However, the idea that it is possible to do without the state was not invented by the anarchists, but has a much older history in Christian theology.

There is a long tradition in European thought, going back to the great theologian and exponent of the theory of Original Sin, St Augustine of Hippo (354–430 AD), which argues that government is needed because human nature is corrupt, and that if it were not corrupt then government would not be necessary. On this view, government is essentially coercive, being there to keep the sinners in line by laying down laws and punishing those who break them. It was an idea still strong in the eighteenth century. Thus James Madison (1751–1836), the chief architect of the American constitution, wrote:

... there is a degree of depravity in mankind that requires a certain degree of circumspection and distrust ... But what is government itself, but the greatest of all reflections on human nature? If men were angels, no government would be necessary.

(*The Federalist Papers*, Nos. 51 and 55)

Neither Augustine nor Madison were anarchists, but this line of thought opened up the possibility that government could be done away with if the evil in the world could be eliminated.

The anarchists asserted that the evil in the world was not caused by Original Sin, but was in fact mainly the consequence of government. If government was taken away human beings would be good and all coercion and domination would be unnecessary.

Individualist anarchism

The first anarchist thinkers in both Europe and America saw themselves as, for the most part, continuing the Enlightenment tradition, emphasising the sovereignty of the individual and the progress of reason.

William Godwin

William Godwin (1756–1836), in his *Enquiry Concerning Political Justice* of 1793, first argued the anarchist case that the state had a corrupting influence on those subject to it and that we could build a better society without it.

Godwin had an optimistic, Enlightenment view of human nature. Our individual natures, he thought, were the product of our environment and upbringing, although that could be improved upon by the application of reason. With the spread of science and philosophy and improved education, there was no doubt in his mind that mankind would gradually improve and that the ills of war, poverty, crime and violence would disappear, since he took it for granted that the consequence of people becoming more rational was that they became more benevolent towards their fellows. He held the utilitarian view that the greatest good was the greatest happiness for the greatest number, and believed that any truly rational person would understand this and behave accordingly; that is, human nature as we observe it would change as the environment which nurtured it changed.

There were, however, certain obstacles on the way to progress, and chief among these was the state. The common belief that the state was necessary for social life was a myth. The state maintained itself by deception and violence, and by keeping the population in ignorance. The process artificially set one above another, and induced competition and greed and conflict, the sources of the ills from which mankind suffered. It was only when the domination of man over man had ceased that people would be able to live a fully rational life. The abolition of all political institutions would put an end to class distinctions and national feeling, and the enviousness and aggression that went with them. It would restore to men their natural equality and enable them to rebuild social life on the basis of free and equal association, governed by their reason alone.

But although a radical, Godwin was not a revolutionary. Revolutions, and for that matter ordinary party politics, polarised society and aroused passions that resulted in the eclipse of reason. Social progress was entirely dependent on intellectual progress, which in turn came from reflection and discussion. The ideal could only be pursued as the entire population was gradually brought to the level of understanding presently confined to the few. It was a lengthy process, although Godwin never doubted the inevitability of its completion.

Max Stirner

The next significant work of a European anarchist was a strange book entitled *The Ego and His Own*, published under the name of Max Stirner in 1843. The author's real name was Johann Caspar Schmidt (1806–56), and he was for a time a schoolmaster, before sinking into misfortune and debt. Schmidt was personally a mild and timid man, but his book is a violent expression of pure individualism that glorified rebellion, crime and violence in the name of the uninhibited free will. The state, society, religion and morality were all denounced for suffocating the free spirit. The assertion of the self, at any cost, was the only good. The state, and all other manifestations of collectivist man, had to be destroyed to make way for a world of unrestrained egoism (that is, selfishness and self-assertion); a world of unique and powerful individuals who would come together and co-operate spontaneously as and when it suited their individual interests. But Stirner did not discuss the kind of social life that would have developed from this. His book shocked society when it was first published, but was then forgotten until the end of the century when it was revived and widely read by anarchists.

Both Godwin and Stirner developed versions of anarchist doctrine based on individualism, but there the resemblance ends. For while Godwin's was an Enlightenment individualism that stressed the capacity of all to participate in universal reason and engage in rational self-direction, Stirner's views were based very much on a Romantic individualism that stressed will and emotion and the assertion of unique individuality. Neither of them founded political movements or had much of a following, and the later trend in European anarchist thinking was towards socialist anarchism.

Nineteenth-century American anarchism

The individualist strand of anarchism continued to develop in America. Here it was perceived by its followers as a logical extension of Lockean liberalism and Jeffersonian democracy, that is, the 'natural rights' of life, liberty and property were sacrosanct, while the state's role as the appropriate vehicle for defending those rights was questioned. American anarchists tried to show that government had 'become destructive of these ends' and therefore ought to be abolished, giving way to a natural harmony,

Godwin's writings were well known in America, but the first important American anarchist, Josiah Warren, was initially a follower of the English socialist, Robert Owen, and was a member of his ill-fated American colony of New Harmony. Its failure in 1827 left Warren convinced of the need to fit society to the individual and not the other way round. He was thereafter a fierce advocate of the absolute sovereignty of the individual, with which no organisation of government had any right to interfere. After the relative success of his 'time store', based on the exchange of promises of labour time, he founded a series of communities based on similar principles, without any regulation or means of enforcing decisions. The first, called the 'Village of Equity', failed because of an epidemic, but the second two, called respectively 'Utopia' and 'Modern Times' lasted for a couple of decades each and convinced their founder of the rightness of his principles.

Warren set out a complicated economic system in his main book *Equitable Commerce* (1852) that was based on people charging for their goods exactly what, in terms of labour time, it had cost them to produce, only modified by taking into account the 'repugnance' of the work involved. In addition there would be free credit, except where a loan involved a demonstrable loss to the lender. This is what he meant by 'equitable commerce'. A society based on honest exchange between free people, he believed, would be harmonious and prosperous, and not need government to run it. Despite the influence of Owen, Warren seemed to have in mind an unchanging society of small farmers, craftsmen and traders, much like that envisaged by Jeffersonian democracy. Some of his followers, however, adapted his ideas to factory conditions. Workers would still be employed by bosses, but both would receive the same wages, related to hours of work, and there would be no return on capital invested. Nor would special talent or skill receive special reward, for that, according to Warren, had nothing to do with the just reward for hours worked. A system of this kind would be quite incompatible with capitalism, and was, as such, regarded as a version of socialism.

There were a number of writers and thinkers who followed Warren and developed ideas of their own, but the most distinguished contributor to the tradition was Henry David Thoreau (1817–62). His attempt to live a life of absolute simplicity in the woods near Concord in Massachusetts (chronicled in his book *Walden*) was rudely interrupted by prosecution and imprisonment for his refusal to pay his poll tax. Thoreau objected to the legal confiscation of his goods for purposes from which he gained no advantage, and which immorally upheld slavery and engaged in wars with other countries. This experience prompted a passionate essay, entitled *The Duty of Civil Disobedience*, which attacked government and insisted upon putting his own conscience above the law. The essay begins:

I heartily accept the motto, 'That government is best which governs least'; and I would like to see it acted up to more rapidly and systematically. Carried out, it finally amounts to this, which also I believe, 'That government is best which governs not at all'; and when men are prepared for it, that will be the kind of government which they will have.

The essay was influential on twentieth-century political figures, for example, Mahatma Gandhi, but Thoreau was ignored in his own time. Besides, he was far too much of an individualist to have a following or to try to start a movement.

Benjamin R. Tucker (1854–1939) was the leading American anarchist of the late nineteenth century. Like Warren, Tucker's ideas were socialistic, although he was much more committed to the free market, and even believed his socialistic anarchism to be consistent with classical liberalism. He argued that the reason why the free market appeared to generate exploitation and huge disparities of wealth was that it was not genuinely free. The market was rigged and distorted by monopolies, for which governments were largely responsible. If the four main monopolies of money, land, tariffs and patents were abolished, then competition in a free market would bring down prices to approximately production costs and interests rates to near zero. In these circumstances anyone could set up a business, land would belong to those who worked it, and no one need be poor or exploited.

From 1881 Tucker published the journal *Liberty*, which became a great forum for radical thought of the period. By this time, Eropean versions of communistic anarchism and theories of violent activism, both of which Tucker detested, were arriving in America. When his printing presses were burnt down in 1907 and *Liberty* ceased publication, the native tradition of individualist anarchism was broken and did not reappear until very recently, in the form of anarcho-capitalism.

American anarchism, although individualist, tended to see

itself as leaning towards socialism in the sense of stressing an egalitarian society of free independent individuals, in seeking to appeal to the common man and in it hostility towards the rich and privileged. On the other hand, American anarchists were not opposed to the market as such, and tended to see human beings as intelligent pursuers of their self-interest. They did not, like Godwin, foresee a change in human nature, but merely the creation of a society where the pursuit of self-interest was more enlightened and mutually beneficial. Their ideas therefore relate to the late twentieth century anarcho-capitalism. Also like Godwin, they eschewed both revolutionary activity and ordinary parliamentary politics, relying on the power of reason, persuasion and education (Josiah Warren promoted his ideas through a journal entitled *The Peaceful Revolutionist*).

The immigrant strand of communist anarchism was the more dominant strand by the end of the nineteenth century. However, before turning to the socialist and revolutionary anarchists, a further strand of the individualist variety needs to be mentioned.

Personal anarchism

Since the end of the nineteenth century, there have always been individualist anarchists who have usually stood apart from the social revolutionaries. They have pursued freedom in their own way: either by campaigning publicly for their beliefs, or by withdrawing from society to live a life at odds with accepted social norms. Their demand has been for freedom from society's pressure to conform; or, as they would express it, freedom from ignorance, superstition and moral prejudice. The kinds of things they have usually had in mind have been artistic freedom, sexual freedom and freedom from religious intolerance. Society, they insist, has no right to impose its norms on these areas: the individual is sovereign.

We now take for granted many of the individualist anarchists' demands. This is partly because there has been a good deal of overlap between their demands and certain liberal ideas of the late nineteenth century which have been extremely influential. This is the kind of liberalism particularly associated with John Stuart Mill (see Chapter Two), who argued that the state had no right to interfere in an individual's way of life, providing he or she was doing no harm to others. In this respect individualist anarchism can be seen as an extreme version of liberalism. The main difference is that all Liberals accept the necessity of law and the state. What Mill advocated was maximum possible freedom within the law, whereas all anarchists reject the law and the state as unnecessary.

Socialist anarchism

The main trend in anarchist thinking in Europe after Stirner was towards socialist anarchism which, while insisting on individual liberty, saw society as based on a network of communities of people working together. A number of thinkers contributed to this increasingly influential tradition.

Proudhon

The first of these was a self-educated French printer by the name of Pierre-Joseph Proudhon (1809–65). If anyone can be said to be the founder of modern anarchism as a political movement it is Proudhon, and he was the first thinker to call himself an Anarchist. Proudhon developed the anarchist case against capitalism in addition to the case against the state. He is probably best remembered for his aphorism 'property is theft', although this does not accurately reflect his views. He did not object to private property as such, but only the possession of such property as gave one man power over another. Indeed, he thought it essential that every individual own his own home, together with the tools and land necessary to do his work. A minimum of property was necessary to maintain independence and liberty, and he objected to communism on the grounds that it took these away. He was fiercely individualistic, writing:

My conscience is mine, my justice is mine, and my freedom is a sovereign freedom . . . To be governed is to be watched over, inspected, spied on, directed, legislated over, regulated, docketed, indoctrinated, preached at, controlled, assessed, weighed, censored, ordered about, by men who have neither right, nor knowledge, nor virtue. That is government, that is its justice, that is its morality . . . Whoever puts his hand on me to govern me is a usurper and a tyrant; I declare him my enemy.

(*General Idea of the Revolution in the Nineteenth Century*, 1851)

Proudhon's ideal was a world of small independent producers – peasant farmers and craftsmen – who associated and made contracts with each other freely for their mutual benefit, and for whom a centralised coercive state was an unnecessary evil.

It is not difficult to see in Proudhon's ideas the reaction of the independent craftsman and peasant proprietor against the new age of industrialism and a longing for a world that was passing away (although he did take factory production into account, believing that this should be based on worker co-operatives), and it was among just such small producers that his ideas took hold. Yet he was more widely influential than this. His followers played an important role in the First International and in the Paris Commune of 1871. On the other hand, Proudhon disliked parties quite as much as any other kind of formal organisational structure, and he also disliked rigid structures of thought in the form of theories or programmes that everyone had to agree to. He refused to call his ideal society a 'utopia' in the sense of a system that once established could not be changed. That would be an intolerable limitation on freedom. Each generation had to be absolutely free to solve its problems in its own way.

This points to a central difficulty in Proudhon's thought. He wanted a society based on mutualism, with free bargaining between individuals and communities. Since such free bargaining was not possible in a situation where some were more powerful than others, he was, therefore, anti-capitalist. On the other hand, he was more individualist than collectivist. He wanted a society based on a voluntary association of independent communes, but also wanted a situation where everyone was equal and could do what they wanted, and each commune could run its affairs as it chose. These elements are potentially in conflict, but he was unclear as to how the combination could be sustained.

Bakunin

Proudhon's most famous disciple was an extraordinary Russian aristocrat named Mikhail Bakunin (1814–76). While Godwin, Stirner and Proudhon confined their rebelliousness to their writings, Bakunin was a rebel in everything he said and did. He scorned all conventions of behaviour and charged about Europe involving himself in every plot, conspiracy and insurrection he could find. He was completely devoted to revolutionary activity, with little thought of his own safety or anyone else's. Despite years of harsh imprisonment his faith remained undimmed and he lived to become the father-figure of European anarchism and inspirer of generations of anarchists.

Bakunin began his revolutionary career by advocating a general uprising of the Slav peoples and the creation of a great pan-Slavonic federation under a revolutionary dictatorship that would lead mankind out of oppression towards freedom and equality. He wrote (rather ironically as things turned out): '. . . the star of revolution will rise high and independent above Moscow from a sea of blood and fire, and will turn into a lodestar to lead a liberated humanity' (*Appeal to the Slavs*, 1848).

He later abandoned ideas of revolutionary dictatorship and pan-Slavonic nationalism, but he always retained an almost mystical belief in violent revolution as a great purifying and regenerative force: 'Let us put our trust in the eternal spirit which destroys and annihilates only because it is the unsearchable and eternally creative source of all life. The urge to destroy is also a creative urge' (*The Reaction in Germany*, 1842).

Bakunin did not, however, believe in mass political parties as instruments of revolution, but in small secret bodies of professional revolutionaries on the Babeuvist model (which later influenced Lenin) who would inspire and lead spontaneous insurrections of peasants and workers.

Bakunin believed that mankind was oppressed by the dual

power of church and state. They both relied on the myth of human selfishness, upon which was based the claim that human beings were not fit for freedom, but needed the guidance of religious and political authority. Science, Bakunin believed, would put and end to religion, but it was only the people who could destroy the illegitimate power of the state.

Like Proudhon, Bakunin believed that anarchism was the logical outcome of the ideals of the French Revolution, and that revolutions were the necessary means by which humanity progressed. Bakunin hoped that ultimately the whole world would be engulfed in a revolution that would destroy the class system and the nation-state. Henceforth property and inheritance would be abolished and mankind would be organised in a world-wide federation of industrial and agricultural communes based on the principle of 'from each according to his ability, to each according to his work' (not according to need as held by Marx and other socialists).

Bakunin's vision was more socialistic than Proudhon's. The basic unit of society was the commune rather than the individual. He argued that since all must be afforded the means to earn their living and not be economically dependent on anyone else, then property rights must belong to the community and not to individuals. Human beings must be free, yet man is by nature a social being who can only flourish in a community of equals. Bakunin's work marked a change in the mainstream of anarchist thought from individualism to collectivism.

But although committed to socialist ideals, Bakunin was an implacable opponent of Karl Marx, whose ideas he believed were inherently authoritarian. Although far less original and far less of a systematic thinker than Marx, his criticisms were prophetic, and were later influential among the New Left Marxists of the 1960s (see Chapter 7).

Tolstoy

After Bakunin the next significant anarchist thinkers were, oddly enough, also Russian aristocrats. One was Count Leo Tolstoy

(1828–1910), the great Russian novelist. Unlike any of the previous thinkers he was a Christian anarchist. After a life of worldly success and pleasure he renounced cultivated society and his art, and tried to live a simple life close to the Russian peasantry.

Tolstoy was a savage critic of contemporary society, which he saw as based on corruption, hypocrisy and false knowledge. Science, he believed, taught nothing of any significance, and he was scornful of the modern world's belief in progress. He rejected all state and social institutions and all organised religion. The honest simple life that was close to the soil and within the family was the source of wisdom and goodness and constituted the best life for man. Tolstoy was a pacifist, believing all forms of violence to be immoral, and consequently did not believe in revolutions. The thing to do, he said, was not to plot and plan for the good society, but to go out and start living the good life.

Kropotkin

In the mainstream of anarchist thinking the last of the major theorists built on the ideas of Proudhon and Bakunin. Prince Peter Kropotkin (1842–1941) was a distinguished Russian scientist and geographer. After a period in the Imperial army followed by scientific work in Siberia, Kropotkin visited Switzerland in 1872 where he was converted to anarchism by some of Bakunin's followers. After returning to Russia he began to promote the anarchist cause, but ended up in prison. He later escaped and spent most of the rest of his life in exile, mainly in London. He returned briefly to Russia before he died, but had little sympathy for the Soviet regime.

Kropotkin was the most thorough and systematic of anarchist thinkers and devoted several books to trying to put anarchism on a firm scientific basis. In the late nineteenth century the scientific theory that caught every imagination was Darwin's theory of evolution. Many social theorists attempted to use evolution as a basis for their own social and political ideas. They were known as 'social Darwinists'; the best known was Herbert Spencer, who used evolution to justify extreme *laissez-faire* capitalism as natural and right, in the sense that free competition ensured the 'survival of the fittest', thereby promoting higher evolution and progress. But instead of glorifying competition, as did most social Darwinists, Kropotkin took precisely the opposite view by arguing that co-operation was the key to evolutionary success, and that human beings were the most successful species because they had learnt to co-operate together effectively.

Thus, as another Darwinian anarchist (and also a distinguished geographer), Elisée Reclus, put it: '. . . if our descendants are to reach their high destiny of science and liberty, they will owe it to their coming together more and more intimately, to the incessant collaboration, to this mutual aid from which brotherhood grows little by little' (cited in D. Miller, *Anarchism*, p.72).

It is not competition, therefore, that is natural and good, but social co-operation and mutuality. The obvious conclusion to be drawn from this, Kropotkin believed, was that the ultimate stage in the evolution of human society was a social life where people freely and naturally co-operated on equal terms, and competition no longer existed. However, man's natural sociability and co-operativeness were obscured and distorted by capitalism and the coercive state. Once these had been removed, by whatever means, human society would be free to achieve its highest stage of development, which was communist anarchism. Society would then be based on a free association of communes, where goods would be produced and distributed on the basis of need (as in Marx) and not labour time (as in Bakunin).

Anarchist terrorism

In the two decades prior to 1914 the Western world was shocked by a series of anarchist outrages. Bombs were thrown into parliamentary assemblies, and into theatres and restaurants where the rich gathered; policemen, judges and other public officials were murdered; most shocking of all was a series of spectacular assassinations, including those of President Carnot of France (1894), Empress Elizabeth of Austria (1898), King Umberto of Italy (1900) and President McKinley of the USA (1901).

The press and the politicians usually portrayed these atrocities as the work of the Anarchist International (or 'Black International'), a vast international conspiracy aimed at destroying Western civilisation. In fact there was no such conspiracy and no such organisation. All these sensational acts were committed by individuals, or very small groups, working alone. Their own justification was that they were striking a blow for the oppressed. The state and the capitalist system constituted organised violence against the people, and terrorism was their only way of fighting back. An assassination was not so much an attempt to overthrow the system directly (though there was always the hope that it would spark off a popular uprising); it was, rather, a symbolic act that would reveal to the masses the true nature of the system and convince them that action to change things was possible. It was, in the anarchist phrase, 'propaganda of the deed'. Many moderate anarchists, like Kropotkin, were appalled by these outrages, but refused to condemn them on the grounds that they were the inevitable products of an unjust society.

The idea of 'propaganda of the deed' had been developed in the 1870s as a reaction against earlier reliance on propaganda and persuasion. The oppressed, it was argued, had neither the time not the inclination to read pamphlets or attend political meetings. They had to be shown by a dramatic and symbolic act against the state and capitalist property, that would highlight their oppression and demonstrate the way forward. What was originally envisaged were acts of insurrection, with anarchist bands moving from community to community, providing the spark that would lead on to a general uprising. The most serious attempts to implement this strategy were in north Italy in the mid-1870s, which all came to nothing. Such failures led to a commitment to terrorism, and the expression 'propaganda of the deed' acquired more sinister connotations.

It might be argued that 'propaganda of the deed' grew out of two other kinds of failure. One was a failure of insight. Anarchists were given to believe (as Marxists often were) that the oppressed masses were ready for revolution, and that all that was needed was the spark that would set alight a revolutionary conflagration across

Europe. The turn to terrorism was a desperate attempt to find the right kind of spark, and no more likely to succeed than previous strategies. But also, anarchists seemed to be neither inclined nor capable of creating the kind of disciplined organisation their aspirations called for. Organisation based on entirely voluntary co-operation and acceptance of decisions could not be effective. The systematic application of anarchist principles to anarchist organisations appeared to condemn anarchism to impotence, even when events seemed propitious (they failed to take advantage of their substantial following in Russia to resist the Bolshevics in the revolutionary period).

The resort to terrorism was itself a massive failure and counter-productive. The masses were not just waiting for the sign to rise in spontaneous insurrection.

Anarcho-syndicalism

Most anarchists believed that the existing order needed to be overthrown by a spontaneous popular insurrection, whether or not it was sparked off by terrorism. There was, however, one strand of anarchism in this period which put its faith in economic rather than political action. This was anarcho-syndicalism (from the French *syndicats* = trade unions), which has been the nearest the anarchists have come to creating a serious political mass movement capable of challenging for power in a modern society.

Syndicalist theory developed in France, and is essentially revolutionary trade unionism. Syndicalism was about class war, using whatever was necessary by way of direct action – strikes, boycotts, sabotage and, where necessary, personal violence – to fight for better conditions and prepare the workers for the revolutionary general strike that would finally cripple and destroy the capitalist system. The syndicalists were deeply suspicious of party politics, and saw the emancipation of the working class as something to be achieved by the working class themselves, and by means of their own institutions.

Syndicates were local trade unions, normally based on an industry, although sometimes a craft or profession. They were under the democratic control of their members and entirely autonomous, and in syndicalist theory must remain so. There were strong links with other local syndicates, and a national organisation for each industry. But these wider organisations were only for purposes of co-ordination. Each local syndicate was sovereign, and joined these organisation and took part in common action on a purely voluntary basis.

Not all syndicalist leaders were thoroughgoing anarchists. For some the main object was destroying capitalism, and the abolition of the state was a minor matter to be settled when that object was achieved. But most were anarcho-syndicalists who did see the stateless society as central to the ideal. The state was not only undesirable but unnecessary, since the federation of syndicates, freely co-operating in the interests of all, would not only create the revolution but were perfectly adequate for running the post-revolutionary world without the need for the state apparatus of oppression. (However, it must be said that revolutionary fervour was confined to a minority.)

Although it never made much impact in Britain, anarcho-syndicalism became a major political movement in several European countries. This was especially so in France, where the movement first developed in the late nineteenth century, as well as in Italy and Spain. In the years before the First World War it was a serious rival to socialism and Marxism. In France, half the work-force belonged to anarcho-syndicalist-dominated unions, and even in America the anarcho-syndicalist union, the International Workers of the World (the 'Wobblies'), had over 200,000 members.

After the war the influence of anarcho-syndicalism waned in most countries. The exception was Spain, where it went on growing as a mass movement and played an important role in the Spanish Civil War. The anarchist trade union, the Confederación Nacional de Trabajo,achieved a membership of over one million in the mid-1930s , and fleetingly controlled large parts of Spain. But with Franco's victory the anarchist tradition more or less died out.

Since then, it has not been a significant political movement anywhere in the world in terms of mass politics. Anarchist theorising has, however, continued along several paths. There was something of a revival of anarchist ideas among the student left of the 1960s, although mainly on the fringes of the New Left which was dominated by neo-Marxism. Since the 1970s there has been the development of 'Green anarchism' and 'anarcho-capitalism'.

Anarchism and Marxism

Curiously, Marx knew all the leading anarchist thinkers in Europe well. Stirner was, for a time, a fellow Young Hegelian in Berlin. When Marx first went into exile in Paris he was on friendly terms with Proudhon, although this subsequently turned to hostility. Finally, it was Bakunin who led the anarchist faction in the First International and was Marx's chief opponent. In the second half of the nineteenth century, and up to the First World War, support for the revolutionary left was divided between Marxists and anarchists.

Differences and similarities

Proudhon and Bakunin objected to Marx's authoritarianism, both organisational and intellectual. Marx wanted the workers to form centralised and disciplined mass parties co-ordinated by an international body led by Marx himself. But Bakunin and other anarchists would have none of this. They were against disciplined parties and intellectual elites possessed of the 'truth'; they thought Marx's theory of the dictatorship of the proletariat suggested a post-revolutionary tyranny not much better than what it had replaced.

Anarchists objected to the whole notion of 'scientific socialism', with its economic determinism and its necessary stages of history, which seemed to suggest that it would all happen automatically anyway. This must, they argued, undermine the revolutionary fervour necessary to overthrow the system. Revolutions were about will and leadership and courage, not about having the correct analysis. Besides, if it was all scientific, that implied a class of experts to run not only the revolutionary party but the post-revolutionary world: only they would know the right moment to act and the right thing to do; they would constitute a new and permanent priesthood.

Another objection was to the role of the proletariat, of which Marx was thought to have too narrow a view. Marx saw the revolution being undertaken by an army of disciplined urban factory workers. Of this the anarchists were sceptical. For one thing they did not believe the working class was the solidly united force which Marxists believed. The top strata of workers was reasonably prosperous and unlikely to participate in revolutionary activity, let alone lead it. Much more likely material, anarchists believed, was the lower strata, the most exploited, the unem-ployed, the poor, as well as landless peasants and other groups. Furthermore, apart from regarding the whole notion of a post-revolutionary dictatorship as inherently wrong, it was completely unacceptable that it should be in the hands of one, narrowly defined social group and not all the oppressed. At best it would rule in the interests of that narrow class and suppress the spon-taneity and creativity of the whole society released by the revolution.

Finally, the notion of the 'dictatorship of the proletariat' was anathema. The means must be consistent with the end. Revolu-tions must be accomplished in accordance with the same values they are intended to realise. To create a tyranny in order to end all tyranny was absurd.

Marxists tended to reply that the anarchists were so disorganised, they would never achieve anything. Nevertheless, despite the rivalry Marxism and anarchism had much in common. They were both equally hostile to capitalism and the bourgeois state. Marx believed that the state was an instrument of class oppression, and that in the future classless society the state would necessarily cease to exist. Thus, Marx's ultimate future (to the very limited extent that he outlined it) was anarchist as well.

Until the First World War the anarchists were the only serious revolutionary rivals to the Marxists, although only in a few places were they of equal importance. But, Spain apart, the anarchist movement collapsed after the war. There were several reasons for this, but one was the success of the Bolshevic revolution, which seemed to show the true and effective way of accomplishing a revolution. In fact the anarchists, both within Russia and else-where, were the Bolshevics' severest critics on the left. Indeed, as time went on anarchists were increasingly clear that all their criticisms and suspicions of Marxism had been well founded, and that the 'dictatorship of the proletariat' had turned into the mon-strous tyranny they had predicted. Their prescience did not, however, prevent the demise of anarchism as a mass movement. Since the suppression of Spanish anarchism by Franco anarchist ideas and aspirations have been confined to small groups of isolated intellectuals, and those individualists who set greater store by living the ideal than transforming society, although there was a renewed interest in anarchist thinking in the 1960s, as part of the broader movement of the New Left.

Anarchism and the New Left

The New Left (discussed in Chapter Seven) was a remarkably disorganised and inchoate movement, with no overall organisa-tion and no clear goals. Theory was fluid and eclectic. Marx and Marxists were the most important figures, but psychoanalysts, psychiatrists, phenomenologists and various cultural critics also contributed. Anarchism was one strand of theory, but also part of the general New Left outlook, as is apparent in the writings of such leaders as Daniel Cohn-Bendit, the French student leader in the Paris uprising. The movement as a whole was profoundly anti-authoritarian, such that one could almost call it 'anarcho-Marxist'. It is Marxist with all the old anarchist criticisms taken to heart. This can be seen in a number of ways.

First of all, the movement's rejection of orthodox communism as a corrupt and bureaucratic tyranny reflected the anarchist pre-revolutionary fears of the idea of a 'dictatorship of the pro-letariat', that were borne out in the experience of modern communism. Neither that dictatorship nor the 'vanguard party' were any part of the New Left programme. There was no national or international leadership and no attempt was made at creating a disciplined party; reliance was placed upon a network of independent democratic groups. Secondly, the New Left rejected Marx's economic determinism and the whole emphasis on the working out of historical necessity. Thirdly, the idea of the proletariat as the instrument of revolution, was abandoned in favour of, as Bakunin wanted, the oppressed and disillusioned, the proletariat itself having, to a considerable extent, been bought off (particularly in the age of consumerism). Finally, the emphasis was on revolt now, leading to liberation now, and a new society now, all based on a transformation of consciousness, and not the juggernauht of historical inevitability being played out in the fullness of time, independent of anyone's will.

Recent developments in anarchist theory

In the New Left there was a kind of merging of the Marxist and anarchist traditions. However, several distinctively anarchist developments remained after the youthful rebellion had died down. These included deschooling theory, feminist anarchism and Green anarchism, which developed in the 1970s. The same period has also seen an entirely new strand of anarchism emerge; this is anarcho-capitalism, which has far more to do with the New Right than the New Left.

Deschooling society

One of the oddest, yet most influential, movements that grew out of the New Left was the 'deschooling' movement, associated with Paul Goodman, Paul Reimer and, most famously, Ivan Illich (*Deschooling Society*, 1970). It was essentially an educational theory, and in fact there is a distinguished tradition of educational theorising by anarchists, starting with William Godwin. Education is central to the anarchist vision. It is the only viable alternative to revolution as a means of creating the anarchist society, and, even where revolution is the means, it would still be essential to the maintenance of the society the revolution had created. However, deschooling theory became a fashionable educational theory for a while, far beyond the confines of radical intellectual circles.

Essentially, deschooling theory argues that schooling as we know it does not in fact educate. All it does is to process and certificate people for modern industrial society, and it is essentially the same process in liberal democratic states as in communist ones. Many spend years being processed and never learn to read or write or do arithmetic. The formal education system needs to be replaced by a voluntary network in which people take charge of their own education, just as in the wider world they need to take charge of their own adult lives. The key to transforming society is the abolition of the schooling system.

Illich in particular emphasises the sheer inability of the compulsory state schooling system to perform the very task it is set up to do, and links this with the inability of massive state bureaucracies to do any of their appointed tasks. Thus we have a defence system that fails to provide security; a social security system that perpetuates poverty; a health service that does not make people healthier, and so on. (This argument is one of the very few links between New Left anarchism and New Right anarchism, although the explanations and remedies are different.) The general reason for this failure, Illich believes, is that people are not, as they ought to be, in charge of their own lives.

Feminist and Green anarchism

Another outcome of New Left anarchism is anarchist feminism (sometimes called 'anarcha-feminism'), where the state is seen as an expression of male dominance, a dimension of patriarchy that must be abolished if women's emancipation is to be accomplished. As with the New Left movement itself, there is among radical feminists generally a specific and self-conscious strand of anarchism, but also anarchist ideas and attitudes have had pervasive influence over the whole feminist movement. There is the traditional anarchist rejection of conventional politics: there has not been (nor is their any prospect of) a Woman's Party. The emphasis is on decentralisation and co-operative small-group democracy, with no national leaders. The same could be said of probably the most important area of anarchist influence today, the Green movement (see Chapter 10 for a fuller account of both feminist and Green thinking).

Murray Bookchin, one of the leading figures of the American Green movement, sees what he takes to be the authentic Green movement, or social ecology as he calls it, as the culmination of the various radical movements of the 1960s, and as fully in the anarchist tradition:

Social Ecology draws its inspiration from outstanding radical de-centralist thinkers like Peter Kropotkin, William Morris, Paul Goodman, to mention a few, amongst others, who have advanced a serious challenge to the present society with its vast, hierarchical sexist, class-ruled, status apparatus and militaristic history.
(Conference paper 1987, cited in Porritt and Winner, *The Coming of the Greens*, 1988, p.236)

He insists that it is not individuals that are responsible for the world's appalling condition, but the racist, sexist capitalist system.

Bookchin is a self-conscious anarchist, but the Green movement has strong anarchist characteristics quite independently of this, and what are clearly anarchist ideals are held by a great many who are entirely innocent of the anarchist tradition of political thought. For a great many Greens, in all countries, the future sustainable society needs to be stateless and composed of a network of self-sufficient communes, based on equality, participation and direct democracy.

Anarcho-capitalism

Although there are socialist anarchists of the old school who are still theorising (see, for example, Colin Ward's *Anarchy in Action*, 1973), the socialist side of anarchism is most flourishing in the Green movement. But while this has been happening, a quite different form of anarchist theory has been developing at what would, at first thought, seem to be hostile territory at the opposite end of the ideological forest, amongst the writers and thinkers of the New Right (see Chapter 11).

The New Right has sought a reduction of the role of the state in favour of the free market (symbolised above all in Britain by the privatisation programme). Some New Right theorists, such as Robert Nozick in his book *Anarchy, State and Utopia* (1974), take the view that the state's function should be reduced to providing law and order. Indeed, Nozick insists that for the state to take citizens' property (in the form of taxes) for any other purpose is positively immoral. And it is only a very short step beyond this 'minimal statism' to downright anarchism. The most important among those who have taken this step are David Friedman (son of Milton) and Murray Rothbart, who argue against there being any form of state at all, leaving everything to free-market capitalism, hence the name 'anarcho-capitalism'.

There are many anarchists of the more traditional variety who would not recognise such ideas as authentic anarchism. They see capitalism as part of the system of exploitation they are fighting against, and rampant unregulated capitalism would be an evil of horrifying proportions. It would reproduce all the horrors of the industrial revolution and worse; poverty, exploitation and squalor would again be the lot of the workers. They see anarcho-capitalism as an aberrant manifestation of the far right's characteristic contempt for the greater part of humanity.

Needless to say, the anarcho-capitalists do not see their ideas in this light. They see their primary concern as human freedom, and like all anarchists, they see the state as its chief enemy. They see capitalism as benign, and any faults it is thought to have as the result of state intervention. State regulation creates monopolies, or reduces the number of producers, in a multitude of ways, and it is in such situations that exploitation takes place. In a stateless situation that is genuinely free, there will be prosperity and opportunity for all; the only differences of wealth will arise from differences of talent and application. Society will be characterised by a spontaneous harmony.

Much of the literature of anarcho-capitalism is devoted to demonstrating how government attempts to help people through collective action end up doing more harm than good, and how the free market could provide whatever was necessary more cheaply and efficiently and to the greater satisfaction of all. This even applies to law and order, the key difference between anarcho-capitalists and the minimal statists.

Anarcho-capitalism is the outlook of a relative handful of intellectuals, who nonetheless are hopeful that their ideas are spreading and will eventually enable people to free themselves from the propaganda that tells us the state is needed, put out by all those in the economy and public sector with a vested interest in its maintenance, and will convince them that the state can and must be dismantled.

Finally, it is not in fact the case (as is sometimes thought) that anarcho-capitalism came out of the blue, without past or pedigree. It has a good deal in common with the earlier American tradition of individualist anarchism, particularly that of Benjamin Tucker. There is also a link with the extreme version of classical liberalism represented by Herbert Spencer and his followers, who saw the role of the state progressively diminishing as free-market capitalism, and therefore social progress, advanced. However, whatever the independent history and standing of anarcho-capitalism might be, its fortunes seem bound up with those of the New Right generally, and will advance or decline as they do.

Fundamentals and criticisms

Anarchism covers such a wide range of beliefs, from extreme individualism to extreme collectivism and from extreme capitalism to extreme Communism, that it could be argued that there cannot be much, if anything, that unites all the strands. The question of whether there are such common principles turns on the question of whether there is a specifically anarchist conception of human nature and its relationship to society, and upon the answer turns the further question of the viability of anarchism as a political doctrine.

Anarchism and human nature

Anarchism can be said to rest upon certain basic assumptions about human nature and its relation to society:

a) Society is based on free association between people and is natural.
b) The state is based on the domination of some by others, is maintained by coercion, and is not natural.
c) Humanity is essentially good, but is corrupted by government.
d) Government cannot be reformed, but must be destroyed altogether.

Anarchists of all kinds agree that human nature is such that it will not flourish in conditions of coercion and domination, especially those represented by the state. Human beings will live more fully and happily once the state has been removed. Only then will humanity's natural sociability assert itself and create a spontaneous natural order superior to any that could be imposed from above.

This, however, is only a partial and initial account of human nature. To complete it we have to see the kind of spontaneous order and harmony that anarchists believe the ending of the state will call forth. It is at this point that different anarchist strands begin to part company. Differing conceptions of natural harmony imply differing conceptions of human nature beyond the initial characterisation.

Thus, Godwin emphasised human rationality and believed in a natural order arising spontaneously if human beings were free to exercise their reason. Kropotkin believed humanity's naturally evolved instinct for co-operation and community would assert itself. The Green anarchists put their faith in man re-establishing a natural harmony with nature, following which everything else will fall into place. Finally, the market anarchists believe that giving free rein to man's natural instinct to pursue his own self-interest will result in the natural order of the market.

Anarchism is open to a variety of criticisms. Some of these apply to anarchism in general while others apply to individual strands within the broader tradition.

Rules and authority

The most fundamental criticism of anarchism is that if we take it to its logical conclusion it simply does not make sense, that is, if we take seriously the idea that 'anarchy' implies without rule or authority. We might imagine an extreme anarchist who, on principle, refused to follow any rule they did not make up themselves. Such a policy could not be pursued consistently, but would be self-defeating. Take, for example, the case of language. If this individual refused to follow the rules of sentence construction, and put words in their own peculiar order, then they would not be able to communicate with the rest of us. A more general point can be made about rules of behaviour. To be part of any community involves shared beliefs and values, as well as shared ways of doing things and ways of behaving. If the individual refuses to share any of this it is difficult to see in what sense they would be a member of the community. Certainly it would not make sense to talk of a community composed of such individuals.

Anarchists are inclined to say that they only reject coercive authority and since nobody is formally punished for using language incorrectly, following generally accepted authoritative rules is unobjectionable. The question then becomes where one draws the line. At this point anarchists divide between individualists and communists. Individualists who are 'doing their own thing' may not be able to work together to form a community, to do the necessary tasks, to get things done. Communists require a high degree of co-operation and authoritative decisions (usually by means of direct democracy), which cannot accommodate the dissenting individual, who may not accept the authority of the majority.

This argument becomes a practical one of what will and will not work. What evidence there is tends to be inconclusive, and usually confined to very limited communities. We are left with plausibility and belief. All forms of anarchy involve a reliance on natural harmony, whether it be the unhindered market or unhindered reason or unhindered sociability or whatever it is, that will assert itself once the hinderance of the state has been removed. Anarchists are sustained by a faith in one or other of these harmonies, while the rest of us tend to be sceptical. The seventeenth-century philosopher, Thomas Hobbes, argued that with the removal of the coercive authority of the state, society would degenerate into a war of all against all in which the life of man would be 'solitary, poor, nasty, brutish and short'. Most people are inclined to believe that the taking away of all forms of coercive authority would lead to conflict. To believe otherwise requires a considerable act of faith.

Problems with socialist anarchism

Socialist anarchism is based on common ownership and distribution on the basis of need. It would appear to presume a considerable degree of discipline and commitment among the members of the community and a good deal of agreement. What happens to people who do not pull their weight; or to those who do not accept the authority or discipline of the community; or who do not agree with the distribution; who want to go off and do their own thing, start a business or whatever? It is all very well to assume that all will share the same values, but if they do not then there will be divisions. There are, therefore, doubts about the practicality of anarchist communities.

The evidence is in fact ambiguous. It is true that there have been anarchist communities that have shared and lived together. These have been of several kinds, and have had different outcomes. The communities of the kind inspired by individualists, such as Josiah Warren discussed earlier, were fairly successful. But they were not communistic; everyone minded their own business and did their own thing, and they gradually evolved into ordinary communities. Communities based on sharing tended not to last, unless there was some religious inspiration. As with the hippie communes of the 1960s, there were difficulties in making sure people did their share of production, and even of chores;

people joined and drifted away as the spirit moved them.

Anarchism has seemed to work best with established communities living a traditional way of life (as in parts of Spain during the Civil War). This tends to reinforce the idea that the appeal of social anarchism is to a lost past of social solidarity, that is quite incompatible with our modern devotion to individualism and personal freedom. The modern version of social anarchism with the most following, Green anarchism, seems to rely on a similar appeal. The social cohesion to make this sort of social solidarity possible is just not there any more. On the other hand, it is argued that we must re-create it if we are to survive.

Be that as it may, it is the case that where anarchism seems to work, if only for a time, is in small, simple, self-sufficient communities. It is not at all clear that it is compatible with modern society, with its high degree of integration and complex mutual interdependence.

Problems with anarcho-capitalism

Modern individualist anarchism, now most forcefully represented by anarcho-capitalism, has its own problems. There are basically three, failure to solve any of which could be fatal to the enterprise. The first is the problem of law and order. As we have seen, Robert Nozick has argued that this is the one essential thing that can not be done better by the free market, but the anarcho-capitalists insist that it can, through private protection and arbitration agencies.

Secondly, there is the problem of public goods. These are goods, like public parks, street lighting, roads, clean air, defence and so forth, which cannot be supplied individually to people who pay for them. We presently pay for them through government taxation. But if there is no government and all things are provided by the free market, how could private firms ensure that everyone pays who uses these things. If they were provided anyway, it would be in an individual's interest to enjoy the good but not pay, to be, as the Americans say, a 'free loader'. Because of free-loading, many would then not pay for others to take advantage, and then the firm providing the good would give up the business and nobody would have it. Again, while anarcho-capitalists offer ways around this, few find them convincing.

Finally, there is the argument that letting capitalism do whatever it wants will lead to mass exploitation and all the horrors that go with it. The anarcho-capitalists deny this would happen, while others are sceptical. In the end, as with all these criticisms of all forms of anarchism, it boils down to faith. This is true of every ideology, but anarchism appears to require a bigger dose of it than most.

7

Marxism

Marxism is a form of socialism, but it deserves separate treatment, for it is a theoretical world of its own, often at odds with the rest of the socialist tradition. It is the most densely theoretical of all ideologies and it has been one of the most influential of the modern world. It takes its name from its founder, Karl Marx, and it helps to understand Marxism if we know a little about his life and how his thought developed.

Hegel, Marx and Engels

Marx was born in 1818 in Trier, Germany, into a Christianised Jewish family. It was intended that he should take up his father's profession as a lawyer, but when he went to university he became absorbed in philosophy and politics instead. At that time, German philosophy was entirely dominated by the ideas of G. F. W. Hegel, who had died a few years earlier. Hegel was an extraordinary thinker whose ideas many people (including some distinguished philosophers) find baffling, but who has influenced other important thinkers, including Marx.

Hegel's philosophy

Hegel was an idealist, which means that he believed that mind or spirit was the ultimate reality and that the physical world could not exist without it. His theory was that 'Mind' (that is, Mind as such, of which each individual human mind is a manifestation) must strive to understand itself, and that the whole of reality and the whole of history has existed so that this can be achieved. To begin with, Mind is unconsciously embodied in physical nature, and only attains consciousness with the advent of human beings. History is the process through which Mind, and therefore humanity, explores its own potentiality, and thereby achieves self-consciousness and freedom. History, therefore, is a single process. Each succeeding civilization is a stage in this process, and each civilization is a totality: ideas, morality, art, religion, laws, institutions, literature, and above all philosophy, are all linked expressions of Mind at a particular stage of its development.

These civilizations each represent stages in a necessary process, which is dialectical. The idea of the dialectic comes from argument, where one person puts forward a point of view (the thesis), another person puts forward a contrary view (the anti-thesis), and in the course of the discussion a third view emerges which combines the best points of the other two (the synthesis). Hegel believed that the human mind naturally developed in a dialectical way, and so does human history. As a civilization develops, he argued, contradictions begin to appear which prevent its further development, and as a result of which an opposite kind of civilization develops, which, in the course of time, gives way to a third that embodies the best of the first two. This third civilization then becomes the basis of a fresh cycle, and so the process goes on.

Hegel believed that human history was exactly like the development of the individual, through babyhood, childhood, adolescence, early adulthood to full maturity; the individual at each stage gaining in capacity, fulfilling potential and growing in self-understanding. Hegel considered that his own world was the final and ultimate stage of history, which had overcome all contradictions, and where the Prussian state, the Protestant religion and Romantic art were the highest possible development of these forms. Crowning all was his own philosophy, which could comprehend all reality and through which Mind could finally achieve full self-knowledge, maturity and freedom.

However, Hegel had a peculiar idea of freedom. For him people were only free when they willingly obeyed the law and behaved morally. He certainly did not see freedom in terms of democracy. His ideal was an authoritarian state that every citizen accepted as right and proper.

Young Hegelians

Hegel's extraordinary conclusion, that his own philosophy was the final culmination of all reality, was accepted by most of his followers, who believed that all that was necessary was to elaborate his ideas in more detail. But a group of his followers, known as the 'Left' or 'Young Hegelians', had more radical views. They thought Hegel was wrong in believing that his dynamic of history was complete. They believed that there was one final, highest stage of history still to come: one that would see the end of all oppression, the dawn of true enlightenment and the final emancipation of all mankind.

Karl Marx became one of these Young Hegelians, believing that a popular revolution in Germany would lead the way for the rest of mankind and begin that final stage of human history. He took up radical journalism and wrote in support of oppressed groups and of radical political action. This brought him into trouble with the authorities and he was forced to leave for France in 1843.

Collaboration with Engels

By this time his views were being influenced by those of another young radical writer, Friedrich Engels, who was to become Marx's lifelong friend and collaborator. Engels came from the Rhineland and was the son of a rich family of manufacturers who owned factories in Manchester. He had spent some time in Manchester learning the family business and observing the industrial revolution at its most advanced. His observations on its impact on the lives of ordinary people was the basis of his first book, *The*

Condition of the Working Class in England (1844).

Engels convinced Marx that the future lay not in raising the consciousness of oppressed classes in backward Germany, but had to do with what was happening in England, and that the key to understanding this was economics. Marx made a detailed study of economics and social history and went on to develop his own theories of economic development and its social impact. He settled permanently in London in 1848, by which time the basic framework of his ideas was complete.

Although they had collaborated on a number of books prior to 1848, it was in that year that Marx and Engels produced the first short, clear but comprehensive account of Marxism with their *Communist Manifesto*. After this Marx spent the rest of his life in London, working mainly in the library of the British Museum developing his theories in a series of books and articles and trying to organise the international working men's movement. He supported himself mainly with occasional journalism and gifts from Engels. He died in 1883 and is buried in Highgate Cemetery. Engels lived mostly in Manchester, managing the English end of the family business. He was able to combine the activity of a successful and prosperous businessman with that of a revolutionary communist for the rest of his life. After 1883 he edited Marx's papers and wrote his own theoretical works. He died in London in 1895.

The Marxian synthesis

Although Marxism was a highly original system of thought, it was shaped by three major theoretical influences: Hegelian philosophy, British economic theory and French revolutionary ideas.

Marx took from Hegel the conception of history as a single process proceeding through a series of necessary stages to a predetermined end, culminating in a final stage when all contradictions and antagonisms will be resolved and mankind will be fully developed and fully free. On the other hand, he rejected the Hegelian conception of history as the progress of Mind towards self-understanding as so much mystical nonsense.

What Marx believed did unite all the elements of human existence was not the 'spirit of the age' but the material conditions of people's lives. It was the economy, and the social structure that went with it, that determined the character of any age, and it was changes in these basic factors that were the driving force of history and responsible for the revolutions that marked the transitions from one stage of development to the next. Marx, therefore, had a 'materialist' conception of history and his basic theory is sometimes called 'dialectical materialism'. His theories are also sometimes referred to as 'scientific socialism', since Marx believed that all his theories were fully scientific, based on the sciences of sociology and economics, and that they 'proved' that the final predestined end of history was the most complete form of socialist society, communism.

To examine Marx's ideas more closely we need to begin with his account of how the various aspects of society are related and how they generate social change.

The analysis of society and social change

Marx believed that the most basic fact about any society is the nature of its economic organisation, its 'mode of production'. This involves two things: the methods of production (the type of agriculture or industry, etc.), and, secondly, the way in which production is socially organised in terms of who owns what and who does which job. The distribution of wealth and work is the basis of the class structure. Although this structure might be quite complicated, Marx insisted that in any society with a class system there will always be a fundamental division between those who own the means of production, and who thereby constitute the ruling class, and those who do the work.

Base and superstructure

For Marx, the socio-economic organisation of society is fundamental because not only does it make all the other aspects of society possible, it also determines the nature of all those aspects. Consequently, in any society the kinds of laws, government, education, religion, art, beliefs and values it has are a direct result of the prevailing social and economic organisation. Marx called the socio-economic organisation of a society its 'substructure' or 'base', while everything else belonged to the 'superstructure' and it is a basic principle of Marxist theory that base determines superstructure.

The crucial link between the base and the other elements of society lies in the need of the ruling class to maintain its power. Thus the state – with its instruments of law, police and armed forces – exists to protect the property of the ruling class, and therefore its control of the economy. But the ruling class cannot maintain its control by force alone; it needs the active co-operation of most of the population. This is where, according to Marx, religion, education and the arts play their role. They help to maintain the position of the ruling class by teaching people to believe that the way society is organised is natural and right and should not be questioned.

The base, therefore, does not just determine the various institutions of society, but also determines the way people think: 'It is not the consciousness of men that determines their existence, but, on the contrary, their social existence that determines their consciousness' (*A Critique of Political Economy*, 1859, Preface).

Marx used the term 'ideology' to refer to ideas, beliefs and values that reflect the interests of a particular class. In any society, he argued, the dominant beliefs and values are always the beliefs and values of the ruling class, while those of the rest of society who accept them (that is, most people most of the time) are in a state of 'false consciousness'. Thus, ideology is also an instrument of class domination, along with all the other elements of the superstructure.

Feudalism and capitalism

We can illustrate these points with the two examples Marx was most concerned to analyse. The feudal society of the Middle Ages was based upon subsistence agriculture. The peasant class did all the work, while the nobility owned all the land. The power of the nobility was sustained by law and custom, and upheld by the king's courts and by force if necessary.

The medieval church was closely bound up with the feudal system and its teachings were designed to maintain the existing order. It taught that the universe was a vast cosmic order, created and ruled by God, in which everything had its appointed place. Human society was part of this order, so that everyone's place in it, from the king to the humblest peasant, had been ordained by God. To try to change the order, or even one's own place in it, was to defy the will of God and was therefore sinful. Medieval art and literature was either religious, and therefore reinforced these teachings, or else was a celebration of the chivalrous exploits of the aristocracy, thereby displaying its fitness to rule.

In contrast, the ruling class in capitalist society is not made up of the owners of land but the owners of capital. This is the bourgeoisie, who control the finance, the factories and the machines upon which modern industrial production is based. Because of this control over the means of production, the bourgeoisie can exploit the industrial workers, the proletariat, just as the feudal aristocracy exploited the peasants. Here again, the state and its instruments support the property and interests of the ruling class, and again the beliefs and values that prevail in capitalist society help to portray the existing state of affairs as natural and right.

The dominant ideology of bourgeois society is liberalism, by which Marx meant the classical *laissez-faire* liberalism of the early nineteenth century, with its principles of free markets, individual liberty, equality of opportunity and limited parliamentary democracy. A society founded upon such principles is portrayed as the good society which works for the benefit of all. In practice, what these beliefs and values do, according to Marx, is to justify the wealth and power of the bourgeoisie, who are seen as having legitimately earned them in the competition of life in which we all have an equal chance. But freedom, equality and democracy are all seen as a sham as long as the ruling class own the means by which the masses earn their living. While the exceptional few might be able to climb the social ladder, the great majority are exploited and oppressed, and the bourgeoisie is able to maintain its economic power over time by means of inheritance.

Religion, although not as important as in the feudal world, also makes its contribution to the bourgeois world view. Protestantism emphasises individuality, and (in some sects at least) views worldly success as a sign of God's grace; while at the same time, as with medieval religion, it reconciles the exploited to their sufferings by telling them that it is God's will and that their reward will be in Heaven. Art and religion also play their part by reinforcing such bourgeois virtues as individuality, freedom and the accumulation of property. Thus, all the elements of the superstructure operate in the interests of the ruling class and consequently are a direct reflection of the socio-economic organisation of society.

The dynamics of social change

These brief and simplified sketches of feudal and capitalist societies pose an obvious question as to how, if the ruling class is so solidly entrenched, one type of society can ever change into another. It is clear from the principle that base determines super-structure that, for Marx, it is social and economic forces that bring about historical change. Great events, such as the Reformation or the French Revolution, do not come about because of changes in people's ideas or because of the actions of great individuals; these are merely the surface manifestations of much deeper sub-structural changes.

Marx's theory of the basic dynamics of historical change is built around four interconnected ideas: economic development, class conflict, the dialectic and revolution. Each mode of production, Marx believed, had its own inner logic of development. Econo-mies change and develop over time through technological innova-tion, new financial techniques or growing trade and prosperity. Such developments give rise to strains and contradictions within the system; a new kind of production evolves along with a new class to exploit it. Eventually, the old structure of society can no longer contain these new developments, and the new class challenges the old ruling class for supremacy. All the contradictions and conflicts can only be resolved by a revolution, since the old ruling class will cling on to its power by any means. But once the revolution is complete, the new ruling class will transform society in accordance with its own mode of production and its own ideology.

This intricate mechanism of change was supposed to explain how the various stages of human development evolved into each other, although Marx only applied it consistently to the latter part of the sequence. The main stages he identified were as follows. Before there was any settled civilization societies were characterised, Marx believed, by a primitive communism, where all property was the property of the tribe. When people settled down and created the first civilization proper, something of this early communal ownership was retained in village life, although the surplus was paid as tribute to a despotic state which organised great public works to irrigate or defend the land. Marx called this the 'Asiatic' mode of production, since it had persisted in Asia while other parts of the world had moved on to later stages of development. The Asiatic mode is succeeded by the 'Classical' mode, which is an economic system based on slavery. This in turn gives way to the feudal mode, which is eventually succeeded by the capitalist or bourgeois mode.

Marx paid particular attention to the transition from feudalism to capitalism. The development of the feudal economy led to a growth in trade, and with trade came towns and, eventually, a new class of merchants, the bourgeoisie. Urban life and the new middle class did not fit well into the feudal social structure. This became increasingly true as the bourgeoisie grew ever more rich on domestic trade, foreign ventures and eventually through the capitalist finance of industry (for example, the domestic system of wool manufacture). The feudal system became an increasing restriction on the development of the capitalist economy, and this contradiction could only be resolved in a new kind of society. The bourgeoisie, whose wealth had come to outstrip that of the feudal aristocracy, eventually came to challenge the power of the old ruling class.

How the bourgeoisie came to take over as the new ruling class varied from country to country. In England it was through the civil wars of the seventeenth century, while in France it was through the most spectacular of all social upheavals, the French Revolution. In each case, revolution was followed by a transformation of society: feudal restrictions and feudal relationships were swept aside; new science and new technologies were inspired by industry and commerce; feudal agriculture was replaced by commercial farming; the old medieval view of the world was replaced by new ideas that were scientific and secular; new art and literature began to flourish; new ideas of liberty and constitutional government began to be advocated.

The capitalist world is not the end of the historical process. By following the dynamic of historical development to its logical conclusion, Marx believed that the transformation of the capitalist stage into one further and final stage, communism, could be predicted. It would necessarily be the final stage since it would resolve all conflicts and contradictions, yet synthesise the best in all previous societies. To understand why Marx thought that this ultimate outcome was inevitable it is necessary to look more closely at his analysis of capitalism.

Capitalism, revolution and human nature

The capitalist system developed through a number of phases and over a number of centuries before reaching its fullest development in modern industrial capitalism. It was only as this final phase was beginning that the theory of how capitalism worked emerged, in the classical economics of Adam Smith and his followers. They were writing at the time when capitalist enterprise was creating the Industrial Revolution, which transformed Britain and would eventually change the entire world.

Marxist economics

Marx admired the classical economists, but believed that their economic laws only applied to a temporary phase of human development, and that as time went on the free market would bring only increasing misery to the majority. He adopted some of their ideas and used them to develop an entirely different theory of his own. The main idea Marx took from the classical economists was the 'labour theory of value', which is an answer to the problem of what determines the value of any object. The theory argues that it is the amount of labour that has gone into producing the object that determines how valuable it is; the more labour has been expended on making or extracting the object the more valuable it will be. This value is a fixed quantity and is different from the price at which it can be bought, which can fluctuate according to the market. (When we think an object in a shop is 'overpriced' or 'underpriced' we are making an unconscious distinction between its price and its value. However, modern economics is based on the idea that the price and value are the same thing.)

In the capitalist economy the workers produce all the wealth and yet remain poor, while the capitalists' wealth grow. Marx used the labour theory of value to explain how this comes about. The workers generate value by turning raw materials into finished products, but only receive a fraction of this value back in the form of wages; the rest, what Marx called 'surplus value', goes to the capitalist as profit. Because he controls the means of production, the capitalist can buy labour cheaply with just enough wages to live on, while keeping most of what that labour has earned for himself. The capitalist, therefore, exploits the workers, and the more he can exploit them the more successful he will be. According to Marx, the capitalist himself adds nothing to the process of value-creation, and so the capitalist class as such is entirely parasitic.

The capitalist, however, has his own problems. Above all he must compete, unlike, for example, the feudal lord. The capitalist economy is based on competition. The capitalist must constantly strive to better his rivals by producing more goods at lower cost. This can be done in two ways: first, by new and better machinery which increases the value-creating power of the worker; and secondly, by reducing the worker's wages. There is constant pressure on the capitalist to exploit his workers more and more, to extract ever greater quantities of surplus value. This fierce competition inevitably produces winners and losers: the stronger capitalists flourish while the weaker ones go out of business. Thus, the capitalist class grows smaller and richer, while the proletariat grows larger and more wretched.

This is the natural tendency of capitalism, although the process is not smooth or continuous. By the time Marx was writing about capitalism the 'trade cycle' had become a recognised feature of economic life. This was the regular progression of boom and slump, of rapid growth and sudden collapse of industrial production. Marx explained the trade cycle in terms of what he believed was the most fundamental contradiction of capitalism.

On the one hand, he argued, there was ever greater production of goods based on ever greater exploitation of the worker, while on the other hand, that same exploitation reduced the workers' ability to buy the goods produced. Consequently, there is always a tendency in capitalism to overproduce, for production to outstrip demand. When this happens, goods go unsold and so workers are laid off and factories close, which reduces demand still further and so more factories close, and so on until the whole economy collapses. There is widespread unemployment and distress, and wages are forced lower and lower. Eventually, wages will be so low that some capitalists will find it profitable to start production again, demand will increase and the economy will begin to recover. But the slump will have driven some capitalists out of business, and only the stronger ones will be left to take advantage of the recovery. With each slump the capitalist class grows smaller as the working class grows larger and suffers more.

The inevitable collapse of capitalism

Marx believed that each successive boom would develop faster and higher, and each successive slump would be deeper and more catastrophic than the last. Eventually the slump would be so great that the impoverished working class would be forced by sheer necessity to overthrow capitalism and establish a worker's state. Thus, the capitalist system is driven to destruction by its own nature, by the working out of its own inner logic.

It is a peculiarity of the capitalist system, Marx thought, that it must train its future destroyer. Unlike other modes of production, industrial capitalism must concentrate its workforce (in factories and workshops) and teach it discipline and mutual dependence. In these circumstances the proletariat has the opportunity to organise and achieve a common understanding of its own experience and what needs to be done; in other words to achieve what Marx called 'class consciousness'.

The progressive enmiseration of the proletariat forces it to see its own situation clearly, undistorted by bourgeois ideology. It will see that capitalist society cannot survive, that the proletariat can and must itself take over the means of production, and dispense with the capitalists whose role in production is unnecessary and parasitic. In short, the working class will come to realise (assisted by intellectuals like Marx and Engels who defect to the proletarian cause) that communism is the true outlook of the working class, and the only hope for the future of humanity. Thus, when the revolution does come the workers will understand what their historical task will be, that is, not only to seize control of the means of production and the instruments of the state, but to go on to build a communist society.

Marx believed that the communist revolution was inevitable. Capitalism could not be reformed, nor the lot of the worker permanently improved. Capitalists cannot change their ways, but must go on increasing exploitation or cease to be capitalists; in this sense they are as much victims of the system as anyone else. The dynamic of capitalist development was so powerful, and its internal contradictions so fundamental, that it must eventually drive itself to destruction. Marx insisted that it was only through a violent revolution and creation of a communist society that all these contradictions could be finally resolved.

Revolution and the dictatorship of the proletariat

Marx believed that the communist revolution would only come when capitalism had reached the full peak of its development.

Consequently, he looked to see the revolution begin in the industrially advanced West, above all in Britain (although he was less certain of this towards the end of his life). But wherever it began it would be a world-wide revolution, because one of the unique features of capitalism was its capacity – through trade and the exploitation of colonies – to bring the whole world within its network. Marx though that nationalism was an aspect of bourgeois ideology, whereas proletarian class consciousness was truly international; that is, workers had more in common with fellow workers in other countries than with their own bourgeoisie. When the communist revolution began in one country, therefore, it would quickly spread to others and eventually the whole world, so that the whole of humanity would be emancipated together.

However, Marx did not believe that the communist revolution would be immediately followed by the establishment of the communist society. There would have to be a transitional period, which Marx called the 'dictatorship of the proletariat', in which the workers would be in control. The state and its instruments would still be the means by which the ruling class overtly maintained its domination, only now the ruling class would be the workers, the majority. The dictatorship of the proletariat has two tasks. The first is to preserve and extend the revolution. The second is to prepare the way for the ultimate stage of human history, the establishment of the classless, stateless communist society, the kind of society appropriate for human nature.

Human nature and alienation

Marx was very suspicious of theories about essential human nature, especially where they appeared to set limits to what was socially and politically possible (for example by depicting human beings as essentially selfish, aggressive and competitive). He believed that human nature expressed itself in different ways in different epochs. In particular, he saw the creation of communist society as involving a transformation of human nature, the emergence of 'socialist man'. However, despite his disclaimers,

Marx did have a theory of human nature that underlay its trans-formations.

For Marx the most crucial feature of humanity, that which distinguished the human being from all other animals, was the capacity to produce. Through social labour, both physical and mental, human beings can make the things they need and build their own world, a world of artefacts and organisations and of ideas. Human needs and the ability to fulfil them develop over the centuries, and they develop socially. Human sociability, the need for the shared life of the community, is another crucial feature of essential human nature, though not unique to the species.

The development of human needs, capacities and social organisation through history has been achieved only at huge cost to the majority of individuals. The price mankind has paid for progress has involved immense exploitation and suffering, the denial of natural human sociability through class, and the warping of the natural creative labour of individuals into the narrow channel of producing goods mainly for the benefit of others. As a consequence, instead of humanity enjoying the world it has created, it is oppressed by it.

In an early unpublished work, known as the *Paris Manuscripts* of 1844 (which only came to light in Russia in the 1920s), Marx described mankind in this oppressed condition as being in a state of 'alienation'. This is a rather strange metaphysical concept which Marx adapted from Hegel. It roughly means that a person's inner self is divided so that they are alienated or estranged from the world, from their fellow human beings and from themselves. This fragmentation and distortion of human personality was, Marx believed, a condition of all societies based on property and class division, but it was at its most severe under capitalism, where human beings are most exploited and where labour is reduced to mindless drudgery. Only in a Communist society will alienation cease, will human beings recognise and be at home in their own creation, and will mankind's fragmented self be restored to wholeness.

Communist society

What, then, will communist society be like? Marx was decidedly vague about this and deliberately so, insisting that communist society was not some utopian blueprint that people must aspire to but the actual society that they would build as they thought best. However, some general features can be given. It will be a world without class divisions and without private property; there will be no more poverty or wealth. It will be a world without the state, at least as we have known it, since Marx sees the state as an instrument of class oppression, so that in a classless society the state will, in Engels' phrase, 'wither away'. For the same reason there will be no more ideology, no more distorted perception, and people will see the world as it really is.

It will also be a world of abundance. Capitalism has taught mankind the secrets of production, and once production is designed to meet human needs and not the need for profit there will be more than enough for all. Consequently, society can be organised on the principle of 'from each according to his ability, to each according to his need'. In other words, everyone will contribute to society according to what their talents and capacities are, and all will take whatever they need from the common stock.

In this society every individual will be able to develop all their talents – physical, intellectual and creative – to the full. In a famous passage Marx wrote:

In communist society, where nobody has one exclusive sphere of activity but each can become accomplished in any branch he wishes, society regulates the general production and thus makes it possible for me to do one thing today and another tomorrow, to hunt in the morning, fish in the afternoon, rear cattle in the evening, criticise after dinner, just as I have a mind, without ever becoming hunter, fisherman, shepherd or critic.

(*The German Ideology*, 1845–46)

This is perhaps a little fanciful, but it does emphasise Marx's insistence on the all-round development of every individual instead of people being restricted to one job. He foresaw a society in which 'the free development of each is the condition for the free development of all'.

Marx believed that many of the divisions in life that we take for granted will have no significance in a future society: the division between the individual and society, between intellectual work and physical work, between town life and country life, and so on. Finally, Marx did not believe that history would come to an end in a kind of static perfection, but merely that all that oppresses and distorts human nature would be thrown off. Indeed, with humanity at last becoming master of its own destiny, genuine human history could really begin.

It should be clear that Marx's ideal was a fully free and creative humanity, which is very far from the totalitarian communism of the twentieth century. But before considering the later development of Marxism, it will be useful to pause and examine some of the objections to Marxism in its original form.

Objections to Marx's theories

Marxism is a powerful and compelling analysis of human society and its development which many people in the modern world accept as fundamentally true, while many others regard it as entirely false. What is certain is that a great many objections to some or all of Marx's ideas have been put forward, some of which are telling and perhaps fatal.

False predictions

The first and obvious point is that Marx's predictions concerning the future development of capitalism have proved false, at least in the short run. In fact, exactly the opposite has happened. Instead of shrinking, the middle classes expanded and diversified with ever greater ownership of capital. At the same time, the working class has become progressively more prosperous, has gained considerable political power, and in recent decades has begun to diminish in size. Furthermore, capitalist society has reformed itself in a manner Marx could not have conceived, with the welfare state and government control of the economy. Finally, Marxist-inspired revolutions have only occurred in undeveloped countries, while the most developed states seem the least likely to follow a revolutionary road.

Although Marxists still believe that capitalism will, before long, collapse under the weight of its own contradictions, they do have to keep adapting their theory to explain away the world's persistent refusal to conform to Marx's projections. This undermines the plausibility of the original theory and calls into question the scientific status it claims to have. Indeed, it has been pointed out (most notably by Karl Popper) that the way Marxist theory is freely adapted to explain any circumstance whatever, means that it cannot be tested against experience. We cannot say what would have to happen to prove it wrong (as finding a metal that shrinks when heated would disprove the law that all metals expand when heated) because it can always explain whatever happens.

Determinism and free will

Another problem is that of determinism. Marx and Engels insisted that their work was thoroughly scientific, and their conception of science was entirely positivist. This means that the social sciences must be like the physical sciences, such as physics, and so based on the assumption that everything that happens, including all human behaviour, is causally determined according to laws of nature. This is a view that has been widely held by social scientists, especially in the nineteenth and early twentieth centuries. However, it has come in for strong criticism. This is mainly because the consequence of this view is that we have no responsibility for our actions, that our belief in our own free will is an illusion, and that human being are little better than sophisticated robots.

Positivism means that everything we do and everything that has ever happened in history had to happen the way it did by necessity and could not have happened in any other way. In fact Marx, unlike Engels, is rather ambiguous about this and does sometimes talk as though human beings do have genuine freedom to choose their actions. Marx may have thought that individual freedom was compatible with historical necessity and natural laws governing the way society behaves (a view known as 'compatibilism'). Nevertheless, the whole thrust of his theory is thoroughly deterministic: necessary stages of history, base determining superstructure, the inevitable collapse of capitalism, and so on. Now if people also have free will then they must be capable of behaving in ways that prevent anything being inevitable. If, on the other hand, there is strict determinism in human affairs then there is something peculiar about the idea that after the revolution we will be free, and that at last mankind will control its own destiny. There is also something odd about writing books to persuade people to work for the revolutionary cause.

Positivist social science has come in for a great deal of general criticism in recent decades. Reasons for this include the fact that no social scientist has ever come up with an empirical law of social behaviour that can be tested; secondly, human actions involve the actor having an understanding of what they are doing, an understanding that cannot be analysed in terms of cause and effect. Human behaviour simply cannot be predicted in the way that the behaviour of physical objects can, and therefore the future course of human history cannot be predicted either.

A further aspect of determinism that is particularly important is Marx's insistence that social conditions determine consciousness and not the other way round. In other words, our ideas and beliefs are determined (and not merely influenced) by our social background. But it is a commonplace that people of the same social background, and even the same family, often have different ideas and beliefs. To take an obvious example, there must have been few people with the same social background as Marx and Engels who thought as they did. Furthermore, if social conditions do determine ideas and beliefs then it is difficult to make sense of Marx's theory of false consciousness, which requires that the exploited class have their ideas and beliefs dictated to them by the ruling class.

Dialectics and history

The scientific status of the dialectic is also dubious. Very few non-Marxists take the dialectic seriously, either as a system of logic or as an explanation of historical development, and least of all as a means of analysing the physical world. It adds nothing to our understanding of historical conflicts to say that they are the result of 'contradictions', or that a resolution of a conflict is a synthesis. The application of such terms is entirely arbitrary. Engels attempted to systematise the dialectic and apply it to the physical world in his book *The Dialectics of Nature*, but produced nothing that would help any scientist to better understand any aspect of nature. To regard ice as the thesis, water as the antithesis and steam as the synthesis tells us nothing whatsoever.

The dialectic is principally an aspect of Marx's theory of historical change. Engels once said that just as Darwin had discovered the law of evolution in organic nature, Marx had discovered the law of evolution in human history. In fact Marx never applied his theory consistently, and there are many instances where it is difficult to see how he could. To take just one example, the end of the classical world was nothing to do with the operation of the dialectic, or with economic development, or with a new class leading a revolution against the old. The classical world collapsed under the impact of the barbarian invasions, which are impossible to fit into Marx's scheme. Indeed, it takes an immense amount of ingenuity to explain all significant historical change in terms of socio-economic developments. Human beings and human societies are far too complex for that. Looking at the sheer variety of modes of human existence, the idea that social development can be summed up in four stages between a doubtful primitive communism and a shadowy future communism is not really very plausible.

These are just some of the objections to Marxism that have been put forward at various times. Needless to say, Marxists have developed a large and elaborate set of counter-arguments, some of which will be discussed in the next chapter.

Revision and revolution

Marx did not confine himself to thinking and writing, but was actively engaged in fostering working-class movements. In 1864 he was actively engaged in setting up the International Working Men's Association (known as the First International), and although this was by no means a Marxist organisation, Marx personally dominated it until its collapse in 1872 (see Chapter 5). Meanwhile, Marxist groups and parties were being set up in various countries, and although Marx's ideas made little impact in Britain they were widely influential in continental Europe, especially in Germany. The major German workers' party was the German Social Democratic Party (SPD), which was fully committed to Marxism. It looked to Marx for advice and guidance, a role taken over by Engels after Marx died.

Bernstein and revisionism

However, after Engels died in 1895 there was no longer an authoritative voice to whom all could defer for the correct interpretation of Marx's ideas and strategy. As a result the Marxist movement began to fragment. The first major division was in the SPD over what is known as the 'revisionist controversy'.

This arose from the writings of one of the party's leading figures, Edward Bernstein. He argued that Marx was essentially a social scientist who had discovered the right way of analysing society, and who had, on the basis of his analysis, identified certain trends, made certain predictions and devised a certain programme of action. But the world had not worked out the way Marx had expected: the bourgeoisie was growing instead of shrinking, while the working class was becoming more prosperous and more politically powerful. The good Marxist social scientist should, therefore, reassess the situation in the light of this new evidence and modify his predictions and his programme of action accordingly. Thus Bernstein believed that the German SPD should abandon its doctrine of the inevitability of communist revolution and its programme of working towards it. Instead it should adopt a doctrine of 'evolutionary socialism' and a programme of working towards socialism through parliamentary means.

Orthodox Marxists were horrified by Bernstein's attempt to 'revise' Marx (hence the term 'revisionism', which became a term of abuse in the Marxist vocabulary roughly equivalent to 'heresy' in religion). The 'revisionist debates' were fierce and bitter, but the final outcome was in fact a compromise. The doctrine and the official programme of the party was not changed, while the actual policies on which it fought elections were more in line with Bernstein's views than with orthodox Marxism.

Bernstein's ideas would eventually triumph in 1959 when the party finally abandoned its commitment to revolutionary socialism at its conference at Bad Godesberg. However, in 1914 the controversy was still smouldering when the First World War broke out. Both Bernstein and the orthodox Marxist leaders argued that this was a capitalist war which the workers should refuse to fight. But a wave of nationalist feeling gripped the working class and the movement's leaders were ignored. By the time the war was over, the focus of world marxism had shifted to Moscow.

Lenin and the vanguard party

Towards the end of the nineteenth century a Marxist party, the Russian Social Democratic Party (RSDP), was established in Russia and began to recruit among the comparatively small industrial workforce. But unlike the German SPD it was not legal, and so was hounded by the tsarist police, its leaders lived in exile, and its effectiveness in organising and supporting the working class was small. This was the party that Lenin (his real name was Vladimir Ilich Ulyanov) joined as a student in St Petersburg. There was already a strong revolutionary tradition in Russia before Marxism arrived, and Lenin was a revolutionary before he became a Marxist (his elder brother had been executed for involvement in a plot to assassinate the tsar).

Lenin's zeal and organising ability soon made him a leading figure in the party and led to his exile. As time went on Lenin became increasingly disillusioned with the RSDP and became convinced that its whole programme and strategy were wrong. The leadership was fatalistic about the possibilities for revolution, believing that Russia must first pass through a long capitalist phase before it was ripe for revolution, which would in any case begin elsewhere first. Lenin disagreed and insisted that the party should work for revolution in Russia as soon as possible, irrespective of what was happening in other countries.

He also disagreed with the strategy of building a mass party on the model of the German SPD. The conditions in Russia were just not the same, the party being illegal, wide open to police penetration and largely restricted to backing workers' demands for better pay and conditions. Lenin's alternative was set out in his most important work, *What Is to Be Done?* (1902). In this he argued that left to its own devices the working class would only develop what he called 'trade union consciousness' and not the necessary 'revolutionary consciousness'. What they needed was leadership from a new type of party which did possess the necessary revolutionary consciousness, plus the theory and tactics to go with it.

Lenin proposed, therefore, the creation of a small party of dedicated professional revolutionaries, trained in revolutionary activity and thoroughly grounded in Marxist theory. The organisation of the party would be based on the principle of 'democratic centralism', that is, open discussion and opinion passing up through the hierarchy, but once a decision had been made at the top it would be rigidly enforced throughout the party. This new party would be the 'vanguard of the proletariat', meaning that it was not separate from the working class, but was its elite, the most class-conscious part of it. Lenin also insisted that whatever was done to further the revolutionary cause was justified, no matter how immoral it might seem. In other words, the end justified the means.

Lenin's ideas split the leadership of the RSDP, and his faction broke away to form their own party that came to be called the 'Bolshevics'. The party he left came to be known as the 'Menshevics'. Some sympathised with Lenin's belief in working for an immediate revolution but could not stomach his dictatorial leadership, most notably Trotsky. (Trotsky had an independent reputation as a revolutionary and a writer, although he returned to the Bolshevics when the Revolution broke out.)

The theory of capitalist imperialism

Lenin's second major contribution to Marxist theory dealt with the problem of Marx's predictions. His solution is suggested in his main work on the subject, *Imperialism, the Highest Stage of Capitalism* (1916). During the late nineteenth century the major powers competed to carve up Africa and other uncolonised parts of the world. Lenin argued that this process constituted a higher stage of capitalism which Marx could not have foreseen. The capitalists increasingly exploited the undeveloped part of the world and used part of the profits to buy off the domestic working class with a higher standard of living. The exploited masses of the colonial world were thus the new proletariat. The First World War was essentially a war for colonial possessions, so that the capitalists of the winning country could extend their exploitation and profits. Consequently, the communist revolution would not necessarily take place in the advanced West.

The country that was in fact particularly ripe for revolution, Lenin argued, was Russia. It was not economically advanced, but then the workers had not been bought off, and its industry, largely financed by foreign capital, was the 'weakest link' in the chain of capitalist imperialism. A revolution in Russia would begin the process, which would spread to the rest of the world and bring the whole system crashing down.

In February 1917 the tsarist regime collapsed under the strain of the First World War, and shortly afterwards Lenin's Bolshevics, joined by Trotsky, seized power in November (October according to the old Russian calendar that was then still in use, hence the 'October Revolution'). Once in power Lenin suppressed all opposition parties, and encouraged the peasants and workers to seize the land and the factories. Despite civil war and foreign intervention the Soviet Union had been established by the time Lenin died in 1924.

Marxism-Leninism

It was Lenin's interpretation and extension of Marx's theory, known as Marxism-Leninism, that became the official doctrine of the Soviet Union and of all subsequent communist regimes (although sometimes with native additions, as in China). It is the version of Marxism that we know as 'communism' and was the only orthodox version until the 1960s. Its reputation as the only authentic Marxism was simply a result of Lenin's success. It was also reinforced by Lenin's creation of the Communist International (known as the 'Comintern') in 1920, which he dominated, insisting that all member parties adopt his doctrines and his system of party organisation, as well as recognising Soviet leadership.

Marxism-Leninism is in fact a rather crude version of Marxism, relying on Marx's later works and Engels' popular expositions. For one thing, it is very mechanical, putting great stress on economic determinism. Democratic centralism is extended from a principle of party organization, where it amounts to rigid control from the top, to a principle of social organisation with party control of every significant area of social activity and where any kind of opposition is suppressed. Thus Article 6 of the Soviet Constitution read:

The leading and guiding force of Soviet society and the nucleus of its political system, of all state organizations and public organisations, is the Communist Party of the Soviet Union. The CPSU exists for the people and serves the people.

The Communist Party, armed with Marxism-Leninism, determines the general perspectives of the development of society and the course of the home and foreign policy of the USSR, directs the great constructive work of the Soviet people, and imparts a planned, systematic and theoretically substantiated character to their struggle for the victory of Communism.

All other communist regimes had similar clauses in their constitutions, which resulted in totalitarian one-party states.

The justification of this in Marxist terms is based on Marx's theory of the 'dictatorship of the proletariat'. Since, in Lenin's theory, the party *is* the proletariat, its vanguard, the party has the right to rule on behalf of the rest of the workers. Various justifications are also offered on democratic grounds. It is said that multi-party systems reflect class divisions, which do not exist in communist countries, and that the Communist Party can alone represent the interests of the people. It was because of arguments like this that communist regimes styled themselves 'people's democracies', as distinct from liberal democracies which were dismissed as a sham because the people had no real power.

On the other hand, while communist regimes claimed to be 'workers' states', they saw themselves as being a long way from achieving a communist society. When Lenin seized power in 1917 he was convinced that his revolution could not succeed unless the workers of other countries followed the Russian lead. This, of course, did not happen. In Marxist terms all communist states are stuck in the transitional phase of the dictatorship of the proletariat (which Marxists, rather confusingly, sometimes refer to as 'socialism' as distinct from the final phase of 'communism') and must maintain a powerful state so long as they are surrounded by hostile capitalist states. Only when the rest of the world has its revolution and catches up, can mankind progress together towards a truly communist society.

Lenin's theory of the vanguard party still dominates wherever communist regimes remain. But since the 1960s it has been criticised as a distortion of Marxism by many Marxists in the West. The theory of imperialism, however, retains its appeal for all Marxists since it overcomes objections based on Marx's failed predictions. It is still widely adhered to despite the end of Western colonialism after the Second World War. The argument is that although overt political control may have gone, the Third World is still dominated and exploited by the capitalist West, only now by more subtle economic means.

The Communist world after Lenin

Following Lenin's death early in 1924 there was a struggle for power in the CPSU (the Communist Party of the Soviet Union, as the Bolshevic Party had now become). Trotsky was the obvious successor, but he was outmanoeuvred by the Party secretary, Joseph Stalin, and in 1929 was forced into permanent exile. Thereafter, Stalin rapidly established himself as the supreme ruler of Soviet Russia.

Stalinism

Through a series of 'show trials' and executions, Stalin virtually wiped out the old Bolshevic party and created a new party in his own image. He ruled through terror, as a result of which millions of people died in labour camps or were executed. Whole nationalities were liquidated, the leading people in every field were frequently 'purged' to eliminate anyone even suspected of dissent, with those that were left reduced to grovelling sub-servience. The history of the October Revolution was rewritten to give Stalin a more prominent place, and he was portrayed as the benevolent father of the nation. The Soviet people were taught to revere him almost as a god, and his portrait was everywhere (a process that became known as the 'cult of personality').

Stalin's policies were summed up in the slogan 'socialism in one country'. This meant concentrating on building up the Soviet Union as a great fortress against a hostile capitalist world, rather than the promotion of world revolution. Stalin was very much a nationalist leader who encouraged patriotism and sought to make the USSR a great power. He was happy to encourage subversion in other countries, but only as a means of promoting Soviet interests; he was quite prepared to abandon fellow communists if it suited him.

At home his first priority was industrialisation, undertaken through a series of 'five-year plans' beginning in 1928, and which eliminated what was left of free enterprise overnight. This was soon followed by the 'collectivisation' of agriculture. These poli-cies caused great suffering and were enforced with great brutality. A whole class of well-off peasants, the 'kulaks', were declared to be enemies of the state and were wiped out; millions were allowed

to starve to death while grain was exported to pay for industrialisation. To ensure that his policies were carried out, Stalin
created a gigantic bureaucracy which came to control Soviet
society in minute detail. By these means, the Soviet Union was
turned from what was essentially a peasant nation into a major
industrial power and by the time of Stalin's death in 1953, one of
the world's two 'super powers'.

Trotskyism

The outstanding communist critic of Stalin was Leon Trotsky
(1879–1940). After his expulsion from the Soviet Union he
devoted himself to writing historical works on the Russian
Revolution, commenting on world affairs and analysing Stalinism.
He also organised a 'Fourth International' of groups in various
parts of the world which accepted his views, although it was not a
significant body until long after his death. He lived in several
countries before settling in Mexico, where he was murdered in
1940 by one of Stalin's agents.

Trotsky's main contribution to Marxist ideas was his theory of
'permanent revolution', which he began to elaborate as early as
1904. He argued that the Russian bourgeoisie was so small and
weak and dependent on foreign capital that it could not carry
through and sustain a bourgeois revolution on its own, as had
happened in Western countries. What would have to happen,
therefore, was that the bourgeoisie would need the assistance of
the proletariat, but once the revolution was under way the working
class would have to keep going until it had created a dictatorship of
the proletariat. In other words, the bourgeois and communist
revolutions would be telescoped into one, and this would stimulate proletarian revolutions in the rest of the world. Although at
first he rejected it, by 1917 Lenin had adopted this theory, and the
events of that year were seen as a vindication of it.

Later, in exile, Trotsky developed the theory further. He
believed that in the underdeveloped world, small and heavily
exploited proletariats would be the force behind nationalist
revolutions to rid their countries of capitalist imperialism. But, as

in Russia, they would not be content with bourgeois democracy but would establish worker's dictatorships. Their success would throw the advanced world into crisis and create the conditions for communist revolution there. The process would not cease until the whole world was under proletarian control, and the movement towards true communism could begin.

Trotsky consistently argued that the primary task of the Soviet Union was to stimulate and aid this process. But, because of Stalin, the Soviet Union had turned its back on world revolution in order to concentrate on building 'socialism in one country'. According to Trotsky, this was not only the wrong priority, but it was not socialism that was being built in Russia either. Stalin had betrayed the revolution. He had destroyed the original Bolshevic party and created a vast bureaucracy that was separate from the workers and which had in effect become a new and oppressive ruling class. He described Stalinist Russia as a 'degenerate worker's state' although some of his followers refused to call it any kind of worker's state, preferring the term 'state capitalist'. Trotsky believed that the proletariat had been robbed of the victory of 1917, so that the Soviet Union was as much in need of a proletarian revolution as the capitalist West.

Although Trotsky is a major figure in twentieth-century communism, his greatest influence has been in the West since the 1950s. By this time many revolutionary socialists shared the general revulsion against Stalin and the system he bequeathed, but there were still Trotsky's ideas to keep alive the idealism of the early Bolshevics. Since the 1950s, Trotskyite groups have provided an alternative to the traditional pro-Soviet Communist Parties (CPs), although they are prone to faction and splits over differences as to the 'correct' political analysis and tactics.

Trotsky's most famous tactical suggestion for his followers in the West was 'entryism', that is, not attempting to change CPs, but secretly penetrating mass social democratic parties to win recruits and eventually control. In Britain today only the Militant Tendency, among many other Trotskyite groups, has systematically pursued this tactic. But whatever their differences, all such groups follow Trotsky in refusing to contemplate any suggestion that

Stalinism was inherent in the ideas of Lenin. Trotsky had, perhaps, a rather romantic idea of the revolutionary potential of the working class and its expression in the pure bolshevism of 1917. He believed absolutely in the Bolshevics' rather crude Marxism and in the concept of the 'vanguard party'. He saw himself as the true heir of Marxism-Leninism. However, despite his standing, none of the extensions of the communist world since 1945 have been inspired by Trotskyism.

The spread of Communism

The Second World War left the Soviet Union with a huge empire in Eastern Europe, which had been liberated from nazi rule by the Red Army. Two other communist states existed by this time in Yugoslavia and Albania. These had achieved their own liberation under partisan leaders, Tito and Enver Hoxa respectively. They were therefore less inclined to take orders from Moscow and soon fell out with Stalin. Albania was, however, to remain true to Stalin's legacy and become the most oppressive regime in Europe, accusing the Soviet regime of 'revisionism'.

In 1949 another major extension of communism occurred when the Chinese Communists, led by Mao Tse-tung, took over the country following a civil war. The Soviet Union was initially friendly and helpful, but this soon turned to hostility and remained so thereafter. By the time of Stalin's death in 1953, the communist world had grown considerably, but it was not the monolithic Moscow-dominated bloc he had wished for. In particular, China had become a rival centre of communist orthodoxy.

Over the next twenty-five years communists came to power in several parts of the world, including parts of Africa, the Middle East, Indo-China, South America and the Caribbean. None of these regimes were dominated in the way Eastern Europe was dominated by the Soviet Union, and many were as nationalist as they were communist. The result was a communist world that was complex and various, and not the solid monolith it was sometimes perceived to be in the West. In particular there was considerable rivalry between the USSR and China for the allegiance of new communist regimes.

Mao Tse-tung

Mao Tse-tung was a Marxist-Leninist, but with significant variations of his own. Soviet communism is built on the proletariat in the orthodox Marxist manner; in China the proletariat played no part in the revolution and Chinese communism is built upon the peasantry. Instead of the Soviet policy of industrialisation at all costs, Mao put much more emphasis on agriculture, upon the revolutionising of consciousness (or 'cultural revolution'), and upon the community. Mao did attempt a sudden dash for industrialisation in the 1950s, known as the 'Great Leap Forward', but this had rather disastrous consequences.

In his writings, Mao was hostile to the Soviet belief that the party had to be omniscient and infallible, and that the 'correct course' had to be imposed on the masses from above. He wrote of his great faith in the wisdom of the masses, and argued that the party was prone to error and must learn from the masses (although how far this did or could happen in practice must be doubted). Mao's China was in fact as totalitarian as the USSR. Nevertheless, it had more appeal to Western youth in the period of the New Left than its Soviet counterpart.

The New Left and after

Following the success of the Bolshevic revolution it was inevitable that Marxists all over the world should look to Moscow for leadership, both political and theoretical. There were some Marxist thinkers in the West who took an independent line, but for most people Soviet communism *was* Marxism. However, the horrors of Stalinism eventually led to a reaction, and the work of some of these independent thinkers became important. In the 1950s and 60s a variety of new Marxisms flourished in the West.

The Soviet version seemed moribund and discredited, having been used for too long to justify a monstrous regime.

Neo-Marxism

Inspiration for much of the new thinking came from Marx's earlier writings, which had not been published and which had only recently became available (particularly the *Paris Manuscripts* of 1844, only discovered in the twentieth century and not widely available until the 1950s). These revealed a 'new', a more humanistic Marx, preoccupied with human alienation, the fragmentation of human existence and the need for liberation. They provided the basis for a fresh interpretation of Marxism that is sometimes referred to as 'neo-Marxism'.

The significance of these early ideas was suggested by a group of German thinkers, including Max Horkheimer, Theodore Adorno and Herbert Marcuse, and known as the Frankfurt School. They had been attempting to take a fresh approach to Marx since the 1930s, and had been convinced that Marx's thought had been distorted by Engels and the Marxist-Leninists, who put too much emphasis on economic determinism, and that Marx himself had been too influenced by positivism in his later years.

More important, they thought, was Marx's analysis of consciousness, and his discussion of human nature and the distorting effects of modern society upon it. They were particularly interested in the relationship between the concept of alienation and modern psychological theories, such as psychoanalysis. Their style of thought is known as 'critical theory', reflecting their aspiration to create a form of Marxist analysis that would reveal the true oppressive nature of modern society, but not based on political economy or class analysis.

When these ideas began to circulate more widely from the mid-1950s onwards they struck a chord, especially among the young. They came at a time when there was not only disillusionment with orthodox Communism, but also a certain disillusionment with the prosperous materialist West. This sparked off a wave of new theorizing which linked Marxism with the ideas of Freud and Wilhelm Reich, with existentialism, phenomenology, black nationalism, 'anti-psychiatry', and with other bodies of thought and social movements (which later included feminism, gay liberation and the ecology movement).

The critique of society

These theorists of these ideas, together with the movements they inspired (above all, the student protest movement of the 1960s), came to be known collectively as the New Left. This was an international movement, though there was little national or international organisation and no fixed body of doctrine common to all. It was all highly anti-authoritarian and displayed a strong anarchist strain (see Chapter Six).

One major theme of the New Left was that modern society, both East and West, was bureaucratic, oppressive and alienating. There was no thought of waiting for capitalism to collapse under the weight of its own contradictions; mankind must be liberated immediately through a transformation of consciousness. Thus in New Left theory economics was largely ignored in favour of the psychology of oppression and liberation, and the critique and analysis of culture.

A major aspect of social oppression was deemed to be sexual oppression, hence the influence of Freud's works, together with those of his more radical follower, Wilhelm Reich. Traditional morality and beliefs were seen as restricting sexuality to joyless conformity, as part of a wider conspiracy to maintain those in authority and keep the rest of us working for the capitalist system. Reich went beyond Freud's theories of sexual repression, and argued that society's systematic repression of sexuality (from the forbidding of masturbation to monogamous marriage) generated unhappy, neurotic personalities and was responsible for aggression and sadism and the desire for power over others. Society's instrument was the patriarchal family, which was based on authoritarianism, was fearful of the youthful instinct for freedom and sexual expression, and which produced the authoritarian personality and ultimately such life-negating ideologies as fascism. Riech put his faith in rebellious youth to liberate mankind from sexual, and therefore political, oppression.

In the 1960s especially, there was a strong sense that all things were possible, even the final emancipation of humanity, if only people had the right understanding. This involved a rejection of conventional lives and conventional morality. The fashion was to 'opt out', into communes, drugs, Eastern religion, and indeed virtually any belief or practice that was deemed to be in conflict with the prevailing order of society.

Heroes of the New Left included Trotsky, Che Guevara and Ho Chi Minh, all rather romantic figures fighting against overwhelming odds. Guevara was a particular favourite, since having played a leading role in the Cuban revolution he refused to be tied down by government and went back to South America to continue the revolution, where he died fighting in Bolivia. Ho Chi Minh was the communist leader of North Vietnam, who had fought the Japanese and then the French and was, in the late 1960s, fighting the Americans for the control of South Vietnam. It seemed a hopeless struggle of a very small and very poor country against an economic and military giant. Intellectual heroes included Jean-Paul Sartre (the existentialist philosopher and Marxist), Frantz Fanon (theorist of anti-colonialism), R. D. Laing (the psychiatrist who thought that it was irrational society that caused mental illness). But perhaps the most characteristic and influential thinker of the New Left was Herbert Marcuse (1898–1979).

Herbert Marcuse

Marcuse had been one of the founder members of the Frankfurt School in the 1930s and had moved with it to the USA after the fascists came to power, later becoming a Professor of Philosophy at the University of California. He was especially concerned to analyse the way in which human freedom, spontaneity and creativity were systematically crushed out of people by modern society. To flesh out his new interpretation of Marx, Marcuse made use of the ideas of Max Weber and Freud.

The attraction of Weber was his analysis of bureaucracy (in *The Theory of Social and Economic Organizations and other Writings*, 1947), which pictured the modern world as increasingly subject to domination and control by bureaucratic structures, so much so that Weber talked of the 'iron cage of modernity'. We all become mere cogs in an ever more elaborate machine, controlled and regulated in ever greater detail of our lives in the name of greater production, efficiency and 'scientific' organisation. Weber wanted to show that both capitalism and bureaucracy were expressions of a particular kind of rationality that was distinctly Western and distinctly modern. This was scientific rationality that assumed everything in reality was subject to rational understanding and control through science, that everything was subject to cause and effect and could therefore be calculated and controlled and that this could be applied to human existence, making ever more complex organisation possible. Weber saw no end to the increasing prevalence of this kind of thinking and its social consequences of ever greater control of social life. He had, therefore, a somewhat bleak view of the modern world and its prospects for the future.

Marcuse shared this view and added his own Marxist twist. The increasing subjection of the world to technical rational control was merely the latest stage in capitalist development. He interpreted science in general, not as a form of objective knowledge and a means of acquiring it, but as a means of domination and control over nature. It was not truth which was the essence of science, but technology. This is used in the capitalist system of the modern world in the form of 'scientific' management and administration, to dominate and control human society. At the same time, in the communist world people were equally oppressed by a bureaucratic monster, spuriously justified by a version of Marxist theory systematically distorted by positivism.

He went on to argue that the alienation of modern man is linked with sexual repression (as analysed by Freud and Reich) and that humanity is in need of sexual as well as economic and political liberation. He further argued that in the modern prosperous

West, capitalism had been clever enough to keep the working classes in their exploited condition, not by overtly oppressive means, but by using advertising to manipulate their desires towards trivial material possessions and satisfactions (such as consumer goods and cheap entertainment) which can easily be satisfied by the industrial system. Through welfare and the consumer society, an artificially-induced sense of well-being, and a spurious freedom and tolerance, diverted them away from demands for economic and political power. This system was so efficient that the capitalist system's grip was becoming unbreakable. It was a comfortable prison reinforced by sexual repression that kept us all in awe.

This rather gloomy picture was the burden of Marcuse's best-known book, *One Dimensional Man* (1964). However, the New Left-student protest movement gave him optimism. The traditional working class had ceased to become a vehicle for revolution. Instead, Marcuse put his faith in those who had not yet been brainwashed and neutered by the system, together with those who missed out on the benefits of the consumer society, that is, the students, blacks, gays, the very poor, and all the misfits and the discontented. These groups together could be a force for revolution and liberation from the tyranny and alienation of the modern world.

Climax and anti-climax

The 1960s was the great age of student protest. Some protest movements were directed against what were deemed to be oppressive governments, as in France. Others supported oppressed minorities, such as the Civil Rights movement in the USA. But the most famous cause, and the one that had most international support, was the protest against the war in Vietnam. It seemed to symbolise America's role as the leader of the racist, capitalist, imperialist system, using its massive military might to crush a poor Third World country that had dared to seek its liberty.

However, much of the student protest seemed to be against

society itself and any kind of social order, and usually (and infuriatingly) without much conception of what they would put in its place. On the other hand, they could argue, as Marx had done, that the revolution itself would transform human nature in ways that could not be predicted, and only after this transformation could a new society be built to suit it.

Student protest reached a climax in 1968. In May of that year riots brought down President de Gaulle. Later the Vietnam war protest ended the presidency of Lyndon Johnson. It merged in a summer of considerable violence in the USA, with major riots in several American cities, and the assassination of, among others, Martin Luther King. But there was no social revolution anywhere, and after 1968 the protest movement all over the Western world began to subside.

The student protest movement died out in the 1970s. The Left took up new causes, such as the women's movement, gays liberation, the ecology and peace movements, but the term 'New Left' no longer seemed appropriate and fell out of fashion. The dream of revolution faded, only remaining strong for those who had become disillusioned with the politics of protest and who had turned to urban terrorism, such as members of the Baader-Meinhof gang in West Germany, the Red Brigades in Italy and similar groups in Japan and elsewhere. These petered out in the 1980s.

Althusser and structuralist Marxism

The change of mood in the 1970s appeared to have much to do with the change in economic climate. In the 1960s people believed that mankind's economic problems had fundamentally been solved and that steadily growing economic prosperity would continue indefinitely but the coming of worldwide economic recession in the mid-1970s put an end to that. Western Marxism changed its emphasis away from a preoccupation with consciousness, alienation and cultural criticism. Once more human beings seemed the victims of great social and economic forces they could neither understand nor control, and so more traditional Marxist concerns with economics and class division appeared to be relevant again.

Orthodox Marxism-Leninism was no longer acceptable, but there was a new version linking Marxism with fashionable theories of structuralism. This new version was principally the work of the French communist theorist Louis Althusser (1918–90). He had in fact developed his main ideas in the 1960s as an antidote to the fashionable neo-Marxism, but it was in the 1970s that his ideas came to prominence.

Structuralism was an intellectual movement that developed in France in the 1960's and which argued that in many aspects of life, our thinking and acting are in fact governed by deep structures of which we are usually entirely unconscious. The movement's most distinguished early figure was the anthropologist Claude Lévi-Strauss, but they could be applied to the study of any aspect of human existence. Structuralism uses explanations in terms of the existence and interaction of underlying structures; that is, instead of agency, of human beings thinking and deciding. Althusser re-interpreted Marx in the light of these ideas.

Althusser dismissed all the recent, humanistic interpretations of Marx by arguing that at a particular point in his intellectual career there was a clear change of direction, an 'epistemological rupture', which left much of his early thinking behind. The early writings, such as the *Paris Manuscripts*, were so much juvenilia that Marx never published because he had in fact abandoned the ideas they contained.

Althusser insisted that what Marx had created in his later work, especially *Capital*, was a new science, on a par with the work of Newton or Darwin. He had penetrated the surface of social life and demonstrated how society worked and changed through the interaction of deep structures. Althusser himself developed these ideas with his theory of 'overdetermination', which says that the determination of the superstructure by the base (in other words, economic determinism) was not a simple determination but much more complex, since different elements of both interacted with each other, so that any given outcome was the result of multiple causes. He also developed ideas about what he called the 'ideological state apparatuses', whereby the state's effective control over the educational system, media and church reproduced the conditions for the continuation of capitalism. All these theories gave the crude economic determinism of Marxism-Leninism greater sophistication and plausibility.

Structuralist Marxism did, however, become less fashionable in the 1980s as post-structuralist theory came increasingly into vogue. This was a philosophical theory that appeared to challenge all theoretical structures, like Marxism, purporting to explain the world in an overall way by showing how the construction of these theories necessarily involved illegitimate metaphysical moves. These theories are thereby 'deconstructed'. Post-structuralism has, therefore, undermined the influence of structuralism in general and Althusser's structuralist-Marxism in particular, although Althusser's own private life, his imprisonment for the murder of his wife, did not help his cause.

Jürgen Habermas

Despite the advent of structuralism and post-structuralism, theorising in the neo-Marxist mode did not cease. In the 1970s, the mantle of the Frankfurt School fell upon Jürgen Habermas (born 1929). Habermas has been an extremely prolific writer, although his work is highly abstract, dense and difficult. He has concentrated particularly on the nature and scope of human rationality and its social consequences.

Like Marcuse, Habermas sees positivist social science and 'scientific' management as the modern means by which the capitalist system controls the population. People are treated as objects of science and in the process are baffled and manipulated. Thus problems such as poverty and disadvantage are treated as technical problems of administration, instead of moral issues over which a public discussion would call into question the justice of the capitalist system. However, because the system cannot solve these problems its credibility is undermined and modern governments consequently face a 'crisis of legitimacy'.

This misuse of science, Habermas believes, is part of a wider distortion of all knowledge and reasoning. His theory is roughly as follows. We have a notion of the ideal human society that is built into the way we communicate as human beings. The simple matter of entering into a discussion with someone implies the acceptance of shared values of mutual trust, respect for truth, the need for assertions to have a foundation in fact, and the recognition that the best argument should prevail. This, however, is an ideal state of affairs that requires all the participants to be equal with each other. Since equality does not prevail in society generally our discussion of human affairs, of how society should be organised and society's problems dealt with, is systematically distorted by the power relations that exist. Public discussion becomes clouded by ideology, which masks and justifies the power differences and the exploitation and oppression that are their consequence. What is needed, Habermas believes, is a 'critical theory', based on dialectical reasoning, that is capable of revealing the distortions of the system and pointing the way to a better society.

In developing these ideas, Habermas has moved further and further away from Marx, to the extent that some would argue that he cannot be properly called a Marxist. However we answer this, it is clear that the intellectual tradition is far from exhausted, and there is still plenty of Marxist theorizing going on. This is despite the collapse of communism in the Soviet empire. Marxists argue that these events in no way invalidate the theory, which perhaps is strictly true, although it will inevitably undermine its plausibility to some degree. There are even some who argue that now a false and distorted Marxism has finally collapsed, the world can progress towards a genuine Marxist revolution in the foreseeable future. This seems hardly credible, but ideological beliefs have a remarkable resilience against mere facts.

The collapse of communism

During the 1960s the Soviet Union was a global superpower and communism was spreading. It seemed that the Cold War would go on indefinitely.

Soviet decline

In the 1970s, communism continued to spread to Asia, Africa and Latin America. Massive resources continued to be poured into Soviet military expenditure, especially into nuclear missiles and the creation of a global fleet. When national security was deemed to be at stake there was no hesitation in taking vigorous military action. Thus, Afghanistan was invaded in 1979 to prevent a communist regime being toppled.

At the same time, the Soviet Union was growing weaker economically. The vast central planning system, GOSPLAN, which controlled the entire Soviet economy and decided exactly who produced how much of what, every price and every wage, was working less and less well. There was immense corruption, virtually everybody lied about what they were producing and there were endless economic dislocations. The economy was grinding to a halt.

Eastern Europe was still under firm control with all dissent suppressed, but Western communist parties increasingly distanced themselves from Moscow, a development known as 'Eurocommunism' in which Soviet policies were criticized, parties became less authoritarian, and increasingly accepted the liberal democratic systems they operated in.

Soviet weakness was cruelly exposed in the early 1980s when America embarked on a new phase of the arms race known as 'star wars', which was based on the latest technology that the USSR could only cripple itself trying to match.

Gorbachev and the collapse of Soviet Communism

Under a new leader, Mikhail Gorbachev, from 1985, the USSR began to change its policies. The Afghan war was ended and talks were begun with the West to reduce nuclear weapons and end the Cold War. This would allow massive resources to be switched from military expenditure to domestic investment, and thereby save the collapsing economy.

Gorbachev also believed that the economy had to be restructured ('*perestroika*') involving more freedom and market forces, and political reform was necessary, with more openness ('*glasnost*') and freedom, and less repression. In this way, Gorbachev hoped to restore the Soviet Union and preserve the Communist Party's power as a modern democratic party instead of an oppressive totalitarian one. These aims were not achieved, partly because the Soviet economy refused to respond to reform, and partly because of events in Eastern Europe.

Among the most rigid of communist regimes was East Germany, which had spent three decades strenuously preventing its citizens from escaping to the more prosperous West Germany, even to the extent of erecting the Berlin Wall and killing those caught trying to cross it. But relaxation of border controls in Czechoslovakia and Hungary allowed refugees to flood to the West. As a result in 1989 the East German regime collapsed and the Berlin Wall was breached amid great jubilation. Other regimes collapsed in rapid succession in Czechoslovakia, Hungary, Bulgaria and Romania. The Yugoslav Federation began to break up in ethnic conflict and even Albanian communism began to collapse.

In the Soviet Union President Gorbachev was prepared to accept the end of Soviet power in Eastern Europe and even countenance the independence of the Baltic states, but he strove to keep the rest of the Soviet Union together. But Gorbachev's unpopularity because of economic failure encouraged a number of hard-line communists still in the government to stage a *coup d'état* against Gorbachev in August 1991. The result was a disaster for the communists. The coup failed and the party was completely discredited. Gorbachev was forced to resign and the President of the Russian Republic, Boris Yeltsin, banned the Communist Party and appropriated its assets. The Soviet Union itself promptly collapsed with all of the republics claiming independence from Moscow. They subsequently formed a very loose alliance, called the Commonwealth of Independent States (CIS) but with no central authority at all. Other communist states have fallen apart under nationalist pressure (see Chapter Four).

China and the wider world

The collapse of the Soviet Union was accompanied by the fall of communist regimes in other parts of the world, including Ethiopia, Angola and Afghanistan. Only a handful of regimes remained, the most important of which was China.

The death of Mao Tse-Tung in 1976 was followed by a change of political direction. His eventual successor Deng Xiou Ping was more moderate and pragmatic and began to move towards economic reform. Mao's collectivization of agriculture had been a disaster and was gradually abandoned, resulting in a big increase in production. The more complex problem of industry was being approached more gradually, when an upsurge of demand for democracy, spearheaded by students occupying Tienamen Square in central Beijing, was put down with great bloodshed and repression in 1989. China became isolated from the world and reform stopped dead. It was several years before changes began again. China is certainly edging towards a market economy, but the government is determined that this will not be accompanied by democratic reform.

Of the remaining communist states, Vietnam is a poor country in need of foreign aid and investment, and is relaxing its orthodox rigour. North Korea has, under Kim Il Sung, become a monstrous tyranny where the adulation and virtual deification of the leader is sedulously cultivated. Whether his son can retain power when the ageing Kim Il Sung dies is open to question. Finally there is Cuba. Fidel Castro has ruled Cuba since he led the revolution in 1959, and has set his face against all change. However, the end of Soviet aid has, many believe, doomed Cuba to economic collapse sooner or later.

Thus communism is not in a particularly healthy state anywhere in the world. Nevertheless, orthodox communism is not yet dead, while Marxism in general is still capable of inspiring belief, support and fresh thinking.

8

Racism and fascism

Racial prejudice is an ancient prejudice, but racism as a formulated doctrine is a product of the nineteenth century. Fascism, on the other hand, is a twentieth century doctrine. There is no necessary link between racism and fascism. Italian fascism, for example, had no interest in racial matters. Nevertheless, there are strong historical links. Both are characteristic of the extreme Right, but more important is the fact that in Nazi ideology the most complete fascism and the most complete racism are fused. Initially, however, we need to examine their separate developments.

Nineteenth-century racism

Racial attitudes, prejudices and beliefs are very old indeed. The ancient Greeks thought of themselves as obviously superior to non-Greeks because they considered their civilisation so much superior. The Chinese regarded Westerners in the same light, while Europeans considered the native peoples of areas they conquered as inferior. Such assumptions were perhaps natural enough in their day; just as in ordinary life, those possessed of power or position are inclined to regard themselves as superior to those who do not have these things. It might be said that in Europe racialist thinking may have been inhibited by Christian assumptions about all being equal in the sight of God, although this did nothing to prevent atrocities inflicted on indigenous peoples of Africa, the Americas and elsewhere by Europeans, nor the persecution of Jews as the people who had 'murdered Christ'.

Early racist theory

However, racist thinking is not confined to relations between continents. Developed racist theory enters European politics at the time of the French Revolution with claims that the French aristocracy had a right to rule because it was descended from the Frankish conquerors at the end of the Roman Empire. It was countered by the argument that the ordinary people of France were reasserting their rights after centuries of unjust and illegal rule by usurpers. Arguments of this kind were, in fact a common feature of French politics in the nineteenth century and continue into the twentieth. A similar point was made by Tom Paine in his *Rights of Man* (1791) where he said that the English aristocracy was descended from 'the French Bastard and his armed banditti'.

Such arguments were based on history, but during the nineteenth century new sources of racial ideas developed that were based on a variety of what were taken to be 'human sciences', growing out of the Enlightenment belief in the efficacy of applying the methods of the physical sciences to the human condition. Anthropology was among the first of the human sciences to classify different human types according to colour and other characteristics. Later this descriptive anthropology became more 'scientific' when an army of fieldworkers, equipped with much ingenious gadgetry, went around measuring all parts of the human body, and relating their data to a variety of specially devised indexes. The most popular of these was the 'cephalic index' for relating head measurements. For much of the nineteenth century academic debate raged over the alleged superiority of dilochocephalic (long-headed) over brachycephalic (round-headed) types.

Racist ideology developed when such classification and analysis was related to wider frameworks that purported to explain the social significance of the scientific conclusions. Among the earliest attempts to put anthropological findings into a wider framework was a version of the old theory of a Great Chain of Being, which linked all known natural and supernatual pheno-mena into a single hierarchy beginning with the elements and reaching up to God, with humanity placed between the animals and the angels. Given a racial twist, a new hierarchy of human types was added, with black Africans a little above the animals and whites a little lower than the angels. Many anthropologists drew explicit political conclusions from their work, directly justifying slavery, or imperialism, or nationalistic assertion, or warning of racial degeneracy through racial mixing.

But perhaps the most significant anthropological contribution to the nineteenth-century debate on race was that of the distin-guished French anthropologist, George Cuvier, who (around 1830) claimed to have demonstrated a consistent and necessary correlation between physical and mental characteristics. The significance of this alleged discovery (later shown to have been mistaken) was that it appeared to prove that it was racial charac-teristics that determined the culture and achievements of a people. Since the superiority of the culture of European peoples was taken for granted (the development of science and tech-nology, arts and philosophy, were all presumed to be superior compared with other races), then it was equally taken for granted that superior racial characteristics were the reason.

Although the jump from anthropology to politics was frequently made, it was not a necessary jump. There were some who did not believe in inherent racial superiority, while others who did make that assumption refused to draw the usual political consequences. Charles White, for example, an eighteenth-century amateur anthropologist and believer in the Great Chain of Being theory, littered his writings with references to the greater intelligence and beauty of the white race, yet he nonetheless insisted that his writings were no justification for slavery. Indeed, he pointed out that many negroes were of equal intelligence and ability to many Europeans and that they were entitled to the same liberty and equality as anyone else. Robert Knox (1798–1862), the famous Edinburgh anatomist and surgeon who had been a student of

Cuvier, wrote a book *Races of Man* (1850), in which he developed a theory that he called 'transcendental anatomy' which, while insisting on the inequality of the races and the vital importance of race for civilization, equally insisted that each race had its natural homeland and should stay there; imperialism, therefore, was mistaken and wrong.

The Aryan myth

The supposed necessary link between physical and mental characteristics also seemed to confirm and justify similar assumptions made in cultural studies. It was quite common to explain differences of art and literature between different countries in racial terms.

Linguistic palaeontology, the study of the origins of languages, took a prominent part in the fashionable passion for the discovery of national origins and identity. It was this field that also gave rise to one of the most potent of racist myths. It was claimed that almost all European languages had a common root in Sanskrit (a language of ancient India). And it was in Sanskrit texts that was found the legend of a noble race of Aryan conquerers. Thereafter the Aryan myth of a splendid race of warriors, who were also the originators of all civilization and all noble values, developed steadily. Count de Gobineau, Houston Stewart Chamberlain and Hitler were the best-known exponents of it, although it was widely used to justify political beliefs of various kinds from the 1850s to the 1940s, with various people claiming their particular nation or aristocracy or other group to be of true Aryan descent.

The most fully developed racist theory of the nineteenth century was that of the French aristocrat, Count Joseph-Arthur de Gobineau (1816–82). He combined various theories from history, anthropology, linguistics and other sources to produce the most comprehensive and complex ideological position of a racist kind in his book *Essay on the Inequality of the Races of Man* (1853–55). He believed that the rise and fall of great empires could be accounted for in terms of race. A people had the vigour and will to create an empire when it was racially pure. But in success were the seeds of defeat, for the inevitable mixing with conquered peoples necessarily produced a dilution of the racial stock, followed by decadence and decline. Miscegenation (racial mixing) debilitated the race and weakened its will and ability to fight.

There was, Gobineau insisted, a definite hierarchy among races. Broadly, the whites came top, followed by the yellows and then the blacks. The whites were noble, spiritual and creative, the yellows were materialistic and only concerned with making money, while the blacks were physical, feckless and unintelligent. He related this in turn to French society, identifying the aristocracy as white, having been descended from the Germanic Frankish conquerors, the bourgeoisie and working class with the yellows, and blacks as the indigenous Gauls. French greatness had declined because of the racial mixing of these groups, and its restoration depended on restoring and maintaining as far as possible these racial hierarchies. Above all, of course, the aristocracy must preserve its racial purity.

Social Darwinism

In the second half of the nineteenth century the scientific debate over race shifted from anthropology to biology, finally centering around the work of Charles Darwin. Despite the fact that Darwin's theory of evolution has no necessary social or political implications whatsoever, it was nevertheless used by ideologists of all kinds to justify quite opposite views (see Chapter Three).

Darwin said nothing about race, but ideologists drew various racial implications according to their prior beliefs. For some, the demonstration of evolution clearly showed that all humanity derived from a common stock and hence were all 'brothers'. But most took a different view and saw in evolution the equally clear demonstration that inequality was 'natural' since some races were thought to be obviously at a higher stage of evolution than others. Various theories of 'social evolution' were developed in which the principle of 'the survival of the fittest' was taken to apply to internal politics, international politics and imperial politics, justifying elite classes, elite nations and elite races.

Success in war, or in other struggles, was deemed a particular mark of racial purity. Such thinking became a standard feature of much political, and especially right-wing, theorising in the late nineteenth and early twentieth centuries. Indeed, various ideologies created racist variations. Even liberalism and socialism, ideologies most committed to notions of universal equality, developed one or two hybrids, though no influential ones. Conservatism and nationalism were the traditions most open to racist thinking.

Anti-Semitism

The age-old prejudice of anti-Semitism was given new force and respectability through this kind of racist theorising, particularly in Germany and Central Europe. Wilhelm Marr argued in a widely read pamphlet of 1873 that all Germany's problems could be traced to the influence of Jews and that such influence had to be eliminated from German life. It was a view given support by Heinrich von Treitschke, the most distinguished German historian of the time. The great composer Richard Wagner vigorously promoted his views that the Jews were an inferior race incapable of contributing to European culture.

Wagner's Germanised English son-in-law, Houston Stuart Chamberlain (1855–1927), produced a similar theory to Gobineau's, although more ferociously anti-Semitic and based on social Darwinism, in his *Foundations of the Nineteenth Century* (1899), which argued for a hierarchy of superior and inferior races with Jews at the bottom and the Germanic Aryans at the very top. He wrote of a great race-war that existed between Aryan and Jew that was coming to a climax, although the Aryans would eventually conquer all because of their 'superior genetic gifts'. Because Christianity had plainly contributed much to Western civilisation he could not accept that Jesus had been a Jew, but must have been an Aryan. His book was widely read in Germany in the early years of the twentieth century.

All these writers and theorists produced an intellectual climate of anti-Semitism that influenced social opinion and politics. The Jews had provided a convenient scapegoat since the Middle Ages, and were blamed for famines, plagues and other disasters. In the latter part of the nineteenth century, a series of crises in capitalism across Europe caused unprecedented distress and unemployment in areas where capitalism was new, and these were blamed on Jewish financiers because people did not know who else to blame.

The growth of national consciousness, especially the aggressive and xenophobic nationalism developed by the conservative Right in the late nineteenth century, also contributed to anti-Semitism, which was in turn a major factor in the development of nationalism in Eastern Europe. In the 1890s anti-Semitic groups and parties were common in Germany, Austria and the rest of Central Europe, while conservative parties, and sometimes governments, adopted policies of discrimination against Jews. Anti-Semitism became distinctive of the far Right in a number of Western Europe countries as well, especially France.

The worst case was in Russia, where anti-Jewish rioting was encouraged by the government in the huge pogroms of the 1880s, 1890s and early years of the twentieth century, in which many Jews died and many more were left with homes and livelihoods destroyed. The result was massive Jewish emigration to North America and Western Europe which increased anti-Jewish sentiment. After the First World War, Russian *émigrés* fleeing from the Revolution put about notions of a mythical world Jewish government, the 'Elders of Zion', who were plotting to take over the world by creating chaos through their control of international finance, and instituting revolutions, beginning with Russia. Austria and Germany, having suffered a humiliating (and in their view unwarranted) defeat in the war, followed by economic disaster, were fertile ground for the propagation of such a myth, as well as other manifestations of anti-Semitism.

Racial thinking was a commonplace of Western thought throughout the nineteenth century and into the twentieth. It was the shock of the Nazi experience that brought all racist thinking into disrepute and stimulated a re-examination of the scientific evidence on race which revealed that no necessary link whatsoever can be established between race and culture or achievement, or even of any clear demarcation between races.

Racism still exists today, but is almost universally condemned by states, international organisations and by educated people everywhere. Where it exists it is usually associated with fascist thinking, although the first fascist thinking was not racist.

Italian fascism

Today the word 'fascist' is used in some circles as a term of vulgar political abuse, meaning 'authoritarian' or 'dictatorial'. In a similar way it is sometimes used to mean 'totalitarian' (where there is one political party which controls everything in society and everyone is told to think the way of the party), hence the seemingly contradictory phrase 'the fascist Left'. But properly used 'fascism' refers to a group of political doctrines that flourished mainly in Europe from the 1920s to the 1940s, most notably Mussolini's fascism and Hitler's national socialism (or 'nazism'). Some have argued that they are two separate doctrines, but it seems more sensible to regard them as two variations of the same thing. Hitler adopted Mussolini's same basic fascist ideas and added a large racist dimension.

Mussolini's career

Fascism was invented by Benito Mussolini (1883–1945) in the early 1920s. He had originally been a Marxist journalist, although, significantly, one who believed in the importance of will rather than economics. But he was disillusioned by the in-fighting among various socialists and communists at a time when Italy was in chaos and plainly in need of strong leadership. The First World War taught him that national feeling was a far more powerful political force than social class. Using a variety of current ideas, he put together a potent concoction of nationalism, authoritarianism and collectivism, which was able to play on people's fears and prejudices and, with skillful propaganda, excite an unthinking mass following. He built a Fascist paramilitary organisation, the Blackshirts, and his followers fought elections using violence and intimidation. Finally, Mussolini himself seized power after an audacious march on Rome in 1922 (which could easily have been frustrated had his enemies worked together). Opposition was then ruthlessly suppressed and Mussolini ruled Italy for the next twenty-one years.

Mussolini's ambition was to build Italy into a major world power. This meant creating a powerful economy as the basis for imperial expansion and European war. An alliance with Hitler, setting up the 'Rome-Berlin Axis' in 1936, seemed initially successful but led to the Allied invasion of Italy and the German army being sent in to prop up his rule. As the Allies advanced he was seized by anti-Fascist partisans and murdered in 1945.

The Fascist state

Like Hitler, Mussolini tended to make up theory as he went along, according to need. Nevertheless, fascism rested upon a fairly consistent body of belief, the core of which centred around the state. The term 'fascism' comes from the Italian *fascio* meaning 'bundle' or 'bound' together, which had implications in Italian politics of an insurrectionary brotherhood. It also comes from the same Latin root as *fasces*, which was the bundle of rods with axe-head carried before the consuls in ancient Rome as a symbol of state authority: the bundle represented the unity of the people under the state, represented by the axe. Mussolini coined the term 'fascism' and used the fasces as a symbol of his regime. (Such Roman symbolism was important to Mussolini, the implication being that he was re-creating the greatness of ancient Rome.)

Fascists glorify the state as representing the unified people, and absolute unity is the ideal. All division and diversity is anathema. Hence fascism is totally opposed to liberal democracy with its divisions of opinion, right of dissent, tolerance, pluralism and party conflict; above all it rejects liberalism's emphasis on individualism. At the same time, the fascist system is claimed to be superior to liberal democracy and capitalism in that it caters for all groups in society and not just those to whom the system gives an advantage. Equally, fascism rejects socialism's egalitarianism and its insistence on the reality of class division and the necessity of class conflict.

Instead, fascism aspires to total unity with discipline imposed and inspired from above. The individual must be subordinated to, and if necessary sacrificed for, the state. People are therefore expendable, for value lies not in the individual but only in the unified whole. Society is an organism and the destiny of the individual is bound up with the destiny of the whole. It is the organism that is important, not the individual. This is fully understood by the great leader, to whose will the masses must be moulded.

Fascism is consciously and explicitly totalitarian, with no organisation capable of resisting the state allowed to exist, the state in complete control of the media and education, and the imposition of ideological uniformity. The term 'totalitarian' was coined in Italy to describe Mussolini's regime, and he adopted it and used it with pride. (Hitler ignored the word, while Communists always indignantly deny that it applies to them.) In 1932 Mussolini wrote:

The keystone of Fascist doctrine is the conception of the state, of its essence, of its tasks, of its ends. For Fascism the state is an absolute before which individuals and groups are relative. Individuals and groups are 'thinkable' insofar as they are within the state ... When one says Fascism one says the state. The Fascist conception of the state is all-embracing; outside it no human or spiritual values can exist, much less have value ... Thus understood, Fascism is totalitarian, and the Fascist state – a synthesis and a unit inclusive of all values – interprets, develops and potentiates the whole life of a people ... This is a century of authority, a century tending to the 'right', a Fascist century.
('Fascism: Doctrines and Institutions' in *Encyclopedia Italiano*, XIV, 1932)

(It is worth noting that Mussolini did not succeed, as Hitler did, in subordinating or intimidating all organizations; for example he could not control the Catholic Church.)

Both Hitler and Mussolini conceived of the state as an organism and its organisation as ideally corporatist. Mussolini wrote: 'Every interest working with the precision and harmony of the human body. Every interest and every individual working is subordinated to the overriding purposes of the nation'.

In Italy this meant that the different aspects of the economy were represented by corporations of workers and employers (in fact dominated by fascists) who planned everything in co-operation with the state. The system is known as 'corporatism'. Mussolini borrowed the idea from the syndicalists (see Chapter Six), but instead of just workers there would be capitalists as well. In practice the workers were disciplined while the capitalists could exploit them as they wished as long as they did what the national plan required. The aim was to build up the Italian economy and make it strong and independent, although in fact it ended up corrupt and inefficient. Economic self-sufficiency was one of the preoccupations of the aggressive nationalism of the late nine-teenth and early twentieth century (as distinct from the liberal belief in free trade). Hitler had similar corporatist aims for much the same reasons, but was rather more effective at achieving them than Mussolini.

Leadership and struggle

As well as the state, fascists also glorified leadership. Mussolini called himself 'Il Duce' and Hitler 'der Führer', both meaning 'the leader'. The leader was the symbol of his people and their struggle. Both Mussolini's *Autobiography* and Hitler's *Mein Kampf* (meaning 'My Struggle') were romanticized versions of their author's lives with which the people were supposed to identify and gain inspiration. It was the great leader alone who could under-stand and articulate the 'true' will of the people. The great leader had the right to hold absolute authority over his people and demand their absolute obedience; it was what Hitler called the 'leadership principle' or *Führerprinzip*. This was absolute dictatorship, but because the leader was supposed to fully express the people's will, the fascists also claimed it to be the purest democracy.

The leader was the best of his people and had proved this by having struggled to the top. This idea came from the social Darwinism that both Mussolini and Hitler embraced. It was the idea that life was a struggle in which only the fittest survived. It was claimed to apply both to the struggle between nations (and between races in Hitler's case) and within nations. Those who rose to the top were *ipso facto* the elite, and he who rose to the very top was the best. Hitler called this the 'natural order', the 'aristocratic principle of Nature'. Mussolini's fascists and Hitler's nazis were thus the elites, the natural aristocracies of their respective peoples, and the fact that they achieved their positions by violence merely confirmed their superiority.

Action, struggle and violence were natural and good, hence the fascist glorification of war. Mussolini wrote:

Fascists above all do not believe in the possibility or utility of universal peace. It therefore rejects the pacifism that masks surrender and cowardice. War alone brings all human energies to their highest tension and sets a seal of nobility on the people who have the virtue to face it . . . For Fascism the tendency to empire, that is to say the expansion of nations, is a manifestation of vitality, its contrary is a sign of decadence. Peoples who rise, or suddenly flourish again are imperialistic; peoples who die are peoples who abdicate.

('Fascism: Doctrines and Institutions' in *Encyclopedia Italiano* V, 1932)

Fascist values reached their highest expression in war. It was in war that the nation was most united, disciplined and possessed of a sense of purpose and national pride. War was thought to 'purify' and strengthen the people; the individual was submerged in the mass, while opportunities existed for individual courage and self-sacrifice for the good of the whole. In war the state was supreme and leadership responded to its greatest challenge. The people forgot their difficulties and conflicts and responded to leadership with a heightened sense of national emotion and participation; it is not surprising that Fascist regimes tended to be highly militaristic.

Fascist ideas and methods tended to be intellectually crude; indeed, Fascists despised intellectuals and sophisticated theory. Instead, they stressed instinct, emotion, will and above all, action. There was, therefore, a strong irrationalist element in fascism: emotion and will were the basis for action, rather than reason

(Mussolini exhorted his followers to 'think with your blood'). In consequence, Fascism is widely understood as a relapse into barbarism, a return to the primitive, and a denial of the basic values of civilisation. It certainly has little appeal to educated people.

Popular dictatorship and socialism

Fascist dictators have not been remote autocrats, but demagogues appealing directly to the people. They have sought to arouse mass passion and maintain a heightened emotion of mass solidarity against those identified as enemies within and without. Some writers have argued that this constant state of emotion and tension is essential for fascism; that it inevitably results in constant war which must eventually end in defeat, and that therefore fascism is inherently and necessarily self-destructive. Certainly, fascist regimes have been characterised by constant mass manipulation through propaganda. Control and use of the mass media (especially radio and film, but also newspapers) was a crucial element in fascism, and helped to make it a peculiarly twentieth-century phenomenon. Emotional rhetoric, especially the rhetoric of hate, played a central part, and Mussolini, Hitler and Goebbels were all masters at manipulating mass audiences.

Great emphasis was put on symbolism and ritual, and flags, uniforms, insignia, rallies, parades, and so forth were used to excite and unify the people with a common emotion. Mass adulation of the leader was generated and sustained, in a way quite different from mere fear of a ruthless dictator. It is an uncomfortable thought that both Mussolini and Hitler were immensely popular when at the height of their power.

One of the curiosities of Italian and German Fascism was their relationship with socialism. Socialism proper was despised and rejected for its emphasis on class conflict and its ideals of equality and universalism. Yet Hitler called his system of ideas 'National Socialism' and Mussolini claimed that his ideas had a socialistic element. Part of the reason for this was that both of them wished to appeal to the working masses and wished to harness the loyalty that socialism commanded. But also, fascism does share with socialism a collectivist approach and an aspiration to solidarity, as against liberal individualism. Capitalism was suspect because it encouraged the pursuit of individual self-interest, which conflicted with fascist demands for total devotion to the collective will. On the other hand, neither Hitler nor Mussolini had any thought of abolishing capitalism and still less of promoting equality. It is in repect of such values that the real differences lie, and from which it is clear that fascism and socialism proper are diametrically opposed and should not be confused. In fact, both Hitler and Mussolini often talked of their systems as a 'middle way' between liberalism and socialism, while transcending both.

Hitler's national socialism

The common elements of fascism – extreme nationalism, social Darwinism, the leadership principle, elitism, anti-liberalism, anti-egalitarianism, anti-democracy, intolerance, glorification of war, the supremacy of the state, anti-intellectualism, and so on – together form a rather loose doctrine. Fascism emphasises action rather than theory, and fascist theoretical writing is always weak. Hitler's nazism had rather more theory, though its intellectual quality was appalling. This greater theoretical content was mostly concerned with race, and it was Hitler's racial theories that distinguished nazism from Italian fascism.

Hitler's career

Hitler was not in fact a German citizen by birth. He was born in Austria in 1889 and studied art in Vienna, where pan-German ideas and anti-semitism were common. He was unsuccessful as an artist but joined the German army in 1914 and won medals for bravery. Like many Germans he thought the German surrender in 1918 was entirely unnecessary and the result of political betrayal, and was bitter and angry at Germany's subsequent humiliation. Against a background of mass unemployment and hyper-inflation, he built up his National Socialist German Worker's Party ('Nazis' for short) into a major electoral force. Its programme and ideology was set out in Hitler's autobiography, *Mein Kampf*. When the Nazis became one of the leading parties in parliament, Hitler was invited to become chancellor (Prime Minister), and he immediately began destroying all opposition and giving himself dictatorial powers.

He then began implementing his programme of uniting all Germans in a single state and creating a German empire in the east, policies which precipitated the Second World War. As to the racial programme, the Jews were systematically persecuted from the moment the Nazis came to power. They lost jobs, had their businesses destroyed, were subjected to endless humiliations and then herded into concentration camps. Hitler's 'Final Solution' was the decision to systematically slaughter all the Jews that could be found. Around six million died, mostly in the gas chambers of Hitler's concentration camps; almost two-thirds of all Jews in Europe perished. Known as the 'Holocaust', it is one of the worst and most obscene crimes in human history. The full horror of the camps was only discovered by Allied troops towards the end of the war. Hitler shot himself in his Berlin bunker in 1945, blaming the German people for letting him down, and still convinced of the truth and rightness of his beliefs.

Nature and race

Like Mussolini, Adolf Hitler had constructed his own ideology in the 1920s using materials around at the time, but he made greater use of social Darwinism and racial theories that emphasised the superiority of the Aryan race. He produced his own synthesis of these theories based on Germany's current conditions and his own particularly virulent brand of anti-Semitism. He often referred to it as the *Volkish* philosophy (*Volk* means 'folk' or 'people').

In Nazi ideology there was much emphasis on Nature and man's part in it. It was not the ordered and rational nature of earlier centuries, but post-Darwinian nature, competitive and brutal. Like every other species, man had to struggle with his kind and with the rest of nature for survival on a crowded planet. This involved struggle within society, but more important was the competition to survive and flourish among the different races or peoples (Hitler used the terms interchangeably). Peoples were in permanent competition: all sought to grow and expand, and needed territory as living space to do so.

Upon this naturalistic picture Hitler superimposed a system of values which he called 'race-values'. To win and to dominate was good and glorious and a mark of superiority. Hitler wrote in *Mein Kampf*:

And so the Volkish philosophy of life corresponds to the innermost will of Nature, since it restores that free play of forces which must lead to a continuous mutual higher breeding until at last the best of humanity, having achieved possession of this earth, will have a free play for activity . . .

Those races that were superior by nature not only dominated but also produced culture. Some races were culture-creating (above all the Aryans), others were culture-carrying (most of the rest), but some were inherently culture-destroying. In the last category the Jews were pre-eminent. They were a people who had to struggle to survive and dominate like any other, and who were just as intent on preserving their race purity. The Jews, however, were special. On grounds that were not very clear, Hitler insisted that there was some kind of natural relationship between the possession and acquisition of territory and the development of culture. What made the Jews different was that they had no territory, no state, and were incapable of creating or defending one.

The Jews were an unproductive people, lacking any race-value, who lived off the races who were productive. They were, in some sense, an unnatural people, and their methods were correspondingly unnatural. They employed not the honest nobility of war, but a more insidious and evil undermining of of the strength of the people they lived among, destroying their race-purity and polluting their race-culture with alien and socially debilitating ideas such as internationalism, pacifism, equality and democracy, while maintaining their own belief and racial purity. The overall purpose of such methods was to dominate the host states (as in Russia and elsewhere) and eventually the world. They would denationalise the world and thereby destroy the meaning of history. Thus, when Hitler spoke of the Jews as 'parasites' it was not only crude abuse but part of his theory.

To make such assertions involved considerable distortions of history. The notion that the Jews could not maintain a state ignored the biblical state of Israel's thousand years of existence. More difficult to ignore was Christianity, an offshoot of Judaism, which undoubtedly had made a very great contribution to Western civilization. The Nazis argued that since Jesus had made a contribution to civilization he could not have been a Jew but must have been an Aryan. Those aspects of Christianity they despised, like universal brotherhood, were attributed to his Jewish followers. Nor were they thrown by the fact that some of the most influential intellectual figures of recent Western history – Marx, Freud and Einstein – were German Jews. Marx was regarded as part of the Jewish plot to conquer the world; Freud's ideas were dismissed as degenerate, while Einstein was simply ignored.

Struggle and history

While the race (or people or 'folk') was the most important entity, Hitler also dealt with the world of individuals within a people. This too was a competitive struggle, within which the equivalent of 'race-value' was 'personality-value'; that is, some were naturally superior to others. In a properly ordered society, a 'just' society, the superior dominated the inferior; the ability to dominate was a mark of superiority. Hitler called this the 'aristocratic principle of Nature'. Politics was a natural struggle for power according to the laws of the jungle. Succeeding in the struggle and dominating all was the Leader, whose task was to ensure that every aspect of social life was controlled that it might subserve race-purity and national greatness. The unjust and unnatural equalising of people in democracy was a Jewish idea designed, like internationalism and pacifism, to destroy the natural vigour of the people.

History was the natural struggle of individuals and peoples to survive and prosper. But it was not a blind and formless struggle (as the Darwinian picture of natural selection would actually imply); for over and above all particular struggles, setting them all in perspective, was the world-historical struggle of Aryan and Jew. Contemporary Germany was the centre of the drama, the home of the Aryan, and the setting for the final act. For this reason the Jews were determined to destroy Germany by means of a world plot embracing both international finance and communism (a somewhat unlikely combination). It was the Germans, or more generally Nordics, who were the true descendants of the Aryans, the purest and finest remnant. They were the 'master race' whose natural destiny was to rule the other 'inferior' races, enabling them to cleanse culture of degenerate influences and reach new and more glorious heights of culture and civilisation. But to do this the Aryans had to be hard and ruthless, suppress compassion and learn to treat lesser people as subhumans to be enslaved or destroyed like vermin.

Jews had betrayed Germany in the First World War, and engineered her humiliation and territorial emasculation. But inspired by a great leader, the German people would rise from defeat, expand territorially to create *Lebensraum* (living-space) at the expense of the inferior Slavs, create a network of alliances with comparable great powers (Italy dominating the Mediterranean and Britain the High Seas), and eliminate European Jewry. Thus, a just and rational world-order would arise with the Aryan dominant and the Jew destroyed, all for the good of mankind and in accordance with nature.

This was Hitler's ideological vision, that he developed in the 1920s. After Hitler's death it was common to suggest that he had no doctrine, that he was an opportunist who simply made theory up without believing it. Others have said that his racial ideas in particular, were simply an excuse to whip up emotion against an internal enemy and were not based on any sincere belief. But this seems unlikely. One obvious piece of evidence here is the fact that Hitler would not release troops from the extermination camps to defend Germany. There now seems little doubt that he believed absolutely in his own doctrine.

Nazi ethics

There is also no doubt that Hitler's doctrine, however repulsive we may find it, was an ethical view of the world, a conception of good and evil. It had the outward form of an objective theory that purports to explain the world, but was in fact the vehicle for a particular set of values and would make little sense without them. There were definite notions of right and wrong, superior and inferior, good and evil, a just society and a justly ordered world. Nazi doctrine glorified racist, nationalist and authoritarian values, while democratic, egalitarian, internationalist and pacifist values were denigrated as evil. These values were built into the theory and consequently into the vocabulary. The central concepts were 'Jew' and 'Aryan', but there were a number of others peculiar to nazism (such as 'folk' and 'race-value') and to fascism ('the Leader' and 'struggle'); and then there were standard political terms given particular Nazi meanings, such as 'justice', 'the state', and so on.

'Freedom', for example, was given a fascist interpretation. Freedom was valuable if it meant the freedom of the nation, or the freedom of individuals to serve the nation, while civil liberties, like freedom of speech and so on, were contemptuously dismissed as 'useless freedoms'. Nazis added to this the ultimate freedom of the 'master race' to subjugate the rest and create civilization. A 'justly ordered world' was one where the superior ruled the inferior, as between races, nations and groups within society, according to the 'iron logic of nature'.

What Nazi ideology did with its theory and its vocabulary was to create a myth, or set of myths, in terms of which Nazi followers could identify their place in the world. They could see themselves as part of Germany's national struggle; as part of the world-historical struggle of Aryan and Jew; and part of the general struggle of life that had been given form and meaning by the personal struggle of the leader, who in *Mein Kampf* has mythologised his own life for just this purpose.

Admirers and followers

Mussolini and Hitler both had their admirers throughout Europe and beyond. They each insisted that theirs was a universal doctrine destined to displace decadent liberalism and its form of government with the state of the future. By the mid-1930s every European country had its fascist party. Fascist governments came to power in Hungary and Romania in alliance with right-wing conservatives. Most, however, came to power in the wake of conquest by the German armies, as was the case in Norway and Holland.

British fascism

The fascist party in Britain was founded in 1932 by Oswald Mosley under the title of the British Union of Fascists. Mosley had been a Conservative, an Independent and a Labour MP (he was expelled from the Labour Party in 1931). He finally came to believe that fascism was the answer to the persistent economic distress and crises of the 1920s and early 30s. Initially he had been an admirer of Mussolini, but increasingly came to see Hitler as his model, and his ideas became more racist as a result. Britain's problems could only be solved by a charismatic leader (himself) substituting authority and discipline and a sense of national purpose for the party bickering and class conflict common to the age.

Free market capitalism, backed by 'international finance', had failed. The world was moving towards protectionism and state intervention, and Britain should do the same. The state should supervise the economy to make sure all parts worked together in harmony like an organism; workers and employers would be reconciled – and all in the interests of the nation. Strikes and lockouts would be banned. Corporatism combined with imperial self-sufficiency was the answer to Britain's economic ills. This meant centralised direction and planning of a capitalist economy. It would be forbidden to import goods that could be made in Britain and the empire would provide everything else. In this way the British empire would be economically self-sufficient.

Mosley believed that the traditional parties ('the old gangs' as he referred to them) and the parliamentary system were useless and out of date. In keeping with his corporatism, he believed that the House of Commons should be elected on the basis of occupational groups. The first Parliament with a fascist majority would grant the government extraordinary powers to introduce the corporate state. Thereafter, Parliament would have only an advisory role, while the Lords would be replaced with a new chamber made up of technical and managerial experts of various kinds that could assist government. The government would then make periodic appeals to the people in the form of plebiscites to confirm its power. The party system could then be dispensed with. Mosley wrote:

In such a system there is no place for parties and for politicians. We shall ask the people for a mandate to bring to an end the Party system and the Parties. We invite them to enter a new civilization. Parties and the party game belong to the old civilization which has failed.

('The Philosophy of Fascism', *Fascist Quarterly*, 1935)

It would then be possible to end all divisions, merge everone into the greater whole and ensure that everything was subordinated to the national purpose.

The nature of British politics, which was very different from that of Italy or Germany, required Mosley to be more circumspect in what he said. His anti-semitism was usually expressed in metaphors ('alien influence', 'international finance') but everyone understood his meaning. He in fact envisaged depriving Jews of British citizenship and deporting any whose activities he did not approve of. Ultimately, he wanted a place set aside for Jews in some barren area of the world to which they could all be sent. Similarly, while he said he would govern with the help of Parliament, and gain it with the consent of the British people, nobody doubted that given the chance, he would establish a dictatorship, or that he would seize power in a coup. Certainly his methods – black-shirted para-military displays, great rallies, beating up opponents, and so on were modelled on his heroes.. He never had the popular support or the support of other groups in society, such as big business, that continental Fascists enjoyed, he made no intellectual impact and since Britain's politics were highly stable (compared to Italy and Germany) he made no political impact either. When war broke out in 1939 Mosley was locked up for the duration.

Spain and Argentina

The utter defeat of Italy and Germany and the revealed horrors of the Nazi concentration camps, completely discredited fascism as a doctrine. In only two places did any kind of fascist regime survive, and this was more to do with the abilities of the leaders than any doctrine they espoused. These were the parties of the Spanish and Argentinian dictators. The most successful of these parties was the Spanish Falange party led by Franco, which came to power in 1936 as a result of the Spanish Civil War, in which it had German and Italian backing. Falange had many of the methods and trappings of Italian fascism in particular, although it was not as thoroughly totalitarian. Besides, the party was, at least for Franco, less important than the army.

Once in power, Franco became less interested in making all Spaniards conform with party ideology, and concentrated on consolidating his personal power. It could be said that Spain evolved away from fascism, and Franco remained a fairly conventional dictator for the next thirty years. His rule was entirely personal, and after his death in 1976 the country returned to constitutional monarchy and liberal democracy.

The fascism of Juan Perón was even more ambiguous than that of Franco. Perón modelled himself on his hero, Mussolini; he created his own party, the Partido Laborista, and was elected President in 1946. He was a charismatic figure who courted the working classes with better wages, conditions and welfare. Together with his first wife, the equally charismatic Eva (known as

'Evita'), he dominated post-war Argentine politics. He used his power ruthlessly to promote his followers to all positions of power and generated mass adulation through his command of propaganda, but he did not create a one-party state, nor try to impose an ideology on the whole population. After the death of Evita in 1952 his regime became progressively more corrupt and he was forced into exile in Spain after a military coup in 1955. Power alternated between the military and Perónist supporters right up to the Falklands War of 1982, although Perón himself only returned briefly to power shortly before his death in 1973.

There is a sense in which that war was a Perónist legacy. True to fascist principles, Perón was an aggressive nationalist, and laid claim to adjacent territories on the borders of Chile and Paraguay, but particularly to the Falkland Islands, which previous Argentine governments had ignored. Perón had all Argentine children learn in school that the Malvinas belonged to Argentina, a practice which has continued, and part of the reason why Argentinians are so passionate about the subject.

However, his main legacy was 'Perónism', which amounted to policies that were a mixture of left and right. Such was the power of his name that virtually all main parties of the post-war period, both left and right, called themselves 'Perónist', even though their politics were diametrically opposed. It was not until the defeat of the Falklands and the subsequent discrediting of the military that a non-Peronist party was elected to power for the first time, which raised hopes that Argentina had at last laid the ghost of Peron and would settle down into being a normal liberal democratic country.

The experiment ended in economic chaos and another Perónist, Carlos Menem, was elected in 1988. He promised strong government and measures to help the masses in true Perónist fashion, but has in fact pursued orthodox right-wing policies of monetarism, privatisation and cuts in public expenditure. Some say that Menem represents the death of Peronism, while others fear he has dictatorial ambitions.

As with Italian Fascism, neither Spanish nor Argentine Fascism were racist. It was the Nazis who preached a doctrine of racial supremacy, and it was the atrocities perpetrated by their regime which discredited racist doctrine in the post-war world. Only South Africa openly espoused a doctrine of racial supremacy, and became an international outcast as a result. Nevertheless, while overt racist doctrine was rare as an ideology, racial prejudice remained common. As a consequence, race remains a factor in the political thinking of the modern world among those groups who have suffered most from such prejudice. This is true of Black Consciousness and Zionism.

Race and ideology since 1945

A racial element appears in several parts of today's ideological spectrum.

Zionism

In the aftermath of war, the world was horrified at Nazi atrocities against the Jews. This gave an impetus to the Jewish dream of a homeland, which they had not had since biblical times. This aspiration is embodied in the political movement called 'Zionism', which is of relatively recent origin. Jews had hoped for assimilation into European society (as opposed to being confined to the ghetto) as a result of the development of liberal ideas that suggested that all human beings were entitled to civil rights and toleration. Certainly there was progress along these lines during most of the nineteenth century. But the growth of anti-Semitism and the persecutions and pogroms towards the end of the century convinced some that emancipation was an unrealistic dream. They argued that Jews would only be regarded as equals in the modern world if they had their own state.

Zionism developed as a movement in the early years of the twentieth century and triumphed in 1948, when the state of Israel was founded in the area of Palestine, with United Nations backing. However, this provoked the hostility of the Arab world over the fate of the displaced Palestinians. It has created massive problems and made the Middle East the most difficult of trouble spots.

Zionism might be said to be a nationalist doctrine with a racial content. It has no necessary racial theory of history or notions of racial superiority or inferiority. It does, however, come in a variety of forms, including socialist, conservative and liberal. In the 1930s and 40s among settlers in Palestine the socialist version was dominant. This represented a revolt against much of Jewish social and religious orthodoxy. It envisaged a regeneration of the Jewish nation through a return to nature and the soil, which the dispersion of the Jews had made impossible. The result would be a new society of producers and farmers, instead of the nation of shopkeepers, traders and capitalists the Jews had become. National regeneration involved social regeneration, with a new society based on pioneering ideals and collectivist values, as expressed above all in the *kibbutzim*, the farming communities run on collectivist lines.

At the other end of the spectrum were the 'revisionist' Zionists, who supported the capitalist and business tradition and also advocated a tougher and more militaristic approach, with the creation of a Jewish army among settlers and the eventual imposition of Jewish sovereignty over the whole of Palestine. This right-wing version came to be represented by the Likud Party.

The Second World War and the Western sense of guilt over the Holocaust gave impetus to the creation of the Jewish state. For its first quarter century, and through three defensive wars, Israel was governed by the socialist strand of Zionism, represented by the Israeli Labour Party. But from 1977 to 1992 it was the right, led by the Likud Party, that was in power. Initially the right had not been a religious right, but after the 1967 war, when Israel conquered substantial Arab lands, there had been increased support for Jewish fundamentalism, which has insisted that these lands be permanently incorporated into Israel, because they were part of the biblical land of Israel given to the Jews by God. It is therefore a religious duty of the Jews to settle those lands and permanently incorporate them into the Israeli state (see Chapter Twelve). Successive Likud governments have allowed settlements, despite international opposition, an opposition that is based on the belief that only the return of the conquered lands, and the creation of a Palestinian state in the West Bank and Gaza Strip, could be the basis of a lasting settlement.

Israel has become the military super-power of the Middle East, and enjoys massive military and financial backing from the United States (where there is a large and powerful Jewish lobby in the American Congress). However, Israel has lost much sympathy in the last decade, beginning with the invasion of Lebanon in 1982, an aggressive, rather than a defensive war, by a regional super-power against a more or less defenceless state. Because of their treatment of the Palestinians it is the Israelis who are accused by some of being the modern racists.

Apartheid

The doctrine of racism only survived after 1945, as anything more than fringe political ideas, in the beliefs of the white elite in colonial or ex-colonial areas, especially in Africa. As most of Africa was given independence with power for the indigenous black or Arab majority, South Africa became the state which almost alone in the world possessed a regime inspired by notions of white racial supremacy. In 1948 the Afrikaaners (that is, descendants of Dutch and German settlers) elected the Afrikaaner Nationalist Party that has ruled South Africa ever since. It is this party that has been committed to the racist doctrine of apartheid.

What the Afrikaans word 'apartheid' literally means is 'apartness' or 'separateness'. The theory is that racial differences are a fundamental and fixed part of human existence. Each race has its own characteristics, and therefore its own 'natural' development. Racial mixing interferes with such natural development and, in consequence, can only be bad. The different races of South Africa must therefore each have their own territory, education and institutions so that they may develop separately. However, the whites must remain dominant, since they are the superior race and have a responsibility to maintain the system as a whole. Many Afrikaaners regard this as a religious duty, a view promoted by the main Afrikaaner church, the Dutch Reformed Church. The Afrikaaners, it is argued, are a special people, chosen by God to perform a purpose in southern Africa and given the land of South Africa as a divine gift. To fulfil their destiny, the Afrikaaners must maintain their distinctive culture and position, and so must remain a race apart.

The policies inspired and justified by these beliefs involved racial classification and segregation for all South Africans. Four racial categories were introduced: Whites, Asians, Coloureds (that is, those of mixed race) and Africans. The latter constituted over 70 per cent of the population yet were denied all political rights in South Africa. Moreover, they were arbitrarily assigned to one of ten tribal 'homelands', such as Transkei, which were pockets of barren land on the fringe of South Africa. On this basis black people could be assigned a homeland thousands of miles away from where they had always lived. Black people living in the 'White' areas (most of the country), such as in the black townships on the outskirts of the great cities, were effectively foreign residents; they were only there by special permission of the authorities, and the system was enforced by the notorious 'pass laws'. Further laws forbade mixed marriages and sexual relations between different races. There was rigid separation of Whites and others in all public places: parks, cinemas, buses, beaches and so on.

As a result of these policies, South Africa became a pariah state, shunned by the world. It is only in the last few years that there has been a government willing to negotiate the end of apartheid and discrimination. However, this is a long process and no one knows how it will end. Certainly there will be fierce resistance from some Whites insisting on white supremacy being maintained. A new Conservative Party was created from the right wing of the Nationalist Party to resist change, while further to the right has been an overtly neo-Nazi racist party, the Afrikaaner Resistance Movement (AWB), led by Eugene Terreblanche, preaching race war.

Black consciousness

Although South Africa is the only overtly racist regime in the world, and although racist doctrines have been anathematised by the world community since the nazi experience, this is not to say that racial prejudice (racialism) ceased to exist in 1945. It remained strong and to some extent still does. Undoubtedly the ethnic group that has suffered most from racialism has been the black Africans. They have suffered not only colonial rule in their own continent, but also suffered mass slavery, so that in the Americas and to a lesser extent in Europe there is a legacy of a transplanted and deracinated (rootless) people whose history has been one of humiliation, degradation and deprivation, who have little of the cultural traditions of their African forbears, and who have been obliged to grow up in an alien society that very largely regarded them with contempt. Consequently, the ending of slavery left appalling problems of racialism, especially in the USA. The American Civil War emancipated the slaves, but the price of reconciling the rebellious South to the Union was a studied Federal indifference to the 'Negro problem'. Negroes remained second-class citizens, a despised underclass.

Real change began in the 1960s, when the Civil Rights movement, led by Martin Luther King Jnr., became active and forceful. It made significant progress in enforcing recognition of legal rights and in outlawing of discrimination. King had been greatly influenced by Mahatma Gandhi and insisted on a strategy of non-violent protest.

But the 1960s was also an age of rebellious youth and the New Left revolt against the materialism of American consumer society (see Chapter Seven). The black cause became part of the general New Left movement, which it also influenced. The New Left was Marxist-inspired, although not the kind of Marxism of communist regimes, being one more concerned with liberation, consciousness and the overcoming of alienation. For many, the mere acquisition of formal legal rights on the same basis as whites, was simply not enough; black liberation had to mean something more. It had to mean the overcoming of alienation and a transforming of consciousness; it had to restore to black people a sense of identity of which they could be proud.

Part of the inspiration came from ideas about African independence. In the 1930s a number of black writers in French Africa (Leopold Senghor and Aimé Césaire were the main ones) developed the idea of négritude (a French word for 'blackness'). The idea was that the black people should rejoice in their African heritage and take pride in the music, art and literature of Africa, which was in no way inferior to white culture. Their main concern was with the policy of French colonial governments to impose French culture on the native population. The idea that subject people did not just need formal freedom, but needed to assert their own identity was strong in the thinking of Frantz Fanon, who was not only an important figure in the liberation movement in French North Africa, but whose writings were an important influence on the New Left generally.

The result was a variety of manifestations of black consciousness, such as the Black Power and Black Muslim movements in America, and various schemes of black assertion and black pride. These included efforts to recover Black history, whether African history or of the slave past, and pride in black cultural achievement in music (jazz, blues, rock and roll, Negro spirituals), as well as in poetry and other literature. There was also a concern with language, with finding slogans and alternative terms to those imposed by whites. 'Black is beautiful' is one example; as is the insistence on the terms 'Black' or 'Afro-American' instead of 'Negro'. Other sources of cultural pride and identity included the wearing of African dress and 'Afro' hair-styles.

The purpose of such symbols was to assert black dignity and self-respect, an antidote to feelings of inferiority and alienation. That alienation manifests itself, so the theory goes, in blacks' acceptance of the externally imposed sense of inferiority, and in the more psychologically destructive form of self-hatred (that is, hatred of white oppression repressed and internally transmuted into self-loathing, a feature of black psychology widely observed by black writers). American psychoanalysts analysed the phenomenon and suggested the concept of 'Black Rage'; that is, rage against white oppressors turned on themselves and each other. This concept, combined with the social effects of poverty and deprivation, is used to explain high rates of murder, crime and drug addiction among the black population in the US. The phenomenon was also analysed by Frantz Fanon in his *Black Skins, White Masks*, (1952), in which he argued that black people could only purge their imposed sense of inferiority and assert their own dignity through violence against the oppressor.

It was thinking of this kind that lay behind the violence of 60s groups like the Black Panthers, whose leader Malcolm X preached race war against whites. Since then, some Black Power radicals have continued to argue that the attempt to gain equality in white society is doomed, that whites are the permanent and inevitable enemy of blacks and that the only hope for black people to live in dignity is in total separation from white society.

Neo-fascism

Despite the discrediting of fascism and racism after the Second World War, and the success of welfare capitalism, there has been a continuing presence of fascism on the fringes of mainstream politics, which is not always easy to explain. One of the most striking features of this neo-fascism has been an almost total absence of those social and economic conditions of the 1920s and 1930s in which fascism first thrived, that is, conditions of political instability, severe economic distress, fear of communism and a widespread sense of national humiliation and thwarted aspirations. The one factor which contemporary fascists thrive upon is immigration, especially where it is exacerbated by economic recession (although, of course, nothing like the economic distress of the inter-war years).

In a number of western European countries immigration has become a political issue, particularly in times of economic difficulty. In these circumstances, which became increasingly common in the 1970s, 1980s and 1990s, people's economic anxieties and racial prejudices can easily be manipulated by parties with affinities with fascism and nazism. Except for one or two cases (such as Italy and Argentina), neo-fascism seems to be little more than politically organised racial hatred. This certainly seems to be the case in France, Germany, the USA and Britain.

Neo-fascism in Germany and France

In post-war Germany there were still substantial numbers of ex-Nazis, which is perhaps not too surprising after the defeat of a movement that demanded and received fanatical loyalty from its followers. The West German government, fearful of a revival of extremism, banned anti-constitutional parties and barred their members from government employment. Despite this, there were many small Nazi groupings, but of no political significance and with a progressively ageing membership. The left-wing terrorism of the Baader-Meinhof group provoked a modest revival in the 1970s, but the more serious recent revival of neo-Nazi activism in the early 90s has been a response to the problem of immigration.

West Germany has had a very liberal immigration policy and has also welcomed many 'guest workers', especially from Turkey but also elsewhere. A rise in unemployment in the 1980s led to the problem of neo-fascism, which fed on fear and resentment of immigration. This was kept under control during the 1980s because the German economy was so powerful and prosperous that most Germans saw the economic problems as temporary.

However, the situation changed because of two related factors. In the first place, the collapse of East European regimes and the economic chaos this left behind prompted a flow, that might eventually become a deluge, of immigrants from bankrupt Eastern Europe towards the rich West. Secondly, the reunification of Germany in 1990 following the collapse of the German Democratic Republic (GDR) was not an instant success. The coming of economic realism caused massive unemployment in the former GDR and threatened the prosperity of Western Germany. It is the presence and the prospect of immigrants combined with economic dislocation that has been the ideal breeding ground for neo-fascism.

There has been a rapid growth of neo-Nazi groups and attacks on immigrants, especially in the former GDR. Although as yet no significant party has emerged to focus all the discontent or to capitalise on the situation electorally, this may only be a matter of time. The new Republican Party emerged as the leading far right party after 1989, although it has not yet become a serious electoral threat. Its programme of repatriation of immigrants, the removal of trade unions and withdrawal from the European Community has very limited appeal.

Similar experiences of immigration and concern for future prospects fuel neo-fascist activity in France. In the French case, as with Britain, much immigration is related to the legacy of empire. There are very large numbers of North African immigrants in France, and with the prospect of many more seeking entry (as a result of famine and civil war in many parts of northern Africa) there is growing anti-immigrant feeling. This has been exploited by the National Front Party of Jean-Marie Le Pen.

Le Pen founded the party in 1972, but it rose to prominence with the coming of recession and high unemployment in the early 1980s, when the National Front won seats in the National Assembly and European Parliament. When unemployment reached three million, Le Pen argued that deporting three million immigrants would solve the problem 'at a stroke'. He spoke of the increasing 'Islamicisation' of parts of France and the consequent threat to French identity and culture. But apart from the over-riding issue of race, the National Front has other right-wing policies, including the restoration of capital punishment, the abolition of taxes on wealth and income, steps to dismantle the welfare state, and, more recently, the compulsory isolation of AIDS victims.

Despite a decline in the electoral fortunes of the National Front, it seems likely that the issue of immigration will be of growing importance and may well be the source of growing support for the far right in the future.

Italian neo-fascism

Italy is the one European state where neo-fascism has been of permanent significance in national politics. The Movimento Sociale Italiano (MSI) has a small but stable following, so that since 1951 it has never gained less than 4.5 per cent of the vote at national elections. It has maintained a block of seats in the Italian Parliament since 1949. At its height, the MSI gained 9 per cent of the popular vote in 1972 (compared with, say, the National Front in Britain, which has never gained as much as 1 per cent of the national vote in a general election). This is because the fascism of Mussolini still has a hold on some sections of Italian society, especially in the more traditional south, among whom the failure of Italian fascism was due to the unfortunate association of Mussolini with the doomed nazism of Germany. As in the time of Hitler and Mussolini, Italian fascism is far less racist than its German counterpart. It is not other races that are seen as the principal enemy, but communism. Fascism had a place in Italian politics as the opposite of the powerful Italian Communist Party, whose very existence provoked the extreme right, who argued that the communist threat could only be dealt with by non-democratic methods.

The MSI was founded in 1946 by former members of Mussolini's Fascist Party. It argued for a 'third way' between capitalist democracy, with its instability, materialist values and its emphasis on individualism; and communism on the other, with its atheism and state control of everything. Fascism offered national unity and stability, the end of class conflict and support for Catholicism as the state religion. Ironically, at least some of the political instability which the MSI continuously emphasises arises from the proportional electoral system, without which the MSI could not survive as a national party. It established some degree of legitimacy after the Second World War because in an era of Cold War and in a country with a large and powerful Communist Party, it could present itself as the defender of 'Christian civilization' against bolshevism, against which liberal democracy was useless.

Initially, the MSI sought respectability and from time to time supported the Christian Democrats in government and forged links with other right-wing parties. However, greater political polarization in the 1960s led to greater efforts to undermine and discredit Italian democracy, and there was involvement in the planning of at least one coup to overthrow the Italian government. Some of the more radical members left and joined underground Fascist groups that were resorting to terrorism in response to the growth of the New Left and its movement to violence. In the 1970s and early 1980s there were both left- and right-wing terrorist acts in Italy, and the MSI appeared to have some links with the latter. But during the 1980s the MSI returned to its earlier search for respectability and left anti-democratic sub-version to other clandestine groups. What its future might be, following the demise of European communism, is difficult to say.

British neo-fascism

After the Second World War there were attempts by Oswald Mosley and his admirers to revive fascism as a national movement in Britain, but without success. Eventually, however, a party was created that managed to attract national support, and which has become Britain's principal fascist grouping. This is the National Front (NF), founded in 1967.

At the levels of both policy and theory, race is central to NF thinking, although there are important differences between the two levels. At the policy level the central theme is black immigration. Black Britons are blamed for every kind of social ill: poverty, crime, drugs, vandalism, bad housing, disease, unemployment and more. Worst of all, it is claimed, blacks are the greatest threat to the British people through the mixing of blood. Thus, a member of the NF leadership wrote:

The greatest danger this country has ever faced is that it has imported millions of aliens who are members of backward, primitive races, and whose large-scale racial intermixture with the indigenous Anglo-Saxons would not only put an end to the British as a distinct and unique ethnic entity, but would produce an inferior mongrel breed and a regressive and degenerate culture of tropical squalor.

(*Spearhead*, October, 1976)

The answer is the compulsory repatriation of black Britons. Other NF supporters have advocated racial laws against marriage between 'Aryans' and 'non-Aryans' in order to preserve racial purity. Beyond this, there are conventional fascist concerns with national assertion and self-sufficiency, such as withdrawal from the EC.

At the level of theory, however, the principal theme is not anti-black but anti-Semitic. It is a slightly modernised version of the old Nazi theory of an international Jewish conspiracy. Thus, both 'international finance' and communism are instruments of a Jewish plot to destroy Western economies and society with recession and communism and to destroy racial purity through internationalism, immigration and other forms of racial mixing. All this is in order to subjugate everyone to a world government based in Israel.

To the great majority of the population, such ideas are puerile and disgusting. Their main appeal in terms of membership is to those blinded by hatred or to ignorant young men with a taste for violence, such as football hooligans. For electoral purposes, much of the uglier side of NF thinking is not made public, and there is a more subtle appeal to fears and prejudices and to 'Britain first', which in times of economic difficulty in the 1970s gave them up to 16 per cent of the vote in certain constituencies.

The National Front was created through an amalgamation of a number of extreme right groups. Their collective membership amounted to around 4,000 in 1967, but rapidly increased to its peak of around 17,500 in 1974. Elections in that year also gave the NF its highest ever popular vote of 113,000, although this was merely 0.4 per cent of the national vote and it came nowhere came near winning any single seat. However, support for the NF began to wilt with the advent of Mrs Thatcher as a Conservative leader, who overtly wanted stricter controls on immigration and firmer policies on law and order and on Ulster. Many right-wing Conservative supporters returned to the fold. Perhaps also the true nature of the NF became better known. But for whatever reason the 1979 General Election was a disaster for the NF. Within a couple of years its numbers were much as they were in 1967. The party split and new groups were set up or resurrected (such as the League of St George, the British National Party and the National Socialist Action Group), producing an array of groups of various degrees of political nastiness.

In 1983 the NF was drastically reorganised, its old guard dismissed, its membership rebuilt and an entirely new strategy adopted. Instead of trying to create a mass political party seeking electoral success, the new NF is a much more secretive organisation that invites people to join it and that is dedicated to infiltration and subversion. It now has wide contacts not only with neo-nazi groups all over Europe and beyond, but with all kinds of terrorist groups, including both sides in Northern Ireland, and black and Arab groups, Arab Liberation, and so on. It seeks to infiltrate all kinds of groups it has little sympathy with, and engages in military training, often at camps in Europe. Indeed, their model is European. They see themselves as 'political soldiers' who use terrorism and subversion as the only way of eventually coming to power. Although the organisation has suffered further divisions, and nothing may come of their increasingly clandestine activities, it is still a worrying phenomenon.

9

The New Right

Arguably the most dynamic ideological force in today's world is the New Right. Some are even prepared to argue that it is the ultimate ideology, the one that will outlast all others and dominate all future politics. What is strange is that there is not much about it that is in fact new: the New Right is really some old left-wing ideas fused with some old right-wing ones. The New Right is a broad movement with a number of components that are more or less essential according to different points of view. However, the one unquestionable essential and dynamic element is what is best characterised as 'neo-liberalism', that is, a revival of the classical liberal thinking of the early nineteenth century (which in those days was a radical doctrine on the left of the spectrum).

As far as practical politics are concerned, that version of liberalism had long since died a death. Its second coming, full of vigour and confidence, has captured a different space on the political spectrum. It is not liberal parties that have espoused this revival, but conservative ones, and it is neo-liberal ideas that have given such parties, for example the Republicans of America and the British Conservatives their intellectual strength and electoral success. In terms of doctrine, therefore, the New Right may be characterised as neo-liberalism in various combinations with older strands of conservatism. These do not always fit well together, but the internal conflict arising from this has not diminished the doctrine's success.

From Swiss chalet to White House

Since the Second World War New Right ideas have risen from complete obscurity to world importance. The most important figure in the early development of these ideas was Friedrich von Hayek.

Hayek's influence

Hayek's *The Road to Serfdom* of 1944 was a book out of step with its time. The post-war world was going to be planned, and have a welfare state; insofar as it was capitalist it would be a Keynesian managed capitalism (see Chapter Two). But Hayek's book argued that any kind of socialism, however mild, any kind of economic planning or state welfare, however well-intentioned, or any kind of interference with the free market, however seemingly sensible, was profoundly wrong. It was a diminution of precious freedom and a step towards a new tyranny and a new serfdom for ordinary people.

Although widely read, *The Road to Serfdom* was widely dismissed as a hankering after a discredited Victorian ideal of *laissez-faire*. (A distinguished Oxford philosopher, Anthony Quinton, later described Hayek's political philosophy as a 'magnificent dinosaur'.) However, Hayek was not only an academic economist and social theorist (he had been a professor of economics at the London School of Economics since the 1930s), he was also an activist who sought to promote his ideas on the widest scale. He found a rich patron to support his projects and he organised a conference in 1947 to launch a society devoted to the kind of free-market ideas he believed in. His patron happened to be Swiss and the conference was held in a Swiss hotel in the town of Mont Pelerin. Milton Friedman and Karl Popper were among those who attended.

It was from these rather humble beginnings that the New Right began as an international movement and from which its ideas spread slowly. In 1957 the Institute of Economic Affairs was established in London in order to promote free-market solutions to problems. Its work was much derided by orthodox economists and it did not make an impact until the 1970s. Other bodies were founded elsewhere.

In 1959 Hayek moved from the LSE to Chicago to join another founder member of the Mont Pelerin Society, Milton Friedman. America was the most free market of all Western societies, especially during the conservative Republican administration of President Eisenhower (1952–60), but that was about to change. In the late 1950s a number of reports were published indicating the existence of extensive poverty in the United States that was being ignored. In 1960 a new young President was elected, John F. Kennedy, with a mandate to tackle poverty and associated problems. He committed the American government to Keynesianism and a programme of state welfare, in line with European practice.

The spread of New Right ideas

The election of Richard Nixon in 1968 marked something of a conservative reaction to the New Left radicalism of the 1960s. His presidency, however, ended in disgrace and led to the Republican Party's defeat in 1976. During this period of the early and mid-1970s New Right ideas were developing, largely outside the Republican Party. They were developing against a background of general disillusionment and doubt. The economy was stagnant; the general social programmes of the 1960s had failed; America's failure in Vietnam seemed to reveal America's weakness in the face of the every-growing Communist threat, and Watergate and other scandals made Washington politics seem corrupt and without direction

In the early 1970s new-conservative ideas began to flourish. Neo-conservative intellectuals such as Irving Kristol, Nathan Glazer, Daniel Bell and others were often former Democrats disillusioned with the 'liberalism' of the Democratic Party and with the failures of the Great Society programmes and other left-wing causes, and wanted a return to more traditional values of family and hard work and country. They operated through journals such as *The Public Interest* and *Commentary*.

Also at this time the religious fundamentalists began to take an active role in politics for the first time (see Chapter 11), with, for example, new organisations like the Moral Majority campaigning against permissiveness and pornography and for other moral causes. Religious leaders such as Jerry Falwell and Pat Robertson became national political figures through their campaigns to 'cleanse America' of the evil ideas of the 1960s and restore traditional Christian values. A number became famour as tele-vangelists, mixing fundamentalist religion and right-wing politics and persuading their followers to campaign against politicians who supported 'liberal' causes like abortion and gay rights.

The early 1970s also saw the formation of the New Right think-tanks such as the Heritage Foundation and the Free Enterprise Institute. Their principal stance was libertarian and new-liberal. In 1974 this kind of thinking received important philo-sophical support with the publication of Robert Nozick's *Anarchy, State and Utopia*, which revived Lockean ideas of natural rights, especially property rights, as the foundation of society, and asserted the illegitimacy of government infringing those rights with high taxation, economic regulation and welfare policies. Nozick's writings gave intellectual weight to neo-liberal thinking just at the time when it was beginning to emerge as a political force in America and Britain. However, it was not theoretical develop-ments that created political interest in new-liberalism, but the course of events, in particular the failure of Keynesian economics.

From the mid-1970s the Western world was plagued byy severe economic recession, triggered off by large and sudden increases in the price of oil. These difficulties were characterised by a new phenomenon called 'stagflation', which was a combination of a lack of economic growth causing unemployment (stagnation) together with rapidly rising prices (inflation). According to current Keynesian orthodoxy, this was not supposed to happen: one could have one or the other, but not both at the same time. This led to a disillusionment with Keynesianism and a search for economic alternatives. For those on the right in Britain and the USA the 'supply-side' alternatives advocated by the neo-liberals had particular attractions, especially in the most narrow form of

Friedmanite monetarism, since it fitted well with notions of minimal government and individual responsibility.

Thatcherism

In Britain, under the leadership of Margaret Thatcher, the Conservatives came to power in 1979 with a clear and consistent neo-liberal programme, which was quite different from the consensus policies all parties had offered for the previous thirty years. Although there have been some modifications and compromises on individual policies, the programme as a whole was pursued with remarkable consistency through the subsequent decade. The central theme of this programme was the reversal of Britain's post-war decline and the restoration of the country's prosperity and economic health. To begin with, this involved a wholesale rejection of the post-war consensus.

The neo-liberal analysis of Britain's post-war failure put the blame on the consensus policies of the managed and mixed economy and the welfare state, which had appeared at the time to give steadily growing prosperity combined with social progress. However, these policies had created massive government with high taxes, endless regulation, state ownership, state planning, state monopolies, state subsidies, incomes policies, regional policies and various other forms of state intervention. Nationalisation, the argument went on, directly diminished the private sector, putting in its place costly and inefficient state enterprises that were a burden on the taxpayer and soaked up investment funds that should have gone to private industry. At the same time, the free enterprise system was being strangled by bureaucracy, weighed down by excessive taxation, intimidated by over-powerful unions, and exploited by inefficient state monopolies.

Meanwhile the independent spirit of the people was being undermined by too much state provision of everything: health, pensions, houses, jobs and whatever else people thought they needed. The welfare state had created a 'dependency culture' where growing numbers of people simply lived off the state, and thought little of doing anything else, while many more depended on the state – (what Mrs Thatcher called the 'nanny state') to fulfil their needs.

All this regulation and provision had necessitated a massive civil service and local government bureaucracy with a vested interested in maintaining consensus policies and which made sure nothing ever changed. (Mrs Thatcher maintained that her favourite television programme was *Yes, Minister*, in which wily civil servants ran rings around their supposed masters to make sure everything stayed as it was. It was supposed to depict things as they were before she transformed them.)

On top of all this, the theory continued, consensus policies created huge government borrowing, easy credit and printing of money in order to increase demand and maintain high employment, despite wages being too high and our industry uncompetitive. All this led to inflation, the great enemy of free enterprise, which ruined savings and investment. Thus Britain had declined economically and was sinking into a condition of dependency on the state for everything.

The overall aim of the Thatcher government's policies from 1979 was the restoration of the country's prosperity by following the classical liberal principles of relying on the free market, minimal government interference and individual liberty and responsibility. The government's strategy was to create the conditions in which free enterprise could flourish by means of policies, which can be broadly grouped into four closely related areas:

- the conquest of inflation
- reducing the size and cost of the state
- providing incentives for hard work and enterprise
- removing restrictions on the operation of the free market.

Defeating inflation was the absolute priority, taking precedence over everything else, although the initial purely monetarist approach was abandoned. Great efforts were made to reduce government spending, although success really only amounted to slowing the rate of growth. The centre-piece of the incentives policy was the reduction of income tax, although other taxes had to compensate for the loss of revenue. Removing restrictions covered many things from reducing trade-union power to the setting up of enterprise zones. But perhaps the most striking policy of the Thatcher revolution was privatisation in its various forms. For neo-liberals it fulfilled all their ideals virtually at a stroke: reducing the role of the state, expanding the free market, providing more consumer choice, and for those who bought shares or council houses, greater freedom and responsibility. Whatever the criticisms of privatisation, it was the most characteristically neo-liberal and Thatcherite policy of all.

Ronald Reagan

Thatcherism has been the fullest expression of neo-liberalism in action, and has been influential around the world (the privatisation programme in particular has been widely imitated). Yet in many ways neo-liberalism's greatest political triumph was to capture the government of the most powerful state in the world. This was the Reagan presidency of 1981–89.

When the Nixon presidency ended in disgrace in 1976 over the Watergate scandal (his former Vice-President, Spiro Agnew, had resigned earlier over a different scandal), the Republican Party was demoralised and in disarray. It was at this point the New Right began to take over the party. The old left wing of the party seemed to shrivel, and New Right thinking became dominant and has remained so since. The New Right soon found a champion in Ronald Reagan, who combined new-liberal attitudes on economics and the minimal state, together with many of the traditional social and moral attitudes of the neo-conservatives and the religious right, and a fierce anti-Communist stance common to them all.

As a neo-liberal Reagan came to power determined to reduce welfare, reduce taxes, reduce bureaucracy and 'get government off the people's backs'. He did all of these things, though he managed only by massive government borrowing (in contrast to Mrs Thatcher who actually achieved the neo-liberral ideal of doing without government borrowing altogether) and leaving America with a very serious problem of government debt. This arose from Reagan's determination to massively increase expenditure on defence, which relates to a different New Right preoccupation – the wish to stem the tide of Communism. There were, therefore, conflicting priorities within Reagan's programme, and one of the features of his presidency was the tendency for different groups to be influential at different times and in different areas of policy.

But whatever the other right-wing elements of Thatcherite and Reaganite policies, underlying the analysis of what was wrong and the strategies for putting it right, lay a strong foundation of neo-liberal theory derived from the writings of Hayek, Friedman and others, and the ideas of organisations like the Institute for Economic Affairs, the Adam Smith Institute and their American equivalents. It is these ideas that we must now examine more closely.

Updating classical liberalism

Neo-liberalism is a modernised version of classical liberalism (see Chapter Two). It consists of the classical liberal themes of free market, minimal state and individualism (that is, individual freedom and responsibility) adapted to modern conditions. The world today is very different to that of the early nineteenth century, and neo-liberalism reflects the intervening experience and theoretical developments, as well as our present day problems. Much of what makes revived classical liberalism different from the original is reflected in the work of the most influential figure in the neo-liberal movement, Friedrich von Hayek.

Hayek and Austrian economics

Hayek's economic ideas were strongly influenced by the intellectual traditions of his native Austria. There are a number of characteristics which distinguish Austrian theory from that of the English-speaking world. For one thing, Austrian economics is less abstract. Instead of explaining the economy in terms of the interaction of large-scale economic forces like overall demand, levels of investment, balance of payments, commodity prices and the like, Austrian economists tend to explain economic activity in terms of psychology and the roles played by economic actors, such as consumers, entrepreneurs, capitalists or politicians. It is consequently less formal and mathematical, and also tends to see economics as a wider subject embracing the whole of society. Secondly, whereas English-speaking economists have tended to ignore the role of the entrepreneur (that is, the creative businessman who pioneers new products and starts new businesses), Austrian theorists tend to emphasise their role as essential to the healthy working of the system.

Finally, Austrian economics has concerned itself with the analysis of socialism and the role of the state in the economy. English-speaking economics has never produced a clear refutation of Marx's economic thinking. It has been simply ignored, for the good reason that Marxism has made very little impact in Britain, the USA or the rest of the English-speaking world. This is not true of continental Europe. Austrian economics has produced a major critique of Marxism and of socialist economics in general, arguing that state control could not be beneficial for the economy or society as a whole.

Neo-liberal theory could be described as a synthesis of classical liberalism, Austrian economics and some later theoretical additions, mostly American.

Markets and invisible hands

Neo-liberals share with classical liberals a limitless faith in the power and benevolence of the free market. No other system, they insist, can satisfy human wants so widely or so efficiently, while at the same time making maximum use of whatever resources a society has and guaranteeing greatest possible prosperity. In a free market the consumer can always choose between rival products, and will always choose what is cheapest and best. A rival product must either improve the original product or sell at a lower price or appear in some version that people want, or else go out of business. Manufacturers are under constant pressure to improve, competition, therefore, ensures the highest quality at the lowest prices, and also that new needs will be explored and new technologies will be developed to produce better and cheaper products.

The market develops an ever wider network in the search to satisfy human wants. Thus we purchase objects made of many components and materials produced in many parts of the world, all brought together in millions of ways by the power of the market in a way that benefits everyone.

Everyone pursues their own interests, yet in doing so this benefits the whole. In a famous passage, Adam Smith wrote of the individual who:

. . . intends only his own gain is led by an invisible hand to promote an end which was no part of his intention. Nor is it always the worse for society that it was no part of it. By pursuing his own interest he frequently promotes that of society more effectively than when he really intends to promote it.

(*The Wealth of Nations*, 1776)

It would not be put in quite those terms today. Rather than somewhat mystical talk of 'invisible hands', Hayek speaks of the market creating a 'spontaneous order' which no one has, or could, design or control. What makes it all possible is the combination of two factors: the price mechanism and the entrepreneur.

The price mechanism is a vast information system which tells everyone what materials, labour, borrowing and finished goods will cost, and therefore their relative scarcity and value to those who might use or consume them. It is the key indicator for those who would invest, providing both information and incentive. Products commanding a high price and high profits will attract investment, which will encourage extra production that will bring the price down, making the product more widely available. In the meanwhile high profits will be attract fresh investment elsewhere. However, this only works if there is competition. It is vital, therefore, that consumers have choice, that they can express their preferences; it is their choices that drive the system. Patterns of consumption emerge, although these are not fixed. Needs change, fashions change, technology changes, as does the availability of resources. The market is, therefore, in a constant state of flux.

The key figure who thrives on the flux, who searches for new needs and new means to satisfy them, is the entrepreneur or 'enterpriser'. Capitalists often invest in standard goods that command a steady income, but some make riskier investments in the hope of higher profits. Capitalists themselves may be entrepreneurs, although more frequently the enterpriser is borrowing in the hope of profit over and above the lender's return.

English-speaking economists from Adam Smith to Keynes have tended to set little store by the work of entrepreneurs, subsuming them within the general category of businessman or capitalist (Adam Smith wrote quite scathingly about businessmen). Indeed, the demise of the entrepreneur was much canvassed (for example, by Joseph Schumpeter an Austrian-American economist in *Capitalism, Socialism and Democracy* in 1943); their role, it was said, had been taken over by the research and development departments of big corporations. It is one of the notable features of the neo-liberal revival that the role of the entrepreneur and small businessman has been emphasised (one might almost say glorified: Mrs Thatcher called them 'these wonderful people').

Given that the market is in a state of constant change, it is not surprising that from time to time things can go badly: there is a dearth of investment, or overproduction, or unemployment, or whatever. The beauty of the free market is that it is a self-righting vessel, and given time will always solve its own problems. Interference only delays recovery. Once restored, the free market will continue its historic task of maximising prosperity for all.

Threats to the free market

Neo-liberals allow no criticism of the free market. All faults flow from the free market not being allowed to work properly, and there are various things that prevent it from doing so. There is monopoly and inflation and, most potent of all, government intervention. Monopoly is bad for the market because it denies competition and therefore distorts both consumer choice and the price mechanism. Monopolists can charge what they like and there is nothing the consumer can do about it, and if competition is impossible there is no incentive for anyone to try to provide a better or cheaper product.

Inflation distorts the price mechanism in a more comprehensive and damaging way. Prices do not go up evenly, but depend on varying wage settlements and a number of other factors. Prices cease to be an accurate indicator of demand, or of likely profit or good investment. The whole economy slows, people will not save, nor make risky investments and so on. Worse still, inflation can get out of hand and destroy an economy, as it did in Germany in the 1920s. Neo-liberals see inflation as a great evil that must be overcome at all costs, and see this is the one crucial role of government in the economy.

However, although inflation is a great evil, it is government intervention that is seen as the most potent threat. In fact, some neo-liberals see government as the root cause of monopoly and of inflation. They therefore see government, and government alone, as the ultimate enemy of economic freedom and consequently of freedom as such, and government intervention is identified with Socialism.

Socialism and the dead hand of the state

Liberals have traditionally identified certain enemies of freedom. In the seventeenth and eighteenth centuries it was the tyranny of priest and king; J. S. Mill added the tyranny of the majority; while today's neo-liberals point to what might be called the 'tyranny of centralised benevolence', that is, governments genuinely seeking to improve the lot of their people by such policies as interfering in the market to 'correct its faults', promoting equality, and trying to alleviate poverty, ignorance and other social problems. The result of these policies, neo-liberals insist, is invariable failure to achieve their objectives, or even to achieve an outcome as good as doing nothing at all.

The growth of collectivism

Neo-liberals believe that in Britain a free society was created in the early nineteenth century, but in the latter part of the century there began a long retreat towards collectivism. It was all benign and with the best of intentions, but it was all a mistake. It began with social policies and proceeded to the economic. However, for the neo-liberal the economic always comes first, so we will begin with economic policy.

During the long depression of the inter-war years, especially after the Wall Street Crash of 1929, the old classical economic orthodoxy of allowing the economy to solve its own problems without government interference, appeared to fail. The thinking behind this policy was challenged by J. M. Keynes, who argued that governments should intervene to prevent both booms and slumps by controlling the amount of demand in the economy (see Chapter Two for a fuller account of Keynesianism). This became the orthodoxy of the post-war world, when governments spent freely to generate demand and avoid unemployment.

Monetarism

Neo-liberals maintain that this strategy was a mistake. Milton Friedman, for example, insists that many myths surround the Great Crash and its aftermath, and that in fact full recovery could have occurred if governments had kept their nerve. This is a highly controversial analysis. More importantly, he insists that the proposed Keynesian cure was in fact worse than the disease. This is because Keynesian policies inevitably lead to inflation, which is the real economic evil, not unemployment.

Friedman is renowned as an economist for his analysis of inflation. Many immediate causes are recognised, but what the most basic cause might be is a matter of dispute among economists. Keynesians argue that a certain amount of mild inflation is an inevitable accompaniment of economic growth (demand runs ahead of production creating shortages, extra demand for skilled labour pushes up wages, and so on), but this can be tolerated. Beyond this, in a situation of full employment unions are in a strong position to bid up wages, causing 'cost-push' inflation, which is more serious but can be controlled by government incomes policies. Friedman disagrees. He argues that unions are too well protected in two respects: by government policies of full employment and by legal immunities: that is, there is no consequence of unemployment if their demands are too high. Furthermore, unions will always strive to stay ahead of inflation.

However, Friedman's fame rests upon his analysis of inflation in terms of an excess of money in the economy. Either governments print too much or allow the creation of too much credit, often in pursuit of Keynesian policies to stimulate demand. In other words, it is government policies that cause inflation, and indeed it is government's sole economic function to control inflation through its control of money supply. His theory is called 'monetarism' and is widely held among neo-liberals (although some are sceptical, including Hayek). It was a key part of early Thatcherism.

Even without monetarism, neo-liberals agree that inflation is the great economic evil and that government economic policy should be aimed at making the free market work as effectively as possible with controlling inflation as the prime economic duty. Government intervention in the economy in other ways is condemned; this includes economic planning, state ownership, high taxation, incomes policies, a minimum wage, regional policies, and a variety of other interventionist policies. They all distort the market, and hinder rather than help in solving economic problems.

This general neo-liberal view of economic policy, of which monetarism is one rather extreme version, goes by the name of 'supply-side economics', to distinguish it from Keynesian economics, which is about manipulating demand. It has been widely influential, even among socialist parties like the British Labour Party (see Chapter Five).

The Welfare State

Neo-liberals are similarly critical of the role of the state in the field of social policy. They argue that attempts to intervene to make up for the deficiencies of the market are invariably counter-productive. Social security systems in Britain and elsewhere are under severe strain. They appear to create legions of the dependent poor on permanent benefit because the problems they are designed to solve just get worse instead of better. For example, aid for one-parent families just creates more one-parent families because the social security system allows people to abandon their families more readily. Or again, unemployment benefit tends to create unemployment because people who can rely on unemployment benefit become more choosy about jobs they will accept. In short, social security institutionalises poverty rather than solves it.

However, neo-liberals disagree about the extent to which the system should be dismantled. Some say the break up should be total and its role left to private charity. Others would prefer to see the social security system greatly reduced, leaving only a last resort for the very few.

In the USA programmes to help the poor have also had little apparent success, particularly in respect of blacks. One black neo-liberal writer, Walter Williams, has argued that they have made the situation of blacks positively worse. Hand-outs have made blacks dependent yet resentful, at the same time disinclining them to work. Many of the jobs they might have done – that is, jobs that employers will only find it worthwhile to provide if they can pay very low wages – have been ruled out by minimum-wage legislation that was designed to help them. Other policies such as 'affirmative action' (that is, positive discrimination) and 'bussing' (bussing black students to white schools to ensure balance) have also been deemed counter-productive.

A British example, according to this theory, is housing. Attempts to hold down rents, and prevent tenants losing their homes at the whim of a landlord, have almost eliminated private rented accommodation in this country. As a result, people are dependent on council housing, which may involve long waiting lists, extreme difficulty in moving, and people living in council houses who could afford private housing while others wait and wait. There is never enough of the right kind of council accommodation, which is normally all family homes, which not all of those in need of rented housing want. On the other hand, in the high-rise block era hundreds of thousands of homes were built that nobody wanted to live in. A completely free-market system, it is argued, would have none of these problems, as was the case before protection began.

Lack of government funds are usually cited as the reason for poor social services in Britain, but neo-liberals insist that this is never a sufficient answer. They claim that other countries have better services, without it spending more by, for example, involving private insurance. Our own state-run services are just not responsive to customer demands as they would be if run by private enterprise.

Public choice theory

Part of the problem with these services, from the neo-liberal's point of view, is that they are not considered part of the market, and market thinking is not applied to them. They are state monopolies where the consumer has little effective choice. As a consequence they are 'producer-led' rather than 'consumer-driven'. In other words, it is a combination of political decision and 'expert' advice (teachers, doctors and other professionals) that prevails and not that of the consumer. It is in the interests of all those on the producer side (politicians, bureaucrats and professionals) to ensure maximum and expanding provision, irrespective of demand. Hence, for example, until recently nobody in the NHS could say what an operation cost in different hospitals, whereas that is a very important guide to efficiency in the private sector. In the NHS efficiency was not a major concern.

It could be argued that the public sector is a different kind of animal from the private sector and that public service has a different motivation from profit. However, neo-liberals maintain that there is a public service mystique that ought to be dispelled. They point out that in America, and increasingly in Britain, there has grown up a body of theory and empirical analysis that makes sense of a great deal of otherwise inexplicable public sector phenomenan by assuming that agents in the public sector, whether politicians or officials or professionals, are as much motivated by self-interest as anyone in the private sector. This body of work goes under the general name of 'public choice theory'.

Of course public sector actors are not motivated by profit. Instead, so the theory goes, they have a number of different objectives according to their role. Put crudely, politicians seek votes, bureaucrats seek departmental expansion and a higher budget, while professionals want power and status. One of the abiding problems of democracy is the tendency of politicians to maximise votes by making expensive promises that require higher government spending and therefore more taxes and inflation, which in the long run undermines the economy. Bureaucrats and professionals have a vested interest in encouraging the politicians in this. But whereas in the private sector there is the check of competition, there is normally no such check on public sector services since they are normally monopolies, so it is producer decision and not consumer choice that decides the nature and level of service. There is, therefore, little incentive to be efficient and a good deal of incentive to be over-staffed and over-funded. Consequently, many neo-liberals see government agencies as necessarily inefficient and inferior to the private sector, and they want to see public sector services privatised or in some way made subject to private sector disciplines.

In all, then, modern state intervention is deemed inefficient to the point of being self-defeating. The most extreme example is the communist states, which have recently demonstrated the effectiveness of full state control by collapsing into poverty and economic chaos.

The neo-liberal free society

Neo-liberals believe that a society based on their principles will not only be the most efficient and prosperous possible society, but will also be morally superior to any other. This is because they believe that their kind of society will be the most free, and freedom is, they believe, the greatest value of all.

Hayek and freedom

The free market is, for Hayek, the engine of progress and civilization. Freedom is the absolute value, and the freedom of the market is the guarantee of all other freedoms, both political and intellectual, as well as the best chance that freedom will spread elsewhere. The way in which economic freedoms underpin other freedoms tends to be argued and illustrated by neo-liberals in a negative way. It is asserted that in socialist societies civil liberties count for little, and that state planning and the effort to maintain equality and 'social justice' must involve stopping people from doing what they would otherwise do, which necessarily impinges on their liberties and is ultimately tyrannous. We only have to look at the experience of communist regimes in Eastern Europe and elsewhere to see the truth of this.

If freedom is the basic value, and economic freedom is the root of all other freedoms, then whatever interferes with economic freedom must be wrong in some fundamental sense. This is the basis of a moral criticism of economic intervention, of the welfare state, and of socialism in general. Hayek insists that state ownership, economic planning and a great deal of regulation and interference is basically immoral because it induces people to do what they would not otherwise do. The high taxes that go along with big government are also an infringement of property rights. Spending other people's money on what is not absolutely essential is intrinsically wrong, and especially so if taxes are used to redistribute wealth. Hence the welfare state is wrong.

In his first major work on social questions, *The Road to Serfdom*, Hayek pictured the development of the welfare state as the unconscious first steps towards totalitarianism, a new serfdom. This was thought fanciful by many at the time and since. However, neo-liberals are given to radically simplifying opposing ideas which advocate state intervention as being merely gradations of socialism, the complete version being communism. Consequently, social liberalism, social democracy, communism and even fascism are indiscriminately lumped together as fundamentally the same thing. Thus Mrs Thatcher once dismissed Neil Kinnock in the House of Commons as a 'crypto-communist', generating a great deal of both mirth and puzzlement on Opposition benches.

The point is that neo-liberals see the growth of the state as a threat to freedom, however limited or benign the initial motivation may be. Indeed, the threat is more insidious for being in the name of what appear to be laudable ideals, such as equality as the means to freedom and justice. However, Milton Friedman writes:

A society that put equality – in the sense of outcomes – ahead of freedom will end up with neither equality nor freedom. . . . On the other hand, a society that puts freedom first will, as a happy by-product, end up with both greater freedom and greater equality . . . Freedom means diversity but also mobility. It preserves the opportunity for today's disadvantaged to become tomorrow's privileged and, in the process, enables almost everyone, from top to bottom, to enjoy a fuller and richer life.

Thus, only freedom matters and anyone who would limit it, for whatever reason, is to be condemned.

Hayek insisted that Adam Smith's 'invisible hand' works not just for the economy but for society as a whole. In other words, if people are left free to deal with each other without government interference, then they will always create a spontaneous order, a 'natural' order, that is both organisationally and morally superior to any that is artificially imposed. This is because the spontaneous order will not be based on any coercion but upon everyone's consent. Societies arrived at in this way will invariably be characterised by inequality, but Hayek will not countenance any suggestion that such a society could be unfair. The notion of fairness or justice, he thinks, cannot be ascribed to society as such but only to individual acts. If people cannot point to where they have suffered from some particular act of injustice for which some person is directly responsible, then they have no grounds for claiming that they are oppressed by 'the system'.

Hayek, however, is prepared to concede a certain bare minimum of welfare provision for the sake of social stability, and Milton Friedman slightly more (with his ideas for negative income tax and educational vouchers). But others are more radical, insisting that even this is completely illegitimate. We have seen that Nozick questions any function for government beyond providing law and order, while the anarcho-capitalists (see Chapter Six) believe that the state has no legitimate functions, summed up by the slogan 'War is mass murder, taxation is theft'.

True liberalism and false

All liberals believe that freedom is the supreme value and human nature cannot flourish without it. However, neo-liberals insists upon a particular definition of freedom which many other modern liberals regard as too narrow. Hayek wrote his major works attacking government management of the economy and the welfare state at a time when these were regarded as a major extension of freedom.

For neo-liberals genuine freedom is 'negative freedom', meaning simply the absence of constraint. But this can mean that although a person will starve if they do not take a job, they are still free because they are able to refuse it. Many modern liberals hold the view that poverty, ignorance and other deprivations limit people's freedom, and that the state can and should step in to alleviate these through collective provision. This view can be broadly called social liberalism (see Chapter Two).

Hayek, Nozick and others reject social liberalism as a false liberalism, and notions of 'social justice' that go with it as so much nonsense. The government, they insist, has no duty to intervene in society to aid the disadvantaged. This would involve taking wealth from others (as taxes) which Nozick argues is an illegitimate violation of their natural rights. Moreover, it means interfering in the market that is the guarantee of everyone's freedom; destroying freedom to make people free is self-contradictory.

The demands for state intervention to provide welfare services and other means of redistributing wealth in the name of social justice are seen as arising partly from the illegitimate demands of newly enfranchised classes in the late nineteenth century, but also partly from false conceptions that had become lodged in the liberal tradition in earlier periods. During the eighteenth century Enlightenment, the authentic tradition of Locke was continued by Adam Smith and the American Founding Fathers. This was a sceptical, empirical, limited liberalism that did not seek to change society, valued the individual and was suspicious of all power, especially political power. But another version developed in continental Europe, through Rousseau and the radicals of the French Revolution (see Chapter Two). This was a rationalistic liberalism that believed in popular sovereignty and equality. It sought to redesign society according to a preconceived rational theory, by capturing political power and using it to create a perfect world.

This 'false' liberalism resulted in the disaster of the French Revolution, whereas 'authentic' liberalism created a great age of freedom and progress in Britain during the nineteenth century, and in America for even longer. Unfortunately, the neo-liberals argue, in Britain 'alien continental influences' and working-class socialism began to permeate and dilute the genuine liberal spirit. The result was social liberalism, which is really a mild form of Socialism, culminating in the welfare state and the mixed and managed economy. As the neo-liberal writer David Green puts it:

By the First World War liberalism had lost its former sway, even to the extent that liberal ideas had been wholly abandoned by the Liberal Party. By the 1930s liberty was barely understood by British intellectuals, and even America had fallen under the influence of socialistic 'liberalism'.

(*The New Right*, 1987, p.32)

Hence the irony that Hayek felt when writing *The Road to Serfdom*: the Allies were fighting a war in order to preserve freedom, while, because of a lack of understanding, they were preparing to abandon it voluntarily at home. It has taken the economic failures of the

1970s to show how mistaken the social liberal path has been, and to stimulate the restoration of genuine liberalism.

We can see this neo-liberal version of liberal history as a variation on the traditional liberal theory of progress, which sees mankind proceeding through the development of freedom and reason towards an ever happier future. In this version we have an additional twist of the truth being lost and abandoned, and only now being rediscovered, but of course the truth must be acted upon if progress is to resume. We also have here the germ of a neo-liberal theory of ideology, which is also slightly different from the conventional liberal view.

Liberals normally define ideology in terms of social thinking that claims to be absolute truth, and which therefore despises toleration, pluralism and discussion as impeding the 'truth' being put into practice. Thus, ideology is the kind of thinking that leads to totalitarianism. The neo-liberal version (perhaps best exemplified by Kenneth Minogue's book *Alien Powers*, 1985) would include 'false' liberalism as well. Ideology is bound up with the false idea that the source of human unhappiness is 'the system' and that vigorous state action can reshape society in order to ensure human happiness. It is an attitude particularly associated with socialism, and the reason why neo-liberals tend to lump together socialism, communism, social liberalism and fascism, as though they were all the same thing.

Neo-liberalism therefore represents itself as 'true' liberalism, that is, liberalism that is above all individualist; that argues that while human beings may be selfish, they are nevertheless rational and therefore entitled to pursue their own interests and their own happiness in their own way, as long as they respect the same right in others. This releases people's intelligence and energy and talent, and their free interplay creates a spontaneous harmony that is natural and right.

Within this broad framework there are some variations among neo-liberals. Where the main variations and complexities lie within the New Right is in the relationship with the more tradi-tional right-wing beliefs.

The New Right spectrum

The New Right is not just neo-liberalism, but has a significant right-wing content as well. It may be wondered what the connection is and why neo-liberalism lodged itself at the right end of the spectrum, rather than in the centre where most political parties calling themselves 'liberal' are to be found. This in fact is only true of the political spectrum in Europe (see Chapter Two). In America the connection is much more natural and obvious. The USA and the United Kingdom need, therefore, to be discussed separately since there are significant differences of outlook and vocabulary between the right-wing politics of America, and those of Britain and the rest of Europe.

The American Right

In America all major parties are liberal in the sense that they believe in individualism and free enterprise, and there has never been a significant political party that has not. Nevertheless, within this consensus there is a broad spectrum of left to right. Traditionally, both Republicans and Democrats had their own left and right wings, although since the 1960s there have been disruptions of this traditional pattern.

On the right are the 'conservatives' who believe in the capitalist system being given free rein, in the complete absence of welfare, and in individuals pulling themselves up by their own bootstraps. In contrast to European conservatives, they have no concern with preserving an hereditary class, although they share other political beliefs such as anti-communism, nationalism, authoritarianism and high spending on defence and law and order. Those on the left of the spectrum are social liberals, who really came into their own in America during the New Deal and the Kennedy–Johnson periods. Rather confusingly, these are known in everyday American politics as 'liberals', and to those on the right they are little better than socialists.

Given the devotion of the American right to individualism and capitalism, it is not surprising that neo-liberal thinking found its natural home in America among conservatives. The writings of Hayek, Friedman and Nozick brought intellectual weight and distinction to a right wing that had been somewhat on the defensive since the 1930s.

However, this took place in the 1970s, when right-wing ideas had a warmer reception in the Democratic Party. In the previous decade the Democratic Party had embraced not only the Kennedy and Johnson anti-poverty programmes, but also the civil rights movement and the causes of other minority groups. This offended the conservative wing of the Democratic Party, particularly in the much more conservative South, which resulted in many conservative Democrats defecting to the Republicans. In addition, there were a number of intellectuals who had embraced the liberal causes of the Democrats, but had become disillusioned at the failure of the anti-poverty programmes, and worried by America's weakness, evident in the defeat in Vietnam and the spread of communism, and related, as they saw it, to the decline of traditional values. Many of these 'neo-conservatives' switched their allegiance to the Republican Party, where they were joined by the growing religious right, who shared their concerns over American weakness and who were especially anxious to halt America's loss of traditional values.

These different groups constituted a considerable expansion of the right in America. Together they captured the Republican Party in the late 1970s, and (like the Thatcherite capture of the Conservative Party in Britain) turned it into a much more ideological party than it had been in the past. From 1980 to at least 1992, the Republican Party was dominated by its left or 'liberal' wing.

However, among the various strands that make up the American New Right there are many differences, some of which are fundamental. Among influential intellectuals there are those who call themselves 'traditional conservatives', 'neo-liberals', 'neo-conservatives', 'libertarians' and other labels, each with its own variations, while the 'new Christian right' has a spectrum all of its own. The most striking contrast is between the libertarians, who would include minimal statists and anarcho-capitalists (see

Chapter 6), and the Christian right. Libertarians think that every-one should be able to do just what they like, particularly in moral matters, so long as they do not hurt others. Some even advocate the legalisation of drugs and allowing parents to auction off their unwanted children. Above all, they do not want the state inter-fering in people's lives. The Christian right, on the other hand, is highly puritanical and would use the powerr of the state to enforce traditional Christian morality (see the discussion of Christian fundamentalism in Chapter 11).

Whether the ideological polarisation of American politics in the 1980s will continue is difficult to say. It may well be that the Republican and Democratic Parties will return to their more traditional position of being able to encompass both left and right wings.

The European right

The right of the political spectrum in Europe is rather different, and the reason why neo-liberal ideas caught on among the right in Europe, as distinct from 'Liberal' parties, is a little more complicated.

Liberal ideas have triumphed in Western Europe as in the USA, to the extent that all are devoted to liberal democracy, free enterprise, constitutionalism and civil liberties. Despite this, most liberal parties in Europe today are small, centre-ground parties. This is because the parties of left and right have managed to appeal to a strong class base, while at the same time sharing the liberal inheritance of ideas between them. Parties of the right appealed to the propertied, while those of the left to the workers and the propertyless. Liberal parties, as in Britain, fell between the two, opting for a middle-of-the-road social liberalism. It was, therefore, towards the parties of the right, the parties of property and free enterprise, that neo-liberalism, naturally gravi-tated. This was particularly true of Britain, where the Con-servatives were never as hostile to liberal ideas as the European right.

Nevertheless, even in Britain there was less of an affinity

between neo-liberalism pre-existing conservatism than was the case in the USA. The adoption of 'Thatcherism' amounted to a revolution in the Conservative Party. While traditional Conservative thought always had a place for free enterprise and individual liberty, these values were held within a wider framework of respect for the past, rejection of politics based on theory, and a hostility towards radical change (see Chapter Two).

Mrs Thatcher had little time for this traditional outlook. It could be said that Thatcherism represents an Americanisation of the British right. Furthermore, she demanded change that was immediate and drastic, according to preconceived neo-liberal theories, and had little respect for tradition for its own sake. As a result, she has left the Conservative Party with something of a split personality.

A curious side-effect of this has been the confusion about what constitutes the far right in mainstream politics. It used to be those who could be described as nationalistic, authoritarian, with little faith in democracy, and so on. Now there is a second, and quite contrary far right that is libertarian and suspicious of any government at all (a current most vociferously represented in the Federation of Conservative Students). Thatcherism, however, has leaned more towards the libertarian side on economic matters and more towards the authoritarian and nationalist side on other matters.

Criticisms of the New Right

Much might be made of the relationship between the new free-market and libertarian ideas, and the old right ideas which have been variously attached to them. Certainly there are conflicts and contradictions here. However, the New Right stands or falls by its neo-liberal core.

Neo-liberalism is a vigorous, crusading ideology, and its critics attack it with corresponding vigour and passion. For many, a return to *laissez-faire* represents a return to barbarism, with society based on the law of the jungle in which the strong survive and the weak go to the wall. It would, so the argument goes, create a society where vast wealth would go side by side with great poverty, squalor and distress; where the lives of a great part of the population would be governed by fear and insecurity, and where greed and rapaciousness would rule and all would seek to exploit everyone else. And if evidence is required, we only have to look at the consequences of *laissez-faire* on Victorian society.

On a more sober level there are plenty of detailed theoretical criticisms to be found for every aspect of neo-liberal thought. To begin with, critics of neo-liberalism point out that its arguments depend on certain assumptions which are open to question. These include assumptions about the beneficence of the free market and the absence of viable alternatives; about the nature of freedom; about natural individual rights; about all non-liberalism boiling down to some greater or lesser degree of socialist totalitarianism, and ultimately, assumptions about the nature of human nature itself.

The Free Market

Neo-liberals will brook no criticisms of the free market. They insist that the free market is the guarantee of maximum prosperity for all, of justice and fairness, and of all other freedoms. Critics point out that with unrestrained capitalism people are exploited and damaged, as was evident from the nineteenth-century industrial system with its children working in factories and mines and so on. Misery is caused on a massive scale, particularly in conditions of slump. From the establishment of the free market there followed cycles of booms and slumps that culminated in the Great Depression of the 1930s, which caused massive distress, dislocation, political instability, and which contributed to the rise of Hitler and the outbreak of the Second World War.

Adam Smith's benign 'invisible hand' is, critics argue, a myth. There is no compelling reason why the free operation of the market will result in the optimum benefit for all. It is more like a random distribution of gross wealth for the few and misery for the many. Furthermore, the notion that state intervention to influence the economy or distribute welfare only ruins the system is nowhere proven. The economic difficulties of the 1970s were due to oil price rises, not government intervention. Besides, the most successful economies, for example Germany and Japan, are certainly not based on a complete absence of government intervention. The main neo-liberal argument against the managed economy – that it is the thin end of a totalitarian wedge – is simply based on prejudice and is demonstrably not true.

The neo-liberal attack on the welfare state is also challenged on the grounds of weak evidence. Certainly there are administrative problems and schemes that do not work, but neo-liberals triumphantly represent these as the whole. All major organisations and administrative systems have their problems, and can be made to look foolish by generalising examples of failure, especially in times of economic stringency. In a similar way, socialists of various kinds have little difficulty, and take equal delight, in finding inefficiency, waste and absurdity in the workings of capitalism.

A narrow freedom

Critics also question neo-liberal notions of freedom and justice. Freedom in particular, they say, is defined far too narrowly. To say that someone is free when they only have formal liberties which they cannot possibly enjoy relies on a definition of freedom that is quite arbitrary. Moreover, it is not at all clear that the neo-liberals have disposed of the social-liberal/socialist case that people who are deprived, exploited and denied education and adequate health and housing because of their poverty, are not genuinely free just because they technically have civil liberties. Neo-liberals argue that a concept of freedom which says that people have a right to be free from these things is contradictory because ensuring such freedom would involve some people losing their liberty. But it is not that black and white. The rich would lose a tiny amount of freedom, of which they have a very great deal, in the interests of greater freedom for the majority. To say that this necessarily involves or leads to totalitarian tyranny is merely melodramatic.

Having defined freedom in an absurdly restricted way, that suits the rich and successful and nobody else, the neo-liberals proceed, critics argue, to illegitimately elevate this freedom to be the supreme value, and the only one of any worth. Other values are either ignored altogether (as with notions of community) or else defined in terms of it. Thus the just society is one where unrestricted freedom prevails, and where social outcomes are entirely determined by the market. Such a society is necessarily just, quite irrespective of whether people are prosperous and happy or starving and exploited. A society where social justice is pursued in the name of a wider notion of freedom is deemed unjust, purely on the grounds that the market is interfered with. There is no reason to accept the insistence of Hayek and Nozick that 'social justice' is a meaningless phrase, or that a situation cannot be unfair if nobody planned it or acted to bring it about.

Natural rights and human nature

Nozick and a number of others who take an extremely narrow view of what government can legitimately do, rely ultimately upon a notion of natural rights, and especially a natural right to property. For Nozick this right is absolute and inviolable. But the idea that such rights exist is extremely difficult to demonstrate. John Locke, who was the first to argue that a natural right to property existed, insisted that these rights had been granted to mankind by God. But the existence of God is not something that can be proved, and by no means all who do have faith believe in a God-given right to property. If we do not rely on religious ideas, then it is not sufficient to merely assert that we have such rights. We need to be able to prove their existence to someone who denies they exist. But there would appear to be no such proof. Certainly Nozick does not supply any.

Another object of criticism is the notion that social liberalism, Fascism and every variety of socialism all amount to the same thing. It is a crucial part of the neo-liberal case against wider notions of freedom, the welfare state, the mixed economy and other aspects of state activity in the modern world. But this lumping together, critics argue, is entirely illegitimate. One can draw a multitude of distinctions and point to a host of differences. Social liberals and social democrats are particularly resentful of being identified with communism and fascism. The notion that a welfare state like Britain's is a giant step on the road to totalitarianism is ridiculous. The point of all this lumping together is to promote the totally false suggestion that the only real alternative to the neo-liberal society is totalitarianism or proto-totalitarianism.

Finally, neo-liberals see human nature in terms of a selfishness and a competitiveness which when given free reign, thanks to some happy contrivance of nature or the divine, always ensures harmony and progress. Critics point out that such selfishness simply contradicts common experience; that, mercifully, human beings have many other qualities. It is precisely these other qualities that make civilised life possible. If people were just selfish and competitive then we could hardly have a social life at all. Silly theories, like public choice theory, simply ignore all the other qualities that produced the public system and make it run; besides, if the theory were true, then it would not have taken political scientists so long to think it up. If anything, human nature has so many facets and characteristics that to pick out one and call it fundamental is to risk looking foolish.

Of course neo-liberals defend themselves against such criticisms. And they have managed to capture parties and governments in major states. On the other hand, these governments have had to be cautious about implementing many neo-liberal ideas. For neither President Reagan or Mrs Thatcher was it politically possible to do away with state welfare. Both Reagan and Thatcher gave way to less committed successors, and while neo-liberal ideas have been influential in many parts of the world, the total commitment of Reaganites and Thatcherites has rarely characterised other governments. All of which gives rise to questions about the future of neo-liberalism. The New Right is in many ways the most vigorous ideology in today's world. It was certainly the ideology of the 1980s, but how long it continues to be in the future remains to be seen.

10

New radicalisms

Most of the ideological beliefs that influence politics in the world today belong to broad traditions of thought that began to take shape around the period of the French Revolution. However, in recent decades there have developed a number of ideological outlooks that stand somewhat apart from the main traditions. These include animal rights, gay liberation, feminism and the ideas of the Green movement.

None of the concerns that lie behind these doctrines are entirely new; it is in their political significance that their newness lies. Gay liberation and animal liberation are entirely modern political doctrines. Green ideas and feminism are of older origin. Concern over what we now call 'Green issues' began to be expressed in the nineteenth century and one way or another since, but the organisation of this concern into a serious political force with a comprehensive doctrine is quite recent. Feminism is both ancient and modern. Some of feminism's ideas were expressed as far back as, inevitably, the ancient Greeks, while its first modern expression came at the time, equally inevitably, of the French Revolution. There have been theoretical writings and there have been campaigns for women's rights, but in every case these can be seen as extensions of existing ideologies, liberal or socialist. It is only with the advent of the Women's Liberation movement of the late 1960s, with its fresh wave of radical thinking, that Feminism can be said to have become a fully independent ideology. Thus, each of these movements has brought something new to the ideological scene and to the politics of our time. We will consider each of them in turn.

Liberation ideology: gay and animal rights

It is possible to see the late 1960s as some kind of watershed in the post-war period. The New Left was a departure from the fixed positions of the Cold War, a move into new territory (see Chapter Seven). Although broadly Marxist in inspiration, it was a highly eclectic movement that brought in new ideas that transformed Marxism into a theory very different to any previous orthodoxy. Economics was abandoned in favour of changing society immediately through a transformation of consciousness.

The New Left and liberation

As a vast, sprawling, inchoate movement, the New Left was doomed to failure. Yet the New Left did develop a distinctive style of thinking that could be, and has been, applied to other things. The result has been an array of 'liberation' movements on behalf of various 'oppressed' groups, often giving new life and a sharper edge to old causes. Such movements have demanded more than just formal equality in the recognition of rights, but demanded an equality that necessitates, to a greater or lesser extent, a new or changed society.

The New Left style of thinking originally saw workers oppressed by capitalists in the traditional Marxist manner, but this was adapted to blacks oppressed by whites, women by men, homosexuals by heterosexuals, and so on. What was especially new about the New Left approach was the notion, derived from Marxian ideas of ideology and alienation, that the oppressed participate in their own oppression through the absorption of their oppressors' conception and evaluation of the world; that is, their oppressors' ideology, beliefs, values and language. Thus, where the workers saw the system as fair and just, and therefore their position as fair and just, so blacks see themselves as naturally inferior; women accept their inferior position as normal and natural and right; homosexuals accept their feelings as 'unnatural', and so on.

A further feature of the New Left approach is that just as the oppressed are seen as participating in their own oppression, so the oppressed must participate in their own emancipation. An essential first step in this process is a 'raising of consciousness', which means to 'confront, criticise and overcome' the alien ideology which is seen as damaging the victim's psyche and from which they must be released. Finally, the oppressors themselves must be seen as alienated and as much in need of liberation as the victims; they too need a change of consciousness, involving seeing the oppressed as fellow and equal human beings.

All this fits in with the New Left theme of liberation through the transformation of consciousness. Much psychological and psychiatric theorising (much of it unorthodox and speculative) has gone into the elaboration of this theory with the aim of establishing a 'psychology of oppression' and the means of overcoming it. Thus, the oppressed self is seen as internally divided, because of feelings of inferiority and even self-hatred induced by the prevailing ideology. Antidotes are seen in terms of techniques whereby the oppressed are able to throw off their feelings of inferiority and build their self-esteem.

Oppressions and political correctness

The first area, beyond the conventional 'class struggle', to which these ideas were applied was that of black rights. Indeed, the black struggle for civil rights in America was a powerful contemporary issue at the height of the New Left, so that black liberation can be seen as part of the New Left movement.

As the first such movement, black liberation became the model for subsequent liberation movements, especially women and gays, but aspects of it have also been used by other groups. We have, therefore, equivalents of racism such as sexism, heterosexism, speciesism, ageism, and so on. Some groups have applied the analysis of self-hate to their own situation and have developed their own techniques, to overcome it. The strategy has been used by a variety of groups seeing themselves or seen by others as oppressed and in need of liberation. The best known are women, gays and animals, but we might also add to this list a variety of disadvantaged groups who feel discriminated against, including the old and the disabled; and others have sought to make a case for children and for the mentally ill. There is also 'liberation theology', a movement among Catholic priests, especially in South America who have applied some of these ideas in self-help organisations for the poor.

These various liberation movements have recently created a controversy in American higher education that may spread elsewhere. The argument is that what is taught in American colleges is male Eurocentric, so that white European male culture is elevated to the detriment of other cultural forms which forebars had originated (such as those of black Africa). The slogan is 'No more DWEM's', that is, no more 'Dead White European Males', such as Plato and Kant and Shakespeare and Beethoven and the rest. Presenting their works as the pinnacle of human achievement is seen as a subtle form of oppression of anyone not white and male. Another aspect of this movement is an insistence on everyone being 'Politically Correct' (PC), which especially applies to language. Thus to use the word 'mankind' is seen as offensive to women and should in all circumstances be substituted by the PC word 'humankind'; the word 'disabled' is not PC, while the phrase 'differently abled' is, and so on.

The PC controversy has often been very bitter, with accusations of censorship and intimidation, but no doubt it will all die down in time. A number of liberation movements are, however, of more lasting political importance and need to be looked at in greater detail.

Apart from black liberation (discussed in Chapter Eight), there are three movements influenced by liberation ideas that have so far been significant. The greatest political impact has been made by feminism, which is by far the oldest movement, given new life by liberation ideology. However, animal rights and gay liberation, although of more restricted appeal, have also had some impact.

Animal rights

The ideas of animal liberation have as much theoretical connection with Green thinking as with liberation movements. Both
Greens and animal liberationists see humanity as out of harmony
with nature and both see the roots of this in the Western tradition
of thought, in contrast to other important traditions. Both point to
Biblical passages that elevate humanity above the rest of creation.
The ancient Greeks are also held responsible, particularly Aristotle, whose view of a hierarchy of nature with inferior species
existing for the benefit of the higher ones (and above all human
beings) was standard Western thinking until the nineteenth
century. Animal liberationists regard the Western tradition in this
respect as intellectually inadequate and, more importantly,
morally flawed.

The animal rights case is almost exclusively a moral one. The
practical aspect of the ideology, in terms of social or economic
improvement of human existence, is of little importance. The
world needs to be changed because it is right to do so, and for no
other reason. Such moral concern for the welfare of animals goes
back to the nineteenth century, and was most significant in
Britain. Victorian reformers campaigned against 'unnecessary
cruelty' to animals (which led to the formation of the RSPCA),
although for most of them there was no serious objection to
vivisection, hunting, or killing animals for food or fur. Only
occasionally was there a voice that suggested that the moral case
was much deeper and that there was no such thing as 'necessary
cruelty'. The most distinguished precursor of modern animal
rights thinking was the utilitarian philosopher, Jeremy Bentham,
who, when discussing slavery, wrote 'The day may come when the
rest of the animal creation may acquire those rights which never
could have been withholden from them but by the hand of tyranny'
(Quoted in Peter Singer, *Practical Ethics*, p.49). A fuller case was
put by Henry Salt in his *Animal Rights* (1892), as part of a moral
justification for vegetarianism.

However, it is only recently that such thinking has been
sufficiently widespread and influential to have inspired a political

movement. There have been a number of contributing thinkers, although the most important has been the Australian philosopher Peter Singer. One of his arguments questions our justification for eating other creatures. The usual argument is that we have reason and speech and they do not. But there are, sadly, some human beings who lack reason and speech; do we therefore have a right to eat them? Singer agrees with Jeremy Bentham when he wrote 'The question is not, Can they reason? nor Can they talk? but, Can they suffer?' (*ibid.* p.50).

Singer has argued that we have no moral right to regard other species as simply there to do with as we please; animals have rights just as we have, and that the many uses we make of animals without regard to these rights is morally indefensible.

It is undoubtedly true that animal rights thinking has had an impact on popular attitudes. This is not just among those such as Greens and vegetarians and others with related interests, but among the general public and especially the young. There is a growing moral repugnance at such practices as vivisection (particularly where experiments are to improve, for example, cosmetics rather than medical research), hunting for sport, the use of animal furs for expensive clothes, the killing of animals for use in dissection in schools, and so on. While it seems unlikely that this will result in human beings ceasing to be carnivores, the movement may well achieve further success in the future.

All these changes in attitude and behaviour could be said to be the positive side of the animal liberation movement, but there is also what is widely regarded as a negative side. This is the resort, by some followers of the movement, to violence and terrorism. The argument is that since animals cannot liberate themselves then humans must do it for them, hence raids on laboratories, shops attacked, fur warehouses set on fire, goods in shops poisoned, and even a recent case where a bomb was attached to the car of a medical researcher (which failed to go off). In some places (most notably in parts of Manchester) butchers have had their shops damaged and their businesses ruined by members of the activist group, the Animal Liberation Front. Many people sympathetic to the cause are angered by such activity. It is perhaps one thing to release animals from where they would otherwise suffer, but quite another to threaten peoples lives and legitimate livelihoods. The activists may well do their movement more harm than good.

Animal rights is an unusual member of the liberation ideology family, in that the 'oppressed group' is not going to have its consciousness raised or participate in its own liberation. But it does fit in in other respects. The oppressors do themselves have to be liberated and overcome their alienation, in the form of 'speciesism' (the belief that human beings are superior and that this entitles them to treat other animals in any way they choose). There is also a certain characteristic use of vocabulary. The use of 'liberation' and 'oppression' for example, and the term 'speciesism' to parallel 'racism', 'sexism' and the rest. On the other hand, if an ideology always offers a key to human salvation, the overcoming of speciesism is not a very convincing candidate. It is perhaps most convincing as a contribution to a wider world-view, such as that of the Greens.

Something similar might be said of gay liberation, which needs to be part of a wider set of ideas to be convincing as the key to human salvation. This is a more conventional liberation ideology. In this case, those deemed victims of the oppression are human and can rethink the world and participate in their own emancipation.

Gay liberation

Homosexuals have long been discriminated against in Western and other societies on the grounds that homosexuality is 'unnatural' and 'perverted', arising from some kind of sickness or malfunction, and provoking a natural repugnance. Gay liberationists insist that it is an unjust oppression which has nothing to do with what is 'natural' but is based, like racial discrimination, on ignorance and prejudice that has long-established roots in Western thought. In this case, it is not the Greeks who were at fault (as they are for animal liberationists, Greens and feminists), for while not as liberal towards homosexuality as is often supposed, ancient Greek culture was not what gay liberationists call 'homophobic'.

The source of Western homophobia lies in religion. Jewish and Christian thought has always been virulently hostile to homosexuality, and insistent that it was unnatural, sinful and an offence to God. (This is also true of Islam. The Islamic fundamentalist regime of Ayatollah Khomeini in Iran was executing homosexuals until quite recently.) In the West, this religious view was standard until the twentieth century. Today, although there has been some easing of legal disabilities, homosexuals are still widely discriminated against in the West, including Europe and North America.

As with black and women's liberation, gay liberation is concerned not just with the assertion of gay rights but with giving gays a sense of worth and self-belief, hence the emphasis on 'gay pride' and 'coming out', the assertion of gays' contribution to history and culture and of working together to overcome the psychological 'damage' of society's prejudices. The internalisation of society's hostility produces the same kind of destructive 'self-hate' that is found among blacks.

The gay movement is also concerned with 'liberating the oppressors' in the sense of combating the common prejudices of a 'heterosexist' society, that is, beliefs about gays being unnatural, promiscuous, sick or whatever. The situation has not been helped by the advent of AIDS. Gay liberationists campaign to end legal discrimination, and this open campaigning as gays is itself deemed a 'therapy' and source of confidence.

In terms of theory, gay liberation is largely an extension of socialist liberation ideology, seeing the divisions of society – male/female, black/white, proletarian/bourgeois, heterosexual/homosexual – as functional to the operation of capitalism, and that ending capitalism is the key to ending discrimination against gays. But like animal rights, gay liberation alone cannot sustain a worldview that can claim to hold the key to mankind's ideal future. It needs to be part of a wider vision, such as feminism. Indeed, there are close links between the two because the lesbian cause overlaps both.

Feminism I: early feminism

In virtually every society in recorded human history women have been accorded a subordinate role, principally confined to the home and excluded from the public affairs of society. From time to time the protest has been made that this is unfair and wasteful, and/or the possibility of an alternative has been articulated (for example in Plato's *Republic*, where he argued that women were as fitted to be philosopher-rulers as men), but it was the advent of liberalism that provided the first vehicle for a sustained tradition of feminist writing and theorising to develop.

Early liberal ideology was based on the notion of natural rights to which all men are entitled by virtue of their reason. The term 'men' was being used generically (that is, meaning 'humanity'), yet for many of the early theorists it was only the male part of humanity that was entitled to the full exercise of those rights which they deemed natural. Locke, for example, did not extend full civil and political rights to women, although he gave no reasons, while the far more egalitarian Rousseau insisted on women's 'sexual nature' fitting them for the role of pleasing men and looking after husband and family. Only with the coming of the French Revolution was there a significant theoretical work to insist that natural rights applied as fully to women as to men.

Mary Wollstonecraft and liberal feminism

The publication of Edmund Burke's *Reflections on the Revolution in France* in 1790 provoked an array of radical responses, and these included the first major feminist work, Mary Wollstonecraft's *Vindication of the Rights of Women* (1792). In essence the work applies liberal values and arguments to the women's case. The view that women's inferior position was God-given and natural, and that their dominant role was necessarily sexual – that is, to please men and look after the resultant family – was rejected. Women's nature was primarily human. Before anything else a woman was a rational being, and therefore entitled to the same rights of liberty and self-determination as a man.

If women often seemed little fit for wider responsibilities, it was because they were not educated or had not had the opportunity to develop themselves, their talents or their character. They had been brought up to be dependent and submissive and emotional because of society's false conception of their true nature. If they could be properly educated, if they could enjoy full civil rights (Wollstonecraft was ambiguous about political rights), and if they could be legally independent of their husbands and exercise their talents in any occupation, then they would be full members of society and fit companions for men.

Wollstonecraft had little doubt that only a minority of exceptional women would pursue independent careers and that the majority would find fulfilment in the roles of wife and mother. Nevertheless, proper rigorous education, the end of legal dependence on the husband, and the demonstrated capacity of women for occupation, even if it was not pursued, would give women the independence and capacity to be effective wives and mothers, and through the exercise of reason and virtue in that role (though not exclusively in that role) to fulfil their nature as human beings.

In not challenging the family, or women's traditional responsibilities within it, Wollstonecraft was at one with most liberal thinkers, feminist and non-feminist. Similar arguments were put forward by a range of both male and female Liberal theorists (the most famous being John Stuart Mill) during the course of the nineteenth century, and they fuelled a growing movement for the extension of women's rights in Europe, America and parts of the British Empire. The result was a steady extension of women's civil rights in the late nineteenth century, including the right to hold property within marriage, and access to higher education and the professions. After a series of militant campaigns, such as that of the Suffragettes in Britain, this was extended to political rights, mostly after World War I.

Charles Fourier and socialist feminism

In the meanwhile, the women's cause was taken up by other

ideologies, most notably socialism and Marxism. From the beginnings of the socialist tradition, most socialist theorists have been enthusiastic feminists. This is perhaps partly because socialists (that is, what we have called 'classical socialists' who have sought the abolition of capitalism) have generally wanted to see the abolition of the existing family. A good example is the 'Utopian' socialist, Charles Fourier (see Chapter Five for a fuller account of classical and utopian socialism). He saw history in terms of a series of progressive stages, and saw the status and treatment of women as the critical indicator of progress: the higher their status and the greater their liberty, the more advanced the stage of civilisation. Ultimately, in the ideal society of co-operative communes which he envisaged, the restrictive family would be abolished and women would be able to develop themselves fully. When that happened, he believed, women would outshine men both in qualities of character and in the performance of any activity that did not depend on physical strength.

Fourier saw both the family and monogamous marriage as oppressive to women. In the future, women and men would choose partners as and when their inclination dictated. In his 'phalanstery' there would be a 'hotel system' with private accommodation and common services, such as eating and cleaning, which would be undertaken by those for whom these were chosen occupations. Similarly, children would be cared for communally by those who specialised in the work, while still leaving room for the exercise of parental affection. This would free women for any occupation (or occupations) they chose on the same basis as men. However, Fourier was unusual in objecting to monogamous marriage, since in most socialist thinking the abolition of the family is not meant to imply the abolition of marriage. The more common argument has been that in capitalist society women may have a formal equality with their husbands, but the reality is of subordination because of the husband's economic power (that is, earning power and control over family property, and so on). In socialist society, these considerations will not arise and marriage will be a genuine partnership of equals.

There were various other socialists who developed feminist

ideas in other directions. For example, Charlotte Perkins Gilman was greatly influential in the USA after the publication of her *Women and Economics* in 1898, in which she developed a social Darwinist version of socialist feminism. She believed that the processes of social development, of differentiation and specialisation, were processes from which women were excluded, and this was simply because men had enslaved women and condemned them to a mindless domesticity. Women were thereby prevented from making their contribution to progress and to the fulfilment of human destiny.

However, the chief contributors to the development of socialist feminism have been the Marxists.

Marxist feminism

Like Fourier, Marx also believed that the status of women was an indicator of progress and that they would only develop to their full potential, equal with men, when released from the bourgeois family. However, Marx himself wrote little on the subject, leaving that to his collaborator Friedrich Engels, who produced the major Marxist work on the position of women in class society, *The Origin of the Family, Private Property and the State* in 1884.

In this book, Engels set out to trace the development of the family and women's place in society through various stages of history. His account of the early stages was based on the speculations of the American anthropologist Lewis Morgan, and saw the early stages of society, before the rise of private property, as based on communal property, matriarchy, group marriage and descent through the female line. But with the development of private property came the dominance of the male, who wished to pass his property to his recognised heirs, hence monogamy (at least for females) and descent through the male line. It was, Engels declared, a world-historical defeat for the female sex, and was followed by millennia of domination and oppression of women by men in differing forms relating to the historical form of society.

The modern bourgeois family, supposedly based on love, is in fact based on a form of prostitution in which a woman must sell herself into domestic slavery in order to live. The man has all the economic power, so that within the home he is, in a sense, the bourgeois while the wife is the proletarian. The family is an economic unit and its whole existence is bound up with property. The communist revolution, by abolishing private property, would remove the economic basis of the monogamous bourgeois family. Housekeeping and childcare would become matters of public provision, and marriage would be genuinely based on love and mutual respect. It was the family and not marriage that was the obstacle to women's emancipation and full entry into society. Women's freedom and equality was, therefore, bound up with the emancipation of humanity and only fully realizable through a communist revolution (see Chapter Seven).

The Bolshevic Revolution of 1917 provided an opportunity to put these ideas into practice. Led by Alexandra Kollontai, Commissar of Social Welfare and head of the Central Women's Department, the new Soviet state began to implement laws giving women a new status and new freedom from the family. However, within a few years the policy was changed and women were exhorted to be good mothers and maintain the family. In a sense they were worse off in that women were expected to be full-time workers and fulfil all their traditional family duties at the same time (although some changes were retained, such as easy divorce).

Achievement and disillusion

As a practical movement to change the condition of women, feminism was dominated by the liberal feminists, who in the late nineteenth and early twentieth centuries secured many important rights for women in terms of the removal of legal disabilities, access to education and the professions and above all the right to vote. New Zealand was the first modern state to give women the vote in 1893. Women over the age of thirty were enfranchised in Britain in 1918, while all American women received the vote in 1920 (although earlier in some states of the Union).

As these gains were secured, feminism as an active movement

went into a substantial period of quiescence, as though the gains had to be experienced and digested and evaluated. There were still women who, through what they did or what they wrote, challenged the prevailing norms. Nevertheless, feminism as a movement shrank to being the preoccupation of a few. Discussion among intellectuals continued and this flourished increasingly after World War II.

Although there was formal equality for women and, in the 1950s and 1960s, there was growing affluence for the overwhelming majority of people in the West, there was also a degree of disillusionment. Despite the gains, the world was overwhelmingly male-dominated and women were heavily discriminated against in almost every walk of life. Two writers in particular articulated these feelings and their books caught the imagination of a generation of women. The work of Simone de Beauvoir and Betty Friedan can be seen as a precursor of the feminist movement that exploded in the late 1960s.

In *The Second Sex* (1952) de Beauvoir gives a long and penetrating account of women's subjection. She argues that women have always been defined in terms of their feminine nature, and therefore in terms of their relationships with men. Men, on the other hand, are defined as free, independent beings, and not in terms of their relationship with women. This asymmetry both expresses and is part of man's domination of women. Since women are defined in terms of their sex and not their human rationality and freedom, they are being classified as incomplete human beings. Men subordinate women in order to guarantee their own freedom, but the price is unsatisfactory relationships.

There is a good deal of existentialist theory in de Beauvoir's analysis, which reflects the influence of her lifetime partner, Jean-Paul Sartre; yet, unlike Sartre, she is not ultimately pessimistic about human relationships. She believes that, while the differences between men and women are more than merely physical, women can assert their freedom and transform their lives, and can achieve satisfactory relationships with men on the basis of equality.

Betty Friedan's book, *The Feminine Mystique* (1963) was significant in changing the direction of liberal feminism, flatly rejecting the taken-for-granted assumption that women were different, had basic characteristics that especially fitted them for domesticity, and just needed formal equality of status. Friedan insisted that this was just not good enough. She insisted that the differences, symbolised in the so-called 'feminine mystique', were overrated, and what women really wanted and needed was to get out in the world, have careers and compete equally with men.

However, despite the importance of de Beauvoir's and Friedan's work, it was in the late 1960s that modern feminism, what is sometimes called feminism's 'Second Wave', really took off. This happened when growing discontent felt by women, especially young women, began to be articulated in terms of the concepts and categories of the New Left.

Feminism II: Women's Liberation

The late 1960s 'new wave' of feminism, or 'Women's Liberation', amounted to virtually a new ideology. Previous feminist theory was always an extension of or special case of among more comprehensive ideologies, but with the development of radical feminism that was no longer the case. Radical feminism became a new strand of feminism in its own right, but also influenced other strands, so that, at least initially, the Women's Liberation movement had a certain unity of outlook. A number of radical writers, like Kate Millet and Germaine Greer, influenced feminism generally, while others, such as Shulamith Firestone, were more strictly confined to the movement's radical wing.

Kate Millet and patriarchy

Characteristic of the new thinking, and widely influential across the feminist spectrum, was Kate Millett's *Sexual Politics* (1970). Like much of the early Women's Liberation theory, it was much influenced by New Left ideas, with its notions of domination and repression and alienation, and the use of psychoanalytic concepts. Nevertheless, the problem she posed and the conclusions she reached struck a chord far beyond radical politics. She simply asked why it is that in a free society, where women have the full range of civil and political rights and all possible educational opportunities, all important decisions in society are made by men, that women have to suffer a subordinate role that men assigned to them.

It was Millett's book that developed the modern feminist's concept of 'patriarchy' to explain women's subordination and oppression. She said it worked by brainwashing women from childhood into accepting a role that was constructed for them by men, and reinforced by law, tradition, language, social 'science' and such aspects of popular culture as television and women's magazines. The main stereotype was the wife and mother: passive and caring, emotional rather than logical, and preoccupied with domestic matters and personal appearance. (The other common stereotype, though not socially approved, was of the whore and temptress. Women were here portrayed as a little more independent and dangerous, but still there for the benefit of men.)

Distinguished social scientists such as Talcott Parsons who was the most influential sociologist of his day, described women's role in society as based on biology, while significantly giving men no such specific role. Women internalised these sex-role stereotypes and came to accept them as natural. In other words, differences of 'masculine' and 'feminine' were treated as sexual differences (that is, deriving from nature), instead of what they really were, which was gender differences based on socially constructed roles. Those women who did not see their fundamental role as domestic and rejected the stereotype, tended to be derided as 'unnatural'; on the Freudian view they were suffering from 'penis envy' (feminists think Freud has a lot to answer for). Thus from all sides there was pressure on women to conform to the stereotype, and in this way women were kept in subjection with no overt coercion being employed.

Millett also developed the notion of 'sexual politics', by arguing that even in the most personal relations between men and women, it was men who controlled the sexual relations, took the initiative and defined and restricted female sexuality in terms of their own needs, leaving women often unfulfilled. This was deemed 'political' in the sense that it was a power relationship, a relationship of domination and subordination, a dimension of the situation where the subordinate exists for the sake of the dominant; in other words it was a dimension of patriarchy. This was the source of the feminist slogan 'The personal is the political'.

Aspects of patriarchy

Many other writers worked along the same lines and developed different aspects of the analysis of patriarchy, such as language, how women appear in history, literature, and in social and political theory. Earlier thinkers discussed in this book (all male), for example, invariably talked in terms of 'man in society', the 'nature of man' and so on. Thus, the *American Declaration of Independence* talks of all *men* being equal, while even figures sympathetic to the women's cause, such as Karl Marx, always talked automatically of humanity in masculine terms, as in 'from each according to *his* need'. While some theorists like Locke and Rousseau did explicitly give women an inferior status, for the most part there was no deliberate denigration of women, it was merely taken for granted that 'man' stood for all human beings. But it was just this assumption to which feminists drew attention. The point being that in a multitude of small cultural ways – such as the generic use of 'man', God always being presented as male, heads of committees always being 'chair*man*', and so on – the male is always the standard, implying that the female is very much the 'second sex'. Women therefore demanded changes in the way we speak and write; although some of the changes demanded by the more radical are less convincing than others, such as 'herstory' instead of 'history'.

There was a general reaction against the notion of women as 'different', that they had different emotions, that they valued different things, that they had different ways of thinking, that they had different needs, including sexual needs. This question was addressed by Germaine Greer in her influential book, *The Female Eunuch* (1970), in which she argued that the traditional conception of female sexuality as being soft and passive, was in fact a stereotype imposed by men, which satisfied them but left women unfulfilled. Women's true sexuality was distorted and repressed to the point of effectively rendering them 'castrated' and sexless, mere 'sex-objects'. Greer was influenced by Herbert Marcuse's analysis of contemporary society as repressive and in need of sexual liberation, applying the idea particularly to women. There was indeed something of a fashion in the late 1960s for aggressive heterosexuality and a rejection of the passive image. More generally, women insisted on being treated as 'persons' and not 'sex-objects'; they resented being patronised and put into categories and told that 'all women think like this'.

This general rejection of 'stereotyping', of how women ought to think or behave or look, was the origin of the notorious 'bra burning' which radical feminists were supposed to go in for, which became part of the popular press image of feminists as bra-burning lesbians. Insofar as any feminists did do such things, it was a comprehensible symbolic act that rejected a stereotyped image of the ideal woman as being of a certain shape which all women were supposed to try to achieve in order to please men. It went along with attacks on pornography and beauty contests.

Lesbianism was considered to have been artificially classified as 'unnatural'. Its condemnation by society was interpreted as part of a general denigration of any female behaviour that did not conform to the male-imposed stereotype, the mould constructed by men into which women's behaviour is forced in order to keep them subservient. In this respect all feminists recognised a common cause with gay men, who were also engaged in challenging the sexual stereotype of their own sex.

The initial feminist ideal was not just a society with no discrimination on grounds of sex, but a society that was 'androgynous', that is, where men and women were not expected to behave differently and have different roles; a society where a woman's 'masculine' characteristics (such as ambition and aggression) and a man's 'feminine' characteristics (such as gentleness and caring)

were not suppressed. Men and women could therefore be themselves, be 'natural' instead of trying to achieve some socially
constructed ideal version of self.

Liberals and socialists

Much of this radical analysis became common across three main
types of feminist thought. There were theorists and groups recog-
nisably liberal in their outlook; others were recognizably socialist,
and there was now a new category of radical feminists. These
broad divisions still remain, although they exist as neat categories
more in the minds of those trying to describe feminism than in
practice. There is great variety and considerable overlapping, and
at the grass roots of the feminist movement a good deal of
eclecticism, taking from different theories and traditions whatever
seems useful. Nevertheless, these divisions have some use in
gaining an initial understanding of a complex field.

Post-1968, liberal and socialist feminism are still flourishing.
The liberal preoccupation with rights has been extended to
making those rights a reality, that is, not merely defending the
right of women to enter the professions, politics, and other traditional male preserves, but also to see women in senior positions.
The British Parliament, for example, still only has a handful of
women MPs (56 out of 631 in 1992), in spite of having had a
woman Prime Minister, and there is a '300 Group' campaigning
for there to be at least 300 women MPs in the future. In America,
the National Organisation for Women (NOW) is the biggest
women's organisation, whose major campaign is for an amendment to the US Constitution that would ban discrimination on
grounds of sex. These are characteristic liberal feminist campaigns.

Socialist feminists often support such campaigns, but often
campaign in addition for working women's and black women's
causes. The vital difference, however, is that while liberal
feminists seek a change in women's situation within an accepted
liberal-capitalist framework, socialist feminists see women's
liberation as part of a more general liberation following the

abolition of capitalism. Theoretically, they have been principally concerned with integrating new developments in feminist thought into socialist theory. As a result, they put less emphasis on the traditional notion that female oppression is part of the mechanism by which the capitalist class keeps the working class divided and therefore less revolutionary, and more on developing the view that women suffer a double oppression, men and capitalism combined. It is a view that rejects the traditional Marxist-feminist belief that the overthrow of capitalism is itself sufficient for emancipation.

Socialist feminists are usually associated with groups and parties on the far left generally, whereas Radicals have gone in more for small group structures, 'consciousness raising' and shared experiences, and are more anarchist in the sense of preferring leaderless, grass-roots, federal organisations, without formal national structures. Some, especially the anarcha-feminists, insist that conventional state and party power structures are essentially masculine. But as well as organizationally, it is the radicals who have been the most innovative and interesting theoretically.

Shulamith Firestone and the primacy of sexual oppression

Although often sympathetic and theoretically close to the socialists, radicals are uncompromising in their insistence that the cause of women's oppression is not class or socialisation or any other social structure or process, but simply and emphatically *men*. Men are the enemy. It is, therefore, just not enough to give women more of the important jobs or facilities for easing the burdens of childcare, or to change the social structure. Women's oppression goes much deeper and its ending requires more drastic change. This argument is an important aspect of feminism's emancipation from other doctrines.

For socialists who follow Engels, women's oppression, like racial oppression, is a special case of class oppression. But radicals argue that, on the contrary, it is the oppression of women by men that is most fundamental, and that other oppressions, of class or race or whatever, are special cases or extensions of the basic sexual oppression. The most sophisticated expression of this view is that of Shulamith Firestone in her book *The Dialectics of Sex* (1970).

Firestone argues that Marxism's historical materialism is correct in form but incorrect in substance, in that it does not recognise that the root inequality and therefore the root oppression is that of women by men. Class domination and exploitation begins with 'sex class', economic class comes later. The origin is biological. Because of women's role in reproduction, and their consequent dependence on men, they are vulnerable and exploited. Women's oppression is, therefore, built into the biological family.

Consequently, the key to revolution is sexual revolution. It is not the overthrow of bourgeois capitalism that is the key to human emancipation:

... unless revolution uproots the basic, social organisation, the biological family ... the tapeworm of exploitation can never be annihilated. We shall need a sexual revolution much larger than – inclusive of – a socialist one to truly eradicate all class systems.

(The Dialectics of Sex)

The obvious question arises as to how this is possible. Firestone puts her faith in science. By means of 'artificial reproduction', and by socialising childcare (that is, sharing the work among all members of society), women's physical and psychological responsibility for reproduction would be eliminated, and their liberation possible.

Although not all radicals accept Firestone's analysis in full (and still less her prescriptions), they do share the belief that the basic problem is men and not society, that sexual oppression is the most basic oppression and that the emancipation of women is the necessary precondition for the emancipation of humanity from other forms of oppression. However, beyond this common outlook there is much controversy over a wide range of issues.

Controversies within radical feminism

Some radicals still hold to Engels' view of a matriarchal golden

age, and it is a convenient morale-raising myth, but few sophisticated feminists now take it seriously. The more common view is
that, whatever the historical origins, what is important is that
women's oppression is now being reaffirmed and reproduced day
after day and generation after generation. This oppression
operates on various levels: economic, legal, psychological and so
on, but there is some controversy over what the root cause is. For
some it is physical violence. For example, Susan Brownmiller, in
her book *Against Our Will* (1976), insists that it is the ultimate
threat of rape that keeps women in subjection, and that every time
a man rapes a women he is doing so on behalf of his whole sex,
reinforcing the fear of violence and violation that keeps them
submissive.

Another source of difference and controversy within the
feminist movement is the question of the nature and importance
of 'feminine characteristics'. In the first flush of 1960s feminism
there was a tendency to regard the 'so-called' feminine characteristics as a myth, or as a set of idealized characteristics, such as
submissiveness or domesticity, imposed upon women as a means
of oppressing them, like the family, and therefore part of the
stereotyping process. Consequently, women who had opted for
domesticity were seen as somehow betraying their 'sisters'. But
since then there has been something of a change of heart among
feminists of all varieties. Many women felt that the early
denigration of the family, the insistence on competing with men
on equal terms and the ideal of the androgynous society, in fact
denigrated and denied the value of most women's experience,
while the career and public role option smacked too much of
having to 'be like men'.

It was argued that while 'women's characteristics' may have
been the result of stereotyping and an immensely long period of
subordination, they are nevertheless the stuff of women's
experience and are the source of values and of a moral vision that
could be the foundation of a better world. In response to such
arguments there has been much more willingness to celebrate
women's experiences and 'feminine qualities' like caring and
co-operation, whatever their origins. This in turn has served as an

impetus to recover women's history and achievements, which have tended to be ignored. The prevailing view on 'women's qualities' is that, while they may have been emphasised in women through socialisation and their socio-economic situation, they nevertheless provide an alternative approach to the world which is at least as valid and arguably superior to that which stems from 'masculine characteristics'.

An important minority of feminists have, however, taken this view much further. They have revived the old view that masculine and feminine characteristics are not the result of socialisation, but are natural and inherent and have some kind of biological origin; in so doing they have rejected one of the central tenets of the modern feminist movement. However, in contrast to the older advocates of this belief, they insist upon the superiority of feminine characteristics, women's values and the female sex in general. Women are morally superior to men and the world will only be safe and civilized when women rule it. Feminist theorists of this kind may be called 'supremacists' and include writers such as Mary Daly, Andrea Dworkin and Dale Spender (see, for example, Daly's *Gyn/Ecology*, 1979, or Spender's *Women of Ideas (and What Men Have Done to Them)*, 1982) . Although a minority position, their ideas, because extreme, do attract much attention and controversy.

The supremacist issue has some connection with the more practical issue of the nature of the feminist movement. Supremacists, as might be expected, abjure dealings with men. Some are lesbians, or 'political lesbians'. Political lesbianism is the view that women should strive to fulfil all their needs, including emotional and sexual, from among themselves. It has been argued that whatever a woman's personal preference may be, a man is not essential for sexual or emotional fulfilment. Any woman may therefore choose to be a lesbian as a political act. Radicals who argue in this way are inclined to see women who choose to have male partners as necessarily incomplete women. They are 'man-identified', in the sense of allowing themselves to be defined in terms of a man, instead of being 'woman-identified' and therefore autonomous and complete.

But lesbianism, of whatever kind, is not a necessary condition of such a supremacist or a isolationist approach. Some argue that women's psyche is so damaged by millennia of male domination that women have to live apart for some time until recovered, before again having dealings with men. This has given rise, at the extreme, to all-women communes (especially in the USA), which try to live with as little contact with men and male-dominated society as possible.

Less extreme and much more common is the building of women's organisations from which various people are excluded. Some exclude women in permanent relationships with men, others just exclude men, however sympathetic to the cause. In fact, small groups of women sharing experiences and giving each other support are a notable feature of the women's movement in general. Liberal feminists tend to be the least impressed by these arguments and are least likely to exclude men from their political campaigns.

Feminism today

Although in total feminism constitutes a considerable movement around the world, national or international organisation is limited. Women's political parties, for example, are almost unknown (in marked contrast to such as the Greens). This would seem to be because compared to the Greens, feminism is much more diffuse and intangible in its goals and priorities, and some feminists are firmly locked into pre-existing ideological outlooks with their accompanying antipathies. Different trends within feminism have developed their own networks of groups, often at odds with each other.

Liberal feminists want women to have their proper share within existing society, while socialist feminists want to overthrow existing society, and see the achievement of liberal goals as merely benefitting middle-class women. Many radical feminists reject traditional formal politics altogether, seeing it as a male-centred political game. Various 'separatists' and 'supremacists' see male power politics as just what is wrong with the world and will not work with any organisation with men in it. These differing strands have tended to grow apart from each other over time.

Time has also thrown up political conflicts. It is the liberal feminists who tend to be best organised and most political (in terms of conventional politics), with campaigns for more representation, child-care support and other issues. But this higher political profile has led to difficulties, the activities of lesbians and other radicals can be an embarrassment when seeking the support of establishment groups. In America, for example, the National Organisation for Women (NOW), fell foul of fellow feminists during their campaign to have women's equality written into the US Constitution (the ERA or Equal Rights Amendment) when they refused to back the abortion campaigns of other feminists for fear of losing support for ERA from the Catholic Church and other organisations.

Partly as a result of these differences, the 1980s saw something of a loss of impetus in the women's liberation movement. Some of the earlier leaders had second thoughts. Thus both Betty Friedan, in her book *The Second Stage* (1982), and Germaine Greer, in her *Sex and Destiny* (1985), reflected in mellower fashion on the virtues of domesticity and motherhood (and have been much criticised by radicals for doing so). There was also in the 1980s something of a reaction, a backlash, against the general radicalism of the 1960s and 1970s. The most obvious manifestation of this was the political and intellectual success of the New Right in Britain and the USA and elsewhere, which insisted on 'traditional values', the virtues of family life, opposed abortion, blamed working mothers for adolescent crime, and so on (a political viewpoint strongly asserted in the 1992 US Presidential campaign, when 'family values' was a major issue).

Nevertheless, the loss of steam in the women's movement in the 1980s was perhaps also partly a result of success. Attitudes had changed a great deal over the previous decade; anti-discrimination legislation had been passed; most people were far more aware of the problem and far more sensitive to sexist assumptions and language; the field of women's studies had grown, and women were generally more confident of challenging male dominance in many areas, such as politics and the professions. There has even been the emergence of the 'New Man', who has shed the automatic assumptions of male superiority, is sensitive to women's needs, recognises the 'feminine' element in his own nature, and accepts domestic responsibilities on the same basis as his partner. The sense of injustice felt in the early 1970s touched all women, but as things were perceptibly improving, crusading zeal and sisterly solidarity were less appropriate. Besides, the great majority of women do not want to overthrow existing society, still less live in lesbian communes.

However, none of this is to say that women's struggle for equality is over, or that feminism's 'moment' is passed. There is, from a feminist point of view, a great deal of injustice and discrimination to overcome. It seems likely that the future will see more of the movement, and there is a permanent legacy of theory and organisation left behind that may form the basis of future movements.

The Green movement

It was the Industrial Revolution, and the huge growth in population and urbanisation that went with it, that provoked the first concerns about the destructive impact of human activity on the environment. Victorian social critics contrasted the healthy natural countryside with the ugliness and squalor of the new industrial towns. Pressure and action to protect the countryside began to develop. One example was the movement in America to create national parks, to prevent areas of unspoiled wilderness from being ravaged for commercial purposes, a concept that has gone around the world. (British national parks are based on the different principle of protecting a landscape created and sustained by human activity.) Eventually such concerns led to comprehensive planning systems in Britain and elsewhere, but it became increasingly clear that this was nothing like enough.

In the second half of the twentieth century, overpopulation, depletion of resources, destruction of the worlds forests, the extinction of species, the poisoning of the land and the sea and the air, acid rain, the thinning of the ozone layer and global warming, not to mention the threat of nuclear annihilation of the planet, all pointed to the likelihood of some global catastrophe engulfing mankind. Such fears prompted the development of an environmental movement right across the developed world, to press for preventative action to diminish the risks. However, for some people it is simply too late to deal with the problems individually, and they think that mankind can only be saved from catastrophe by a total transformation of human society and consciousness. Those who hold this view, and work to bring such changes about, belong to the 'ecology' or 'Green' movement.

Green politics

Ecology is one of the biological sciences that studies how living things interact and live together in a given environment. The ecology movement is not a movement of biologists, but of those who take the idea of ecology to have profound social and political implications for how people live and think about reality.

Many came into the Green movement from the New Left in the early 1970s, attracted by the radicalism of the cause. Indeed, many felt that Green ideas were a natural extension of New Left ideas (see Chapter Seven), which rejected both capitalism and communism; were suspicious of all bureaucracy and large-scale organisation; strove to transform modern consciousness, and experimented with alternative ways of living in communes and small anarchist groups, based on sharing and without domination or alienation. Not all of the early Greens came from the New Left, but some of the leading thinkers did, such as the German former Marxist radical, Rudolph Bahro, and the American anarchist, Murray Bookchin (see Chapter Six). There are also important connections with other post-New Left causes, such as feminism. Bookchin has argued that 'authentic' Green thinking is the culmination of all the radical movements of the 1960s and 70s, although this is a rather extreme claim.

The Green movement began with small groups and local

parties in several countries. The first national political party, significantly called the 'Values Party', was formed in New Zealand in 1972. Britain's first Green party was formed the following year. It was initially called 'PEOPLE', then changed to the 'Ecology Party' and finally, in 1985, the 'Green Party'.

It was the German ecologists who started to call themselves 'Greens' (*Die Grünen*) and the name has now been almost universally adopted. The Green movement is now worldwide, with parties in just about every country. The most politically successful (in the narrow sense of winning elections) have been the German Greens. Although only founded in 1981, the party astonished Europe in 1983 by winning 28 seats in the Bundestag, as well holding seats in many provincial and local assemblies. The party thus became a major force in Germany, Europe's most powerful economic nation, virtually overnight; it went on to win 8.3 per cent of the vote and 42 seats in the 1987 general election. This success has, however, created problems of how to relate to other parties, which led to internal conflict and electoral failure in 1991.

Many countries in Europe and elsewhere now have Green MPs. Britain does not have any, although there are some Green local councillors. In the 1989 British elections for the European Parliament the Greens gained a remarkable 15 per cent of the vote, but no seats. Support is nothing like this in general elections, but the result did show the potential support for Green policies, and there might be more support in general elections if Britain's electoral system did not penalise small parties. After electoral failure in 1992 the party began to break up in some bitterness. It would be wrong to say that the Greens are now a major factor in world politics, but it is true that the environmental movement as a whole, of which they are part, has put the environment firmly on the agenda of world politics.

Traditional attitudes to nature

Although the newest of ideologies, Green thinking claims to be discovering an ancient wisdom concerning the human being's place in nature. Philosophies of ancient India, China and elsewhere have emphasised the need to live in harmony with all natural things. It is implicit in a famous passage (much quoted by Green writers) in the reply of the Red Indian, Chief Seattle, to the request of the US government to be allowed to purchase some of his tribe's traditional lands:

How can you buy or sell the sky? We do not own the freshness of the air or the sparkle of the water. How then can you buy them from us? Every part of the earth is sacred to my people, holy in their memory and experience. We know that the white man does not understand our ways. He is a stranger who comes in the night, and takes from the land whatever he needs. The Earth is not his friend, but his enemy, and when he's conquered it, he moves on. He kidnaps the earth from his children. His appetite will devour the Earth and leave behind a desert. If all the beasts were gone we would die from a great loneliness of the spirit, for whatever happens to the beasts happens also to us. All things are connected. Whatever befalls the Earth, befalls the children of the Earth.

(1855)

What is important here is the sense of humanity as not separate from nature but merely one part among others, as contrasted with the characteristic western attitudes which it rejects. Greens insist that an understanding of this contrast is the beginning of genuine wisdom.

In contrast to the words of Chief Seattle are those of the Bible on the question of how human being relate to nature 'And God said, Let us make man in our image, after our likeness: and let them have dominion over the fish of the sea, and over the fowl of the air, and over the cattle, and over all the earth . . .' (Genesis I.26).

This sets humanity apart and above nature, giving it dominion over nature and conceiving of the natural world as existing solely for human benefit. It was a view reinforced by Aristotle, whose account of the natural world largely dominated Western thinking until the nineteenth century. However, no very evil consequences for the environment could flow from this attitude until humanity had vastly increased its power over nature. In all parts of the world and in all kinds of habitats, people adapted to their physical environment and of necessity lived in some kind of balance. It was when Western civilization acquired unprecedented powers over nature that balance was lost.

The impact of modernity

The process began with the development of physical science and an accompanying materialistic outlook, the eventual outcome of which was the Industrial Revolution. This gave human beings the potential to destroy nature as never before, and there were, in the West at least, no religious or ideological restraints on the process. Greater production, greater exploitation of resources and greater profits all became gods of the new age, and have continued to be so since.

The outcome is today's consumer society with its conspicuous consumption, massive waste and appalling consequences for the environment. Capitalism bears much of the blame, with its ethos of profits at any cost. But the communist world has been no better in its attitude to production. The Third World has been bullied or persuaded to participate, industrialise and compete in world markets. And despite the fact that the world is beset by social ills such as poverty, starvation, unemployment and urban decay, even to the extent that some think that modern industrial society is breaking down, the panacea of all contemporary ideologies, proposed by those in power, is economic growth, which is, Greens insist, the root cause of all the problems anyway. Humanity is rushing towards an abyss and all that the world's politicians can suggest is that we rush ever faster.

The super-ideology of industrialism

Although Greens are perfectly aware of the differences between the main ideologies, they are more concerned with what they have in common. Conservatives, liberals, social democrats, democratic socialists and communists, are all and everywhere preoccupied with economic growth and technology and what they like to term 'progress'. For this reason Greens are inclined to see them as differing manifestations of the same 'super-ideology' which they call 'industrialism'. The main features of this industrialism are:

- a devotion to economic growth and industrial expansion and continuous technical innovation
- a belief in the overriding importance of satisfying people's material needs
- large-scale centralised bureaucratic control
- scientific rationality is the only kind of reasoning that matters
- large-scale units – in industry, administration, etc. – are most efficient ('big is beautiful')
- patriarchal and an emphasis on 'masculine' values of competition, aggression and assertiveness predominates
- an anthropocentric view that sees the earth and all that live on it as simply there to be exploited for any human purpose
- a hierarchical social structure where power and wealth is concentrated at the top
- economic considerations predominate in society and moral, social and artistic values are of lesser importance.

Within this common framework, the predominant systems of East and West have their own horrors. Communism suppresses human freedom in the name of an inhuman system. And although communism appears to be a dying system, rivalry between them has produced a stock of nuclear weapons that could destroy the planet many times over.

Western capitalist democracy has become triumphant within this 'super-ideology'. But while compared to communism it has much to commend it in terms of liberty, it is even more ruthless in its destruction of the environment. On top of the industrialist feature it shares with communism it adds its own destructive characteristics. It is an outlook that favours aggressive individualism, competition and selfishness, that finds expression in a free-market economy given free rein to make profit irrespective of the damage it causes. Profit is given priority over all things. The modern consumerism that the free market has created positively encourages people to buy what they do not need and throw things away as soon as possible. Continuous consumption is deemed desirable, as good for the economy, no matter what resources it wastes. Free market capitalism has also created a world market which has encouraged the Third World to industrialize and compete in world markets, despite their severe disadvantages and the destruction of their traditional ways of life.

The most basic assumption – that economic growth, with ever greater production and consumption, is the solution to all ills – is the most destructive. We are so imbued with these assumptions, Greens claim, that it requires a considerable feat of imagination to break free of them. But break free we must if disaster is to be avoided.

The Green alternative

The first step is to realise that there is an alternative. The Green perspective is not just a set of solutions to environmental problems but a complete theory of the human and the social. There are variations, but all Greens would subscribe to the following analysis.

First of all, human beings are part of nature and must live in harmony with nature or risk destruction. Green thinking is not anthropocentric but biocentric. What is good is not what is good for humankind in isolation, but good for the earth and all that live on it. Consequently, protection of the biosphere and the conservation of finite resources is a first priority; to achieve this, international co-operation must replace competition and aggression between nation-states. There must be an end to both economic growth and population growth. Economic systems that recklessly exploit the earth's resources as though they were infinite are inherently wrong.

The giving up of such wasteful systems will necessitate a lower standard of living, with less growth and, for example, fewer cars and other consumer goods. Industrial society is breaking down, as evidenced by such symptoms as chronic unemployment, inner city decay and general alienation. It needs to be replaced by a simpler and more satisfying way of life, one based upon more spiritual values than the material ones that dominate our world at present.

Most Greens would add the following principles. Patriarchal

characteristics and aggressive and competitive values must become much less important beside 'feminine' values such as co-operation and caring. There must be a massive redistribution of wealth, and not just between rich and poor within a society, but between continents and between generations (that is, we must not use up the earth's resources that future generations could benefit from). The Greens are not against private property as such, but against excessive wealth and power. Greens insist that any kind of decent society must be characterised by 'social justice', and be without discrimination or inequality. A world built upon such principles, it is argued, would be free, safe, humane and just.

Upon these broad principles Green base their ideas as to what would be an ideal society, an 'ecotopia'. These vary, but generally they include a basis of small communities, where people know each other, where direct democracy can operate, and where everything is on a human scale. It would involve an economy based on small-scale organic farming, small-scale industry and crafts, and based on co-operation rather than competition. All such industry would be labour-intensive and use the minimum of non-renewable resources. Great emphasis is laid on self-sufficiency for community and region, as far as possible. No one would be poor or disadvantaged.

Shades of Green

However, it must be said that while there is a good deal of consensus about what Greens are against, there is much less agreement about what Greens are for. There are considerable differences over detailed policies, strategy and tactics, and also over the kind of world that would be possible or desirable.

Greens differ a good deal among themselves as to the exact place that humanity has in nature and its ideal relationship with the natural world. For most, Green thinking must involve a spiritual element, and the salvation of mankind must involve some kind of spiritual renewal (see, for example, Jonathon Porritt's or Sara Parkin's writings). For some, indeed, Greenism is a new religion. The earth is a goddess, Gaia, with whom we must be in tune, and so on. The most famous exponent of this view in Britain is David Icke, a former television presenter and leading spokesman for the Green Party. He astonished everybody in 1990 by announcing his religious beliefs (that he was the son of God and had a mission to save the world and so forth), which most people found eccentric to put it mildly. However strange Icke's beliefs may be, there is a background to this kind of thinking, especially in America.

Other Greens see the need only for a greater reverence for nature, and greater humility in its presence, without any need for spirituality. Others still dismiss all this as dubious metaphysics and emotionalism, and see nothing beyond the science of ecology as necessary for a Green vision of the world.

There are other disagreements about what kind of world might be possible if and when humanity comes to its senses. What, for example, should be the role of technology? Some see our modern faith in science and technology as the root of our present crisis. Salvation lies, it is argued, in rejecting high technology and developing 'low-tech' solutions to practical problems that everyone can understand and operate. Yet others see modern information technology as the key to a decentralised social life where people can work at home and live in small communities.

A major source of division in the Green movement is the development of various hybrids that synthesise Green ideas with older ideologies. Some have reworked traditional Marxist ideas to argue that capitalism is inherently the enemy of the environment, and that some form of communism is the only solution. Others have argued the feminist categories are the key to understanding the situation. Thus male competitiveness and aggression, essentially side-effects of patriarchy, are the source of the problem, and is female qualities such as caring and co-operativeness must be the basis of a solution.

In many ways anarchism seems to have most affinity with Green ideas. The trend of Green thinking is towards smaller, self-sufficient communities as against large-scale modern industry organisation and urban life, yet it is strongly reminiscent of older anarchist ideas of federations of small communities, which occur in the writings of Proudhon, Kropotkin and William Morris, as well in the more recent anarchism of the New Left (see Chapter Six).

On the other hand, Green ideas do not necessarily preclude quite different ideas that involve hierarchy and authority. What for some may be a desire to create a viable post-industrial society, may for another be a desire to recreate a pre-industrial society based on social hierarchy and discipline. Writers like Edward Goldsmith, in *Blueprint for Survival* (1972), see a Green programme in terms of preserving an essence of traditional Englishness in its rural purity. Then again, Green ideas can be consistent with fascism. One dimension of Nazi ideology was its notion of 'Blood and Soil', imbued with nostalgia for a rural past of sturdy peasant life.

Support for Green ideas may thus come from very different and incompatible directions, but such differences usually matter little so long as the Greens do not hold political power. Once they do, differences tend to come to the fore. This has happened in Germany, where their electoral success has put them in a position of influence, and has forced them to make hard political choices about who they can support. This had led to rows and splits within *Die Grünen*, and the British Greens have recently followed suit. Nevertheless, there are differences over strategy. The Green Party, for example has deliberately pursued a policy of trying not to behave like other parties. They do not have a single leader, party conferences consist of a series of seminars, and so on. The point is to show that the Greens are not a party like other parties – that they are 'an anti-party party'. But some Greens feel such tactics are counter-productive, and considerable recrimination and acrimony followed the party's poor showing in the 1992 general election.

The variations and differences within the Green movement may be exacerbated by the tendency to take on board radical causes which may not always fit with Green thinking. Unilateral nuclear disarmament and animal rights are causes that fit well. But Greens also tend to support feminism, gay rights, holistic medicine, the legalization of cannabis and a good many other causes which may not fit quite so well and can result in dissension.

Criticisms of Green ideas

However, the main criticism levelled against the Greens is not so much their variety and eclecticism, as their other-worldliness. The idea that we can simply de-industrialise the world and create some rural idyll, borne of nostalgia and a romantic imagination is, so it is claimed, a fantasy. We cannot forget science and disinvent industry. Greens counter this by insisting that we either do something drastic along these lines or we destroy ourselves. Besides, Greens insist, there is no desire on their part to recreate some mythical bucolic past. New technology is fine in its place, although not all Greens agree with this view.

Perhaps a more telling criticism of Green ideas concerns the difficulty of reconciling the freedom and equality that Greens insist upon, with the drastic transformation of society that they insist upon even more strongly. What if people do not want to live in small communities or change their lifestyle or co-operate with their neighbour? Will they have to conform? Will they be forced to be free?

Will there not need to be severe restrictions on people's economic activity? And who will enforce them? Many Greens reject the modern state. Yet possibly it is only the strong state that could enforce Green policies, and it would certainly have a better chance of doing so than a network of self-governing communes. Greens often talk as though it is only necessary for people to understand the environmental dangers to stop them wanting to make money by polluting rivers or destroying forests, or to stop them wanting cars or other goods. But the idea that all will be well once everyone sees things the right way, is one of the oldest of political illusions. How to stop people behaving in ways deemed to be undesirable is a particular problem for Greens, who reject authoritarianism.

Whatever answers to these problems Greens come up with, it seems likely that Green ideas will become more important in the future, although it is difficult to predict whether the future of

Green parties will be one of greater strength and political success. It may turn on whether the Greens can agree sufficiently on their ideas and learn to play the political game successfully, or whether their ideas and energies will be dispersed among other parties and beliefs: Green socialists, Green liberals, Green conservatives, Green Marxists, Green Christians, and the rest. Either way, Green ideas seem set to make a major impact across the ideological spectrum.

11

Religious fundamentalism

It is broadly true that since the French Revolution religion has been in retreat. This has certainly been the case in Europe, but also in the rest of the world as European influence has spread. Modern ideas of freedom, equality, democracy and nationalism are not necessarily inimical to religion, but they have generated enthusiasms that in many cases have replaced or diminished religious commitment. Where religion remained politically important, as in Austria and Spain, it was often as a bulwark supporting a traditional authoritarianism. Instances of religion in partnership with modernising influences are relatively rare.

However, the seemingly relentless trend towards secularism has suffered something of a reverse in the late twentieth century. In recent decades there have been a series of revivalist movements among the world's great religions that have had important political implications. Islam, which has become a major force in world politics since the Iranian revolution of 1979, is the most striking case, and the one to which most of this chapter is devoted. But Jewish, Hindu and Christian fundamentalists have also had a significant political impact in particular countries.

'Religious fundamentalism' is something of an umbrella term. The growth of religious fundamentalism around the world has occurred under so many different circumstances and taken so many different forms, from the affluent suburbs of America to the desperate slums of Beirut, that it may not be appropriate to look for common features or common causes. However, there is one connecting theme which these disparate phenomenan would seem to share, which is some kind of rejection of modernity and a harking back to past certainties, past values and past authority. This is certainly true of Islamic fundamentalism, which has made by far the greatest impact on world events.

Islamic fundamentalism

Islamic fundamentalism as a modern political movement dates back to the 1920s. On the other hand, Islam has always been the most political of the world religions from its very beginning.

The origins of Islam

The Prophet Muhammad (670–732 AD) founded the first Islamic state and led its early expansion. He was, therefore, a political and military, as well as a religious, leader. This is in striking contrast to the founder of Christianity, who was not a political leader, and still less a military one. Christ left no guidance on political matters beyond the injunction to 'render unto Caesar the things that are Caesar's and unto God the things that are God's', which implies a clear separation between church and state. The Islamic ideal has always been the unity of political and religious authority. It has always been a conquering, proselytising faith, and within a couple of centuries of its foundation possessed an empire stretching from Spain to India. Towards the end of the Middle Ages the leadership of Islam passed from the Arabs to the Turks, who for a time threatened the conquest of much of Europe.

Islamic thought on politics did not centre around the state but around the idea of the community of all Muslims led by the *Caliph*, or successor of the Prophet, who was a political and religious ruler to whom the entire Islamic community owed allegiance. The caliph would rule with the advice of the *ulama*, the body of religious scholars who were experts on the *sharia*, or divine law found in the Koran (conceived, like the Bible, as the direct word of God) and in the sayings and deeds of the Prophet.

When the Ottoman Turks came to dominate the Islamic world, the Turkish ruler, the Sultan, also became Caliph and claimed the loyalty of all Muslims in the world (from Morocco to southern China). Arab Muslims did not have much choice since the Turks had conquered their lands, but Muslims of India and beyond also came to look to the Turkish Sultan for leadership as they became increasingly subject to European control. After the heyday of Turkish power in the sixteenth and seventeenth centuries Europe came to dominate the world economically and militarily. This was resented by many Muslims who regarded their civilization as greatly superior to that of the European.

On the whole, Islamic political thinking under Turkish leadership was extremely conservative, traditionalist and quietistic. While Europe had been swept by major intellectual movements such as the Renaissance, the Enlightenment and the democratic and nationalist ideas of the French Revolution, these had all passed the Islamic world by and its thinking had changed little for a thousand years. But the European conquest of large parts of Islamic Asia, and then North Africa, with Turkey itself becoming weak and vulnerable as the 'sick man of Europe', provoked fresh thought, which began to appear in the late nineteenth century.

Broadly, there were two main responses to the success of the Europeans. One was to say that the Islamic world had fallen behind, and that it needed to learn from Europe and modernize its thinking and its way of life. The other response was to say that the Europeans had only succeeded because the Islamic world had become lazy and slack and neglectful of religion. Only by restoring the true faith to the centre of life would the Islamic world restore its former eminence.

Fundamentalism and the state

The second of these responses belongs to the Islamic fundamentalists. However, there was one aspect of the modern world that fundamentalists accepted as much as the modernists, and this is the nation state. The fundamentalists have not sought to recreate the worldwide Islamic community as a single political entity led by a caliph (although for some this may be an ultimate ideal). Their energies have been directed at turning existing national states into Islamic states, that is, to restore the unity of religion and politics, but within a modern political framework.

The question of whether to Islamicise or westernise is a dilemma facing all Islamic societies in the modern world. Yet in some ways it is a modern form of a long-standing tension within Islamic thought and practice as to the proper relationship between religious and political authority. The Prophet and his immediate successors are deemed to have held them in perfect balance, but historically the political has usually predominated and the religious authorities have been subservient to it. Modernising nationalism would keep it that way and learn from the non-Islamic world. Fundamentalism is about 'restoring the balance', although in practice it means subordinating the political to the religious. (Islamic fundamentalism is not about asserting the literal truth of the Holy Book, as it is for Christian and Jewish fundamentalists, for all Muslims believe this as a matter of course.) However, the choice between these two alternatives, to westernise or Islamicise, remained largely academic until the fall of the Ottoman empire.

The collapse of the Turkish empire in World War I marks the beginning of modern Islamic politics to a considerable degree. Under Kemal Atatürk (1881–1938), the Turks themselves moved decisively towards the creation of a modern Western nation-state. This involved the overthrow and abolition of the sultanate and caliphate (ending the traditional fusion of political and religious authority), along with the introduction of Western law, the emancipation of women, and the suppression of traditionalist Islamic opposition.

Among the Arab peoples newly independent of Turkish control, the Turkish model of modernisation was favoured by nationalists. For the more traditionalist, the end of the nominal religious leadership of the caliph left the way open to develop the idea of the Islamic state, that is, a modern territorial, centralised nation-state, but one inspired by Islamic ideals and based upon the divine law. It is this latter view that has been the particular province of Islamic fundamentalism, which first appeared as a modern political movement, in the sense of a political party seeking power, in the late 1920s in Egypt. Oddly enough, the first Islamic fundamentalist state was being founded around the same time, not through modern political methods, but more in a manner characteristic of the Middle Ages and the methods of the Prophet himself.

The creation of Saudi Arabia

Abdul Ibn Saud was the hereditary leader of one of the tribes of the Arabian peninsular, which since the eighteenth century had also been the home of a particularly puritanical version of (Sunni) Islam. The Turkish withdrawal left a vacuum in the area which needed to be filled. Like the Prophet, Ibn Saud was a charismatic leader who united some of the tribes around him, and, by a mixture of political manoeuvering and force of arms, conquered the Arabian peninsula and made himself king. His new kingdom included the two most holy sites of Islam, Mecca and Medina, which enabled Ibn Saud to claim a religious significance for the whole of the Islamic world as the guardian of the Holy Places. They also brought great wealth because of the religious duty of all Muslims to go on a pilgrimage (the *haj*) to the holy places at least once during their lifetime. However, the 1930s, being a period of world depression, was also low on pilgrimages and Ibn Saud signed an agreement with Standard Oil of California for the exploration and exploitation of oil reserves. The combination of oil and pilgrimages has made the Saudis immensely rich ever since.

Nevertheless, Saudi Arabia is a deeply religious country where Islamic practices are strictly observed. The *ulama* (the body of religious and legal scholars) control a religious police who enforce the prohibition on alcohol, the wearing of traditional female dress and much else. Saudi society is extremely conservative. When the introduction of television was proposed in the 1960s, the *ulama* were opposed on the grounds that it clearly involved magic and was therefore the work of the devil. Only when the king arranged for an experiment in which passages from the Koran were transmitted did religious objections cease, on the grounds that the Devil would not allow the transmission of the Koran. Saudi Arabia is still an absolute monarchy (although the *ulama* are consulted on legislation) with no political parties. One might say that the extremely large royal family amounts to a party on its own; Ibn Saud, the founder of the dynasty, had nearly 300 children of his own.

However, despite its adherence to Islamic codes, its religious standing and its generous patronage of Islamic causes, the Saudi royal family has been subject to criticism by fundamentalists. The major objects of criticism have been the close alliance with the USA and the lifestyle of the royal family, especially since the 1970s oil crisis, as a result of which the Saudis became even richer. The idea of royal princes living a high life in the fleshpots of the West, while avoiding their religious duties at home (such as fasting for the month of Ramadan) has been very damaging.

Saudi royalty has been vilified as currupt and un-Islamic by the Iranians since their 1979 revolution and this has led to conflict with Iranian pilgrims to Mecca. But much the most serious trouble has been home grown. In 1979 a group of fundamentalists captured the Great Mosque at Mecca and were only removed with considerable difficulty. They had believed (mistakenly) that the king would be there, but in any case they hoped that their action would inspire a general uprising against the ruling family. This did not happen, but their removal took several days and a great deal of bloodshed. Those captured alive were subsequently beheaded in various public squares around Saudi Arabia, as a lesson to all. Yet the incident was a serious blow to the prestige of the royal family. It was not enhanced by its need to rely on the Americans and their Western allies to protect Saudi Arabia against the threat of invasion by Iraq in 1990–91.

The Islamic Brotherhood

The entry of Islamic fundamentalism into conventional political activity followed from the formation of the Islamic Brotherhood in Egypt in 1928. Egypt at the time was firmly under British control, with a subservient king and establishment. It was the most westernized of Arab countries and Western dominance was much resented. This expressed itself in two forms. There were the modernizing nationalists and there were traditionalists. It was one of the latter who founded the youth movement, the Islamic Brotherhood, which in the 1930s became the first fully-fledged fundamentalist political party.

The founder of the Brotherhood, Hassan al Banna, believed that the Islamic world had become corrupted by Western ideas and needed to be purified. A restored faith must then be placed at the centre of the nation's life. The *sharia* (divine law) must resume its central authority, and Islamic principles be applied to all aspects of social and economic life. The result would be an Islamic society that was neither socialist nor capitalist. This would come about as the result of a *jihad* or holy war, which would destroy the colonial power and liberate Egypt and then the rest of the Islamic world.

The post-war years were characterised by increasing political instability and violence in which the Brotherhood had a leading part. It culminated in the overthrow of the monarchy by a group of colonels, one of whom, Nasser, eventually took control. Initially the Brotherhood co-operated with Nasser's modernising nationalist government, but eventually they went into opposition. Nasser cracked down severely and many went into exile, spreading Islamic fundamentalist ideas throughout the Arab world. However, the catastrophic defeat of Egypt by the Israelis in the Six Day War of 1967 forced Nasser to compromise, attempt to appear as a good Muslim and allow the Brotherhood more scope, and many returned from exile.

There seemed more likelihood of closer ties with the fundamentalist with Nasser's successor, Anwar Sadat, who appeared to be a more genuinely religious man than Nasser, and who was initially hailed as the 'believer president'. However, his decision to ally himself with the Americans and allow the considerable commercialisation of Cairo in an attempt to attract American investment outraged the fundamentalists. They took to rioting and an orgy of destruction in Cairo's night-club district in January 1977.

But they where further incensed by Sadat's peace with Israel, signed in 1979. Islamic fundamentalism grew and many more extreme groups than the Brotherhood emerged, one of which assassinated President Sadat in 1981. His successor Hosnay Mubarak has had to tread a difficult course to prevent the flare up of fundamentalism, which has included making a number of concessions to religious sentiment.

The Brotherhood and its offshoots are to be found in many countries. In Syria, for example, fundamentalists have formed the only significant opposition to the otherwise absolute rule of President Assad. On several occasions during his rule, fundamentalist uprisings have been put down with considerable bloodshed. He too, despite leading a secular Ba'ath Party, has had to make concessions to religious sentiment and be wary of provoking fundamentalist action. Meanwhile many other states have become 'Islamic' in the sense of adopting the Koran as the standard for laws including mutilation of thieves, rules on women's dress and occupation, the prohibition of alcohol, and so on. States that have adopted the fundamentalist course include Sudan and Pakistan.

The most recent case is Algeria, and this illustrates much about how the West influences the growth of fundamentalism. Algeria became free of French rule in 1962 under the leadership of the National Liberation Front (FLN), who went on to rule the country as a one-party state. This was a nationalist party devoted to modernization, westernisation, industrialisation and socialism. Like similar regimes, it became part of the Western economic system and suffered badly in the recessions of the 1970s and 1980s. Furthermore, nationalisation and other modern ideas simply did not work, while attempts at creating a modern industrial economy produced a new urban working class who suffered particularly from economic failure. Bad times produced much poverty and disillusionment and an excellent recruiting ground for the fundamentalists. Western pressure to democratise then gave the fundamentalists the opportunity for power. Failed attempts at the creation of a modern industrial economy produced a massive pool of urban poor, amongst whom the fundamentalists have recruited large numbers.

At the end of 1991, the first democratic election since independence produced a huge vote for the fundamentalists, leading to
the cancellation of the second round of elections and an army
take-over. This was something of a relief to surrounding regimes,
including Morocco and Tunisia, all of whom fear their own
Islamic fundamentalists. In Libya Colonel Quadafi has suppressed the fundamentalists with great ferocity, although claims,
rather doubtfully, to be one himself.

Shia fundamentalism

All the versions of fundamentalism touched upon so far have
belonged to one of the two main branches of Islam, the Sunni
branch. Sunnis do in fact constitute about 85 per cent of the
world's one billion Muslims. The other 15 per cent are Shias. Yet
it is Shia fundamentalism that has produced the most spectacular
and aggressive version of fundamentalism, that of Iran and its
admirers. To understand the particular nature of this fundamentalism we need to see something of the difference between the
Sunni and the Shia versions of Islam.

Sunni and Shia Islam

Muslims are divided among a number of different sects, but the
two most important are the Sunnis and the Shias. These two
branches of Islam parted company at an early stage over the
succession to the Prophet. Shias were the followers ('shia' means
'follower') of Ali, the son-in-law of the Prophet, who was pious
and idealistic and who refused to become Caliph on the terms
offered him, although he did eventually become Caliph on his own
terms. One of Ali's sons, also revered by the Shias, chose to suffer
martyrdom rather than renounce his claim to the caliphate. This
self-sacrifice and standing on principle is characteristic of
Shiaism. Shi'ites tend to be more puritanical, more fundamentalist and more devoted to martyrdom, to holy war and to the
fusion of religion and state than the Sunnis. Although by no

means without their fundamentalists and puritans, the Sunnis on the whole tend to be more pragmatic, more ready to adapt to the modern world and more ready to accept the secular state.

Shiaism tends to be the more emotional and inspirational, and also the more anti-establishment form of Islam, putting greater emphasis on social justice. As such it is often found as a minority sect which appeals strongly to the poor and dispossessed. Sunnis are followers of the *Sunna*, the Beaten Path or Tradition, and Sunnism is usually the establishment religion. In most Sunni states, the religious leadership is part of the establishment, and the law, education and preaching are all practised under the aegis of the state and the *ulama* receive state salaries. The Sunni clergy have often acted as the mouthpiece of the state. The Shia clergy, even in Shia states, have a separate organisation from the state and have traditionally had a more critical role.

Furthermore, Shiaism has a messianic dimension that Sunnism lacks. Sunnism sees human history in terms of a perpetual tendency of the Islamic community towards corruption, and needing a periodic restoration of purity by a charismatic religious leader, but beyond this, history has no overall direction. For Shias history does have a final end. Sunnis believe a caliph to be merely a fallible interpreter of the Koran, whereas Shias believe a true caliph is an *Imam*, a divinely inspired and therefore infallible religious leader in true descent from the Prophet and Ali. The true descent of the Prophet has been lost, but, Shias believe, will eventually be found again. Ultimately, it is believed, there will be a restoration of the rule of the Prophet with the return of the 'hidden Imam' who will one day lead the Islamic community to a final paradise, when all injustice will be banished and the oppressed will inherit the earth.

In most Islamic states Shiaism is a minority sect. Iran is the most important of the few states where this is not so.

The Iranian revolution

Hostility between the state and the Islamic leadership has a long history in Iran. The recent history goes back to the period after World War I when the Shah, backed by Britain, proceeded to strip the religious leadership of much of its power, financial, legal and educational, and began a vigorous programme of westernisation. Everyone had to acquire a Western-style surname, and Western dress was required. The Shah forbade Shia religious rituals, such as self-flagellation, and even forbade the pilgrimage to Mecca.

His son pushed ahead with westernisation and developed close links with the USA. This alienated even the most moderate clerics. The Shah's actions were fiercely attacked in public by Ruhollah Khomeini, a junior cleric, who became the hero of the more religious part of the population, while the more affluent and westernised supported the increasingly autocratic Shah. When Khomeini was arrested in 1963 there were massive riots all over Iran, which were put down with great violence and up to 10,000 demonstrators were killed. But Khomeini continued to attack the Shah fearlessly, especially over Iran's increasing dependence on America, and was eventually sent into exile.

From his base in Iraq, Khomeini launched bitter and vituperative attacks on the Shah and the whole concept of monarchy. He argued that the *ulama* (the body of religious scholars and jurists) should not just give advice on laws and government actions, as is their traditional function, but should actively participate in the overthrow of repressive governments and lead the regimes that replace them. The ideal Islamic state was, therefore, a theocratic state, one with which hereditary monarchy was incompatible.

As economic difficulties added to the regime's problems in the 1970s, there was an increasing gulf between the Shah and the people, and an increasing reliance on the armed forces and on American support, which alienated the westernised middle class. All groups looked to Khomeini for support, and he was careful to play down aspects of his thought that offended educated groups (like the treatment of women; he stressed his fierce nationalism, and the need to abolish the monarchy (despite its boast of a continuous existence for over 2,000 years), which tended to bring all together. The regime became increasingly oppressive, so that 'Death to the Shah' was a popular cry and riots and bloodshed were common. Eventually the army became discontented and the situation could no longer be controlled. In January 1979, the Shah fled into exile and the Ayatollah Khomeini returned in triumph.

The Iranian revolutionary state

Immediately upon his return to Iran Ayatollah Khomeini established his legitimacy by holding a referendum on the creation of an Islamic republic. The new constitution put the ultimate leadership of the country in the hands of a leader who (pending the eventual return of the Messiah, Hidden Imann or Mahdi, who would lead the faithful to paradise) had to be a leading religious scholar or jurist, who would be head of state and officially appoint the elected President, as well as control the judiciary to ensure that divine law prevailed. Khomeini was give this position for life. The President (who must be a male Shia Muslim), aided by a Prime Minister, would be in charge of the day-to-day running of the country, implementing the constitution and executing the laws passed by parliament.

The system is democratic, although within limits. The parliament and the president are both elected, along with, when necessary, the council of 'experts' whose task is to choose a successor to the leader. However, there are also means of ensuring that whatever the Islamic republic does is 'in conformity with the will of God'. In the first place, the *sharia* or 'divine law' (as found in the Koran and the works of the Prophet) is incorporated into the constitution. Secondly, the leader appoints a Council of Guardians, composed of religious scholars, to make sure that no laws passed by parliament are in conflict with divine law. Thus the people are sovereign within the wider 'sovereignty of God' as interpreted by the religious leadership.

Initially, Khomeini's leadership and the aspiration towards an Islamic republic were acceptable to most parts of Iranian society that were not fundamentalist. Khomeini swept to power on a wave of enthusiasm that was at least as much anti-Shah, nationalistic and anti-imperialist as it was Islamic. Khomeini sought to bring along others, who were not his immediate supporters, who in turn thought that an accommodation was possible with the new order.

But as time went on, Khomeini's supporters became more and more dominant and others felt undermined. The regime became more clerical, more intolerant and totalitarian. Enforcement of Islamic law became more vigorous. Women were harassed for not wearing Islamic dress, and were forced out of occupations and education. Not only enemies of the regime were executed in large numbers, but also drug dealers, adulterers and homosexuals.

Iran became isolated, even within the Islamic world. Having created an Islamic republic, Khomeini assumed that Iran was now the leader of not only Shia Muslims, but the entire Islamic world. It condemned other regimes and encouraged Moslems to over-throw their leaders. In particular, Khomeini insisted that heredi-tary kingship was incompatible with Islam, and that the mon-archies such as those in Saudi Arabia and Kuwait were corrupt, tyrannical and in the pocket of the hated America, which he called 'the Great Satan', in other words, the source of corruption in the world.

Such sentiments did not endear the Iranians to their neigh-bours. Saudi Arabia was particularly resentful of the regime's pretensions to leadership, a position it had tended to assume by right. Relations reached rock bottom with the *haj* (pilgrimage to Mecca) of 1987, when a large number of Iranian pilgrims chanted political slogans and waved pictures of the Ayatollah. The con-frontation with Saudi police provoked a riot and stampede in which over 400 people were killed, mostly Iranians. Khomeini insisted that it was a deliberate Saudi massacre inspired by the Americans. Khomeini also offended many in the West with his *fatwa* ('judgement') in 1989 condemning the British writer Salman Rushdie to death for allegedly making offensive references to the Prophet in his novel *The Satanic Verses*. The Ayatollah died the same year, but such was his stature that nobody has been in a position to reverse his decision and the unfortunate Rushdie has had to live in hiding under police protection ever since.

Only with the death of Khomeini and the advent of a more moderate leadership under President Rafsanjani, who was con-cerned to rebuild Iran following a long destructive war with Iraq, has there been a change of mood. Rafsanjani has had to move cautiously since the radicals are still a major force, but he has begun to restore relations with the West (despite the Rushdie affair). A condition was Iran exercising greater control over its followers in Lebanon.

Iranian influence

Shia influence outside Iran is relatively limited. However, it is influential in a number of important trouble spots. There is an important Shia presence in the southern republics of what was formerly the Soviet Union; there is a Shia majority in Iraq, although the Sunnis have always ruled; however the most important influence has been in Lebanon.

After 1975 Lebanon collapsed into civil war among its different religious and ethnic groups. Among these, the Shias have always been the poorest and least well represented community in Lebanon. Lebanese Shias had long looked to Iran for inspiration, but following the 1979 revolution the fundamentalists have been especially strong, and have seen the community as engaged in a holy war against the Israelis, encouraged by Iran. But it was only with the Israeli invasion of 1982 that the militias have come to the fore. Their suicide attacks on the Israelis and against the peace-keeping forces of the Americans and French shocked the world. (300 US marines were killed in an incident in 1983). Even more shocking to the West was the capture of Western hostages, who were kept prisoner and ill-treated for up to six years.

The Shia militias saw the West and Israel as all the same, and their activities were blessed by the Ayatollah Khomeini as contributing to a holy crusade to liberate the Islamic holy city of Jerusalem from the Zionists. Death in this struggle was martyrdom and ensured instant access to heaven. It was only after the death of Khomeini, when the Iranian regime wanted better relations with the West that it was able to persuade the Lebanese Shias (the Hezbollah and other groups) to release the Western hostages (for example, Terry Waite and others) in 1991. The Shia fundamentalists are still, however, an important factor in the politics of the area.

The importance of Islam

There are about one billion Muslims, or about one in five of the world's population. Islam is important for that reason alone. But also, the centre of the Islamic world, the Middle East, is one of the most tangled, fraught and dangerous of the world's trouble spots. The area's conflicts are complicated by the fact that the rest of the world has a profound interest in the region's oil supplies. The industrial world is heavily dependent on oil, and more than half the world's oil reserves are to be found in the states surrounding the Persian Gulf: Saudi Arabia, Kuwait, Iraq and Iran, all of which have been involved in major wars in the region over the past decade. It was because of the West's interest in oil that America, Britain and France engaged in war with Iraq in 1991 to liberate Kuwait (an American politician cynically remarked that if Kuwait had produced carrots instead of oil nobody would have given a damn).

Conflict with Israel

However, the most potent source of conflict in the region is not between Islamic states, but between the Arabs and Israel. All Arabs believe that Israel was artificially created out of land that belonged, and still rightfully belongs, to an Arab people, the Palestinians. In addition, all Muslims believe that the Palestinian cause is a cause for the whole Islamic world, since Jerusalem is the third most holy place for Muslims after Mecca and Medina. To complicate matters, the USA (the most powerful country in the world, militarily if not economically) is both dependent on the Middle East oil that is entirely under Arab control and is the main supporter of Israel, which could not survive without American support.

The situation is, to say the least of it, difficult. Conflict in the area always threatens the West. The Yom Kipur War of 1973 and the oil price rise that followed it was responsible for the recession and mass unemployment in the West in the mid-1970s. Something similar happened in the early 1980s following the Iranian revolution. There was yet another threat to the West's prosperity in 1991 when Iraq invaded Kuwait, a threat only averted by the speed with which the allied powers forced defeat upon Iraq. Before the collapse of the Soviet Union, it was often said that if a third world war was going to start anywhere it would be in the Middle East, where a local conflict would suck in the 'superpowers'. With the end of the Cold War this is now unlikely, but the area remains extremely dangerous. These dangers are increased with the continuing spread of Islamic fundamentalism.

Rejection of liberal values

Some have even suggested that the Cold War between the Communist bloc and the liberal democracies was really a local family conflict, and that the really significant conflict, between the West and Islam, is just about to begin. This may be unlikely, but it is certainly true that Communism and liberal democracy, despite drastic differences in practice, have shared ideals and aspirations, and common roots in Western thought going back to the Enlightenment and even to ancient Greece.

It is also true that while it may embrace democracy, as in Iran, fundamentalist Islam is the most significant alternative to Western liberal values, which are the values we associate with modernity. In this sense there are a number of ways in which pure Islam could be said to be in conflict with the modern world; examples include the position of women, sexual morality, punishment for crime, the problem of usury and relations with the non-Muslim world.

Women are accorded great respect in Islam, more so than when the West was dominated by Christian ideas (in such matters as, for example, the ownership of property). But Islamic society is nonetheless highly patriarchal. Men may have several wives. Contraception is strictly forbidden. Women's role is largely confined to the home, and their traditional education accords with this. To the traditionalists, it is not appropriate that women should have the same education as men, or follow careers. Neither should they adopt Western dress, but should be covered from head to toe in the traditional manner. Westernised women have been attacked and intimidated and female university students harassed.

Sexual morality in Islamic law is strict and inflexible. Extra-marital sex is strictly forbidden, as are homosexual acts. In some fundamentalist countries, such as Iran, adulterers and homosexuals have been executed. There are also severe punishments for the drinking of alcohol. The traditional punishment for thieves is the amputation of the hand.

To many modern Muslims much of this is medieval and barbaric, and they see no reason why the morality of sixth-century Arabia should be imposed on people today. Like modern Christians, they see the need to interpret the teachings of their religion in a modern context. To fundamentalists, however, this is a dangerous attitude. Modernity tends to mean westernisation, corruption and the undermining of Islam. Western influence and decadence is deplored and there is a tendency to isolationism. Modernists see this as absurd in the modern world, and see the necessity of at least learning from the West, if only to avoid being left backward and vulnerable, as the Islamic world was in the past. A strong Islamic world needs modern technology and other modern products and techniques.

An interesting conflict between Islamic traditionalism and modernity lies in the question of usury. As in medieval Christianity, it is banned by Islamic divine law. Strictly interpreted, this would forbid the existence of a banking system, which is one of the essential ingredients of a modern economy. A conflict over this matter arose in Pakistan. General Zia, who ruled Pakistan as a military dictator until his assassination in 1988, sought to give legitimacy to his regime by presenting it as an Islamic state. He set up a commission of religious scholars to examine the country's constitution to make certain that all its provisions were consistent with Islamic law. The result was that the Commission (some time after Zia's death) pronounced usury, and therefore banking, to be against Islamic law, thereby throwing much of the economy and a number of major civil projects into confusion, and dividing the by then civilian government of ordinary politicians and Islamicists.

But apart from the workings of the free market and capitalism, there are more basic differences in values. Liberal societies are founded on freedom of the individual, based on civil liberties that are protected by constitutions. Thus we largely take for granted freedom of speech, freedom of association, freedom of religion and related civil liberties, and underlying all them is the liberal value of toleration, the willingness to respect views different from our own. Islamic fundamentalists (and indeed other religious fundamentalists) see no virtue in such values and liberties. They conceive of themselves as possessing the truth and see no reason to give opportunities for falsehoods to flourish by allowing people to say what they like, nor to triumph through democracy. Truth must prevail above all, and only when that is secure can democracy be permitted to contribute to decisions that do not involve that truth.

There is, therefore, a profound gulf between Western values and attitudes and those of the Islamic fundamentalists. Conflicts between Islamic traditionalism and modernity are to be found throughout the Islamic world.

Other religious fundamentalisms

Islam has not been the only one of the world religions to see a revival that has had political importance; it has also been true of Judaism, Hinduism and Christianity. However, these have had less impact than Islam since in each case their influence has been confined to a single country. Jewish fundamentalism is significant only in terms of Israeli politics (although Israeli politics does have a wider international significance – see the discussion of Zionism in Chapter Eight), and Hindu Fundamentalism in terms of the politics of India. In both cases there is a strong link with nationalism. In the case of Christianity, there is a long and complicated relationship between various Christian churches and the political order that is still significant in some parts of the world. But in terms of fundamentalism it is really only in the USA that it could be said to be a significant force.

Christian fundamentalism

Christian fundamentalism in the USA shares with other religious fundamentalisms a common rejection of 'liberal attitudes' to morality, lifestyles and politics, in favour of traditional values of social morality, social order and old-fashioned nationalistic patriotism. For American fundamentalists 'liberal attitudes' had led to the anarchy, atheism and moral degeneracy of the New Left and the permissive society of the 1960s. This outlook put the fundamentalists firmly on the right of the political spectrum, as one of the major strands of the New Right that emerged in the 1970s.

The fundamentalists are on the evangelical wing of American Protestantism, who often call themselves 'born-again Christians'. They believe in the literal truth of the Bible, reject Darwinian evolution, uphold traditional religious values in personal and social matters, and bitterly oppose Communism as an atheistical system opposed to everything Christianity and America stands for. In many ways their outlook is authoritarian and is in direct conflict with the libertarian wing of the New Right (see Chapter 9).

Although levels of religious belief and observance are much higher in the USA than in Britain, there has nevertheless been a general decline in religious commitment in America since the Second World War. The great exception to this has been among the various fundamentalist churches, whose following has grown. Churches, and federations of churches, such as the Southern Baptists, Seventh Day Adventists, Mormons, Assemblies of God, Jehovah's Witnesses and Pentecostalists, have all grown substantially since the 1950s, so that by 1980 they had some thirty million followers, or roughly one third of all American churchgoers. This is partly, no doubt, because the fundamentalists offer simplicity and certainty in a complex and uncertain world. They are also zealous and proselytising in their approach, embracing radio, television and the latest communications technology. But only since the 1970s has some of their crusading zeal been applied to politics. Hitherto these groups have traditionally stood aloof from political activity and even from voting.

What occasioned this change was a reaction to the age of permissiveness and the general rejection of traditional values by American youth of the 1960s, and what they saw as the continuing abomination of feminism and the gay movement. These challenged the traditional family and its values, and what they understood to be the natural patriarchal order of things. For many the culminating event of America's spiritual decline was in the Supreme Court decision of *Roe versus Wade* of January 1973, which gave American women limited rights to abortion. The fundamentalists felt that their values had to be defended politically and that America had to be 'cleansed'.

This led to the creation of a multitude of crusading organisations led by Protestant ministers and pastors, campaigning on a variety of issues such as 'pro-life', ending sex education in schools, against homosexual rights, pornography and so on. Organisations like Moral Majority and Christian Voice were religion-inspired general campaigning groups, created to campaign on these issues and persuade voters to rid Congress of all who supported 'liberal' causes.

The concentration on family values chimed with other elements within the New Right, such as the neo-conservatives, and indeed seemed to speak to many people not of their religious persuasion. This even included the Catholics, against whom Protestant fundamentalists were traditionally hostile, and who had been traditional supporters of the Democrats. In the early 1970s Catholics and extreme Protestants found common cause on many moral issues, especially abortion, and a common enemy in 'liberals' who believed in such things. The fundamentalists' ideas fitted less well with the libertarians on moral issues, but did find common ground in other areas, such as hostility to Communism and a passionate defence of American capitalism. Thus the Reverend Jerry Falwell, the leader of Moral Majority, wrote:

The free enterprise system is clearly outlined in the Book of Proverbs in the Bible. Jesus Christ made it clear that the work ethic was a part of His plan for man. Ownership of property is biblical. Competition in business is biblical. Ambitious and successful business management is clearly outlined as part of God's plan for His people.

(*Listen America*, 1981)

The fundamentalists also shared with the conservative belief in individual responsibility and hostility to state welfare.

The fundamentalists thus became part of a wider New Right spectrum that found its champion in 1980 in Ronald Reagan, who openly declared himself to be a born-again Christian, spoke of the USSR as the 'evil empire', talked of 'family values', and opposed the feminist campaign for equal rights to be written into the US Constitution. In office Reagan did not, perhaps inevitably, deliver all that the religious right wanted, but they nonetheless campaigned vigorously for him in 1984 and, with a little less conviction, for his successor, George Bush. They were particularly influential in the 1992 Republican campaign, when 'family values' and related issues were a major part of the Republican platform.

Despite the heavy defeat of George Bush in 1992 (some say the influence of the religious right was more a hinderance than a help) it seems unlikely that the religious right will give up politics and return to the more traditional fundamentalist stance of non-participation. They have built up an infrastructure of organisation, journals and institutions, as well as a following that has become experienced in political campaigning (and possibly leaders who still have political ambitions). But also their vigorous campaigning activities in the 1970s and 80s have provoked a response among religious groups who do not share their views, who have moved, albeit more quietly, into political activity. It is unlikely that the fundamentalists will leave the field to their religious rivals.

Jewish fundamentalism

There have always been those in Israel who have insisted upon a strict observance of traditional Jewish codes, and there have always been political parties to cater for this. These parties have grown in importance since the 1970s, partly because of the nature of the Israeli electoral system and party balance, where governments have needed their support to remain in office.

What has grown in recent years is the demand for the annexation of the West Bank on the grounds that it is the part of ancient Israel that was Judea and Samaria. Fundamentalists insist that this land is the historic land given by God to the Jews, who thus have a religious duty to settle it, defend it and make it fertile. They see the founding of Israel and the collapse of Communism as part of God's plan for the return of the Jews to their homeland. But Jews must play their part and fight for what is theirs. There must be no compromise with the Arabs. Indeed, some fundamentalists believe that it is religious duty to recover the site of Solomon's temple, which would mean destroying the Al Aqsa mosque one of Islam's most holy shrines. Jewish fundamentalism is, therefore, aggressive and nationalistic.

Since the creation of a Palestinian state is the only conceivable basis for a peace settlement between Arabs and Jews, the fundamentalists are making demands of greatest importance to peace in the region and the world. Their determination to create new settlements in the 'Occupied Territories' (which infuriates the Arab states) has been supported by the Likud party, which was in government in Israel from 1977 to 1992. The election of a Labour government in 1992 has raised hopes that building settlements will stop and peace may have a chance. Nevertheless, despite small numbers (only about 10,000 in all) the Jewish fundamentalist have had a big impact on Israeli and world politics.

Hindu fundamentalism

Aggressive nationalism is also characteristic of India's Hindu fundamentalists, whose growth has been one of the most significant developments in India in recent years. The movement is associated with the Bharatiya Janata Party (BJP) or Hindu Revivalist Party. This is an authoritarian, right-wing party, which believes that Hindus need to assert themselves against non-Hindus (especially Muslims) and that the state should be overtly

Hindu and should have a more aggressive foreign policy.

The BJP's most infamous cause has been the demand that an ancient mosque in Ayodhya in Uttar Pradesh should be demolished to make way for a Hindu temple to the god Ram, who, they believe, was born on the spot. The result of this provocative demand was months of rioting in late 1990 and early 1991 in which more than 1,000 people died and over 4,000 were injured. Trouble broke out again in 1992 when Hindu extremists demolished the mosque. The government promised to rebuild it, but this did not prevent massive riots and much bloodshed. The potential for conflict seems endless, since many mosques erected in the time of the Moghul emperors were bult on the former sites of Hindu temples. This particular dispute remains unresolved, but the government has since passed legislation making it impossible for such a dispute to arise elsewhere.

Although the BJP insists that it is dedicated to reviving traditional Indian culture many see it as distorting Indian tradition and feel it has more in common with a Fascist Party. For one thing, the god Ram is a minor deity in the Hindu pantheon. He is given such emphasis by the BJP because he was a warrior god who, in the mythical past, helped to drive alien invaders out of India, and can therefore be presented as a nationalist god. Furthermore, although it has fought wars in recent times (against Pakistan and China), modern India has conceived of itself as possessed of a particular vocation for peace and tolerance. In the Cold War, for example, it was a powerful advocate of non-alignment. This is partly the legacy of Mahatma Gandhi who was dedicated to bringing about change by peaceful methods, and to tolerance (he was assassinated by a Hindu fanatic just as India became independent). There is also, however, a strong strand of pacifism in Indian culture (see the discussion of Indian nationalism in Chapter Four).

The BJP is not traditionalist in that it has no such commitment to peace and tolerance. Nevertheless, it has gained considerable electoral success. In the general election of May-June 1991 (during which the Indian Prime Minister, Rajiv Gandhi was assassinated) the BJP emerged as the second biggest party and the main opposition.

The influence of religious fundamentalism seems to be growing in world politics. Whether or not this is a temporary phenomenon is difficult to say. Much will depend on the future of
ideology in general, which is the suject of the final chapter.

12

Conclusion: the future of ideology

Previous chapters would suggest that ideology is alive and flourishing. However, it has been forcefully argued on two occasions in the recent past that ideology, or at least ideological conflict, is about to cease permanently. The first occasion was in the 1950s when an argument was put forward known as the 'end-of-ideology' thesis. The second occasion has produced the 'end-of-history' thesis, which first appeared in 1989 and is still the subject of fierce debate. Examining these ideas briefly, and their confusions and limitations, may help us to better understand ideology and give some indication of its future.

The end of ideology

The end-of-ideology thesis became fashionable among American political scientists in the 1950s. Its best known proponents were Seymour Martin Lipset (*Political Man*, 1959) and Daniel Bell (*The End of Ideology: On the Exhaustion of Political Ideas in the Fifties*, 1960). The argument was roughly as follows. Ideology expressed in extreme form the frustrations and aspirations of people for freedom and a decent standard of living. They were doctrines that inspired mass movements that were dedicated to achieve these things. However, in the West at least, the means had been found to satisfy these aspirations for the vast majority of people. The modified free market with a mixed economy, Keynesian economic management and the welfare state, was eliminating poverty and giving freedom, prosperity and opportunity for all. As a consequence, there was a general consensus among political parties over the broad framework of policy, thereby eliminating the need for ideology, and reducing politics to the process of deciding the best means of policy implementation. The rest of the world would eventually follow this path, but the intellectual battle had already been won.

The age of ideology, therefore, was over. Seymour Martin Lipset wrote:

This change in Western political life reflects the fact that the fundamental political problems of the industrial revolution have been solved: the workers have achieved industrial and political citizenship; the conservatives have accepted the welfare state; and the democratic left have recognised that an increase in over-all state power carries with it more dangers to freedom than solutions for economic problems. This very triumph of the democratic social revolutions in the West ends domestic politics for those intellectuals who must have ideologies or utopias to motivate them to political action.

(Political Man, p.406)

Within a few years, however, the theory was looking doubtful because of the advent of the New Left. Not only was that movement a revival of ideology which had not been predicted, but it happened among the most well-off and privileged youth of the richest Western countries, who were demanding an end to the very materialism that was supposed to be killing ideology off.

More importantly, their concept of ideology was questionable. It was equated with extremism and fanaticism, which was then contrasted with the 'rational' politics and political principles of those who shared the political scientist's own beliefs. It was in fact a partisan view (see Chapter One), which is clear from Seymour Martin Lipset's remark that contemporary liberal democracy was 'the good society itself in operation' (p.404).

One of the consequences of adopting a more neutral view of ideology that includes all political beliefs, is that it rather undermines the notion of an end to ideology, the idea that at some point all false thinking will cease and give way to the true. The modern version of the end-of-ideology thesis does not, therefore, argue that all ideology has finished, but instead argues that one ideology, the 'right' one, has finally, absolutely and permanently, won the conflict of ideas and will dominate human thinking in perpetuity. This view is known as the 'end-of-history thesis' and has been put forward by Francis Fukuyama.

The end of history

In the summer of 1989 Fukuyama, who was then a little-known official in the US State Department, published an article in a rather obscure foreign policy journal, *The National Interest*, entitled 'The End of History?'. In it he wrote:

What we may be witnessing is not just the end of the Cold War, or the passing of a particular period of postwar history, but the end of history as such; that is, the end point of mankind's ideological evolution and the universalisation of Western liberal democracy as the final form of human government. ('The End of History', p.3)

The article caused something of a sensation and the intellectual world has been vigorously discussing it ever since. Fukuyama subsequently published a book setting out his ideas in more detail, *The End of History and the Last Man* (1992), in which his conclusions are a little more tentative, but the thesis remains essentially the same.

The whole idea of history having an end is taken from Hegel (whom we met at the beginning of Chapter Seven). Hegel believed that human history had passed through a series of necessary stages or civilizations, each of which developed internal conflicts or 'contradictions' which undermined it and could only be resolved in passing on to a new and more advanced civilization, which in turn had its own conflicts, and so on. History is 'ended' when we reach a form of society where all conflicts have been resolved and humanity will have discovered the form of society best suited to its nature: 'Hegel believed that history culminated in an absolute moment – a moment in which the final rational form of society and state became victorious' (*Ibid.*, p.4).

When this happens, history will not be finished in the sense that there will still be great events and achievements (or crimes) worth recording. What will have ended will be the process of social and political evolution and the conflict of ideas that this generated.

Fukuyama claims (incorrectly as a matter of fact) that Hegel recognised liberal democracy as the ultimate society, following the French Revolution, but that it would take the best part of another two centuries before his insight was universally recognised. Liberal democracy had to contend with a series of rivals, but in winning the Second World War the challenge of fascism was defeated, while the end of the Cold War signalled the defeat of communism. With those gone there is no serious challenger to modern capitalist liberal democracy. There is religious fundamentalism and nationalism, but Fukuyama insists these present no adequate alternative.

However, this is not mere triumphalism. Maximum individual freedom in a consumer paradise does not provide much spiritual satisfaction. In a rather bleak and ironic closing passage Fukuyama writes:

The end of history will be a very sad time. The struggle for recognition, the willingness to risk one's own life for a purely abstract goal, the worldwide ideological struggle that called forth daring, courage, imagination, and idealism, will be replaced by economic calculation, the endless solving of technical problems, environmental concerns, and the satisfaction of sophisticated consumer demands. In the post-historical period there will be neither art nor philosophy, just the perpetual caretaking of the museum of human history.

(*Ibid.*, p.10)

Despite the sting in the tale, Fukuyama believes that free-market liberal democracy is the society which alone can provide humanity with maximum satisfaction and fulfilment. And that given the failure or weakness of alternatives, and the globalisation of communications so that all can see and aspire to what others have, its triumph is inevitable. There are, however, objections to this analysis.

Objections to the end-of-history thesis

Fukuyama seems to believe that the world will become increasingly like America, since all peoples aspire to American prosperity and freedom. Yet it could be argued that if people want prosperity, better models can be found in Asia.

Japan is the greatest economic superpower and her South-east Asian neighbours have seen the most spectacular economic growth of recent years. The great economic success of countries like South Korea, Singapore, Taiwan and Hong Kong were not the result of liberal democracy, but the combination of free markets with various degrees of authoritarian rule. (Lee Kwan Yu, the British-educated leader of Singapore, has declared that democracy would inhibit his country's economic success, while it is also true that South Korean economic growth has been less spectacular since it began to move towards more democracy in 1986). It would seem that China is attempting its own version of this authoritarian model rather than the liberal democratic one.

One of the features of Asian economic success is thought to be the absence of Western individualism. People work for the group rather than for themselves. Family and community ties are much stronger. This is true of Japan, where there are powerful group loyalties that bind workers to their firms. While Japan is constitutionally a liberal democracy (imposed on them after 1945), a single dominant political party has overseen Japan's formidable economic success, and no particular virtue is seen in periodic changes of government. Furthermore, the Japanese economy is a much more state-guided version than free-market advocates in the West think desirable.

The values of community and loyalty that are so strong in Asia are relatively weak in the USA, and Asian people find its decadence, moral decay, crime, drugs and other problems deeply offensive. The economic success of the East, especially combined with the relative economic decline of the West, could convince Asians that liberal democracy on the Western model, with its self-indulgence and lack of discipline, is a questionable ideal.

A rejection of decadent Western society is also a major factor in the revival of Islam, which for example sees Western music, dress and manners corrupting Muslim youth. It may be unlikely that a revived Islam will conquer the world, yet there are around one billion Moslems in the world (about 20 per cent of the world's population) who may reject the west and find their own alternatives.

There is then the possibly related question of the 'spiritual emptiness' of modern consumer society, which Fukuyama himself points to. He says that the filling this can be a wholly private matter, but this hardly answers the case. People feel the need for a common cause, something greater than themselves. New ideologies may arise to fulfil that need. This might mean more religious fundamentalism and certainly new or revived ideological causes.

Green thinking is one area of ideology posing a threat to liberal-capitalist ideas that Fukuyama does not take sufficiently seriously, although it may be increasingly important in the future. In the meanwhile, the other ideologies we have discussed are not just going to go away. They represent ideas and values that can still have great appeal. It seems unlikely, for example, that socialism will not be reformulated. Its ideals of community and sharing and its condemnation of greed and individualism are too strong to be ignored indefinitely.

Capitalist societies have huge social problems that show little sign of disappearing and may well become worse. The free market will no doubt give us more economic growth in the future, but it is also subject to great slumps as well. Free market capitalism is all the rage, but then so it was in the nineteenth century under *laissez-faire*. Its failure then led to the development of collectivism, and we may have to relive the consequences of its failure again. The likelihood is that if capitalism falters there will be a demand for fresh thinking, and new ideas will surely arise.

Fukuyama takes no account of future creativity. Even in the unlikely event of the present world hardly changing for a long time, new ideas will develop. In fact all kinds of changes will certainly come. The idea of the end of history carries with it notions of a static ideal, but this is hardly possible if capitalism is to be the basis, for of all economic systems, capitalism is the most dynamic, the most open to change and the most effective in changing society. It is driven by change and in turn drives change, indeed at an ever faster and bewildering pace. Who can say where economic and social change will end, if it ever does end, and no one can presume to say that such change will not have its impact on ideology.

It is simply not plausible that political change will cease under capitalist liberal democracy or any other system. We only have to contemplate the wider course of human history, when certain political systems and ways of life have lasted for hundred and even thousands of years. But all in the end succumb to change. Capitalist liberal democracy, even if it spreads to the entire world, will generate change and probably more readily than any other system. Compared to the empires of China, Rome or ancient Egypt, liberal democracy has been around for the merest fragment of time, a mere two hundred years. History would suggest that no system, let alone liberal democracy, will last for ever.

Progress and relativism

Finally, something might be said about Fukuyama's whole enterprise. The end-of-history thesis is plainly a theory of progress. Such theories have been much out of fashion in the twentieth century, and with the horrific bloodbath of World War I, the nightmare of Nazi Germany and the prospect of the Cold War leading to the annihilation of mankind, this is perhaps not surprising. There are, on the other hand, good intellectual reasons for being sceptical about such grand theories of history, which Fukuyama ignores.

The idea of progress is bound up with values. If we are making progress then we are moving towards things we think are good, and away from things we think bad. But, of course, people's values differ. As we have seen, some see Fukuyama's ideal of America as the very home of self-indulgence, decadence and immorality. Others see America as symbolising the end of civilised values, swamped in a bland mass culture that appeals to the lowest common denominator. For others still, America is the bastion of capitalism, which is the great block on the road to any kind of human progress. Indeed, some believe that history is very opposite of progressive. The great modern poet, T.S.Eliot, to take an extreme example, admired medieval Christianity and believed that Western civilization had been in steady decline since the Renaissance.

Furthermore, people can always interpret the world according to their own ideas. Jehovah's Witnesses, and other Christian fundamentalists, see in current world events plain evidence of the biblical prophecies of the end of the world coming true. Someone who believes that deep in the human psyche there is a 'death wish' that will eventually end in humanity's self-destruction will find plenty of evidence of this belief in the daily news. The selective reading of history and current events will furnish evidence for an infinite number of contrary theories. It all depends on what people believe, and believe *in*.

Even if we believe, like Fukuyama, that things are generally getting better, there is no reason to suppose, as he does, that they must go on getting better, and that there is some mechanism at work that ensures in the long run we will create the best possible world for people to live in. We may go on improving our science and technology, but that does not say that society and human behaviour will also improve, or even that we will put our discoveries to best use. There are some, indeed, who argue that science is not progressive.

Some years ago, an American scholar, Thomas Kuhn, wrote a study of scientific history entitled *The Structure of Scientific Revolutions* (1962), in which he argued that each major scientific theory is not an improvement on previous theories but merely a different view of things, and that consequently our belief in scientific progress is illusory. Since then some thinkers have taken a more radical view. There is now a fashionable and influential body of theory, developed mainly by a number of French thinkers such as Michel Foucault and Jacques Derrida, and known as post-modernism, which claims that there are a multitude of differing ways of looking at the world, historical and scientific and religious and practical, each with its own kind of truth, and we simply do not have the means of judging between these different versions of what is true.

If the postmodernists are correct, then it rules out the grand historical theories of the Kuhn type, let alone Fukuyama's, making any sense. More importantly, postmodernists question the whole of what they call the 'modernist project'. This is the belief, beginning with the Enlightenment, that human reason can master all reality and with that knowledge can create a more rational world. All truth is relative, not merely to different historical periods and cultures (as some people have argued in the past) but to different theories, religions, outlooks, fashions and even ideologies.

Postmodernism is a rather bewildering and disturbing analysis, although it is vulnerable to the old argument against relativism, that if nothing is absolutely true, then relativism cannot be absolutely true either. But whether we are impressed by the post-modernist case or not, Fukuyama's ideas do look rather naive and simplistic. Yet having said all that, even if we find Fukuyama's arguments unconvincing, it is nevertheless possible that eventually ideolgy, or ideological conflict will die out.

Can there ever be an end of ideology?

If we have a neutral concept of ideology that encompasses all kinds of political belief about what society we ought to live in and how it can be achieved, then there is reason to suppose that an eventual end of ideology altogether is unlikely. However inadequate they may be as intellectual constructions, and whatever the conflicts and dangers they bring in their wake, we nevertheless seem to need beliefs of this kind. They embody our aspirations to solve mankind's problems and live a better life. They help to satisfy a widely felt need to believe in something greater than ourselves, offering shared values that every community needs; in doing so they help us to determine our identity and place in the world.

It may be that eventually one ideology will triumph, or at least do so for a very long time, although this is not necessarily so. If one ideology does eventually prevail it will probably be the one that is most satisfying to most people. But that prospect would seem to be a very long way off. In the meantime we will remain in a world of ideological conflict, where different beliefs contend for the allegiance of the mass of people. In other words, we will still live in the age of the French Revolution.

Hitler and Mussolini both believed that they were putting an end to that era, and that fascism constituted a new epoch for humanity when all the world would be fascist. Hitler's chief of propaganda, Joseph Goebbels, expressed it with characteristically brutal simplicity when he said: 'The year 1789 is hereby eradicated from history'. Happily this proved to be premature. Chou En-lai, the long-serving first prime minister of Communist China, was more shrewd. When asked what he thought the consequences of the French Revolution were, he simply replied that it was too early to tell.

Select bibliography

Introduction and general

I. Adams, *The Logic of Political Belief: A Philosophical Analysis of Ideology*, Harvester-Wheatsheaf, 1989.

I. Adams & Bill Jones, *Political Ideas in Britain*, PAVIC, 1992.

T. Ball & R. Dagger, *Political Ideologies and the Democratic Ideal*, HarperCollins, 1991.

T. Ball & R. Dagger, *Ideals and Ideologies: A Reader*, HarperCollins, 1991.

L. P. Baradat, *Political Ideologies: Their Origin and Impact* (4th ed.), Prentice Hall, 1991.

D. Bell, *The End of Ideology: On the Exhaustion of Political Ideas in the Fifties* (2nd ed.), Free Press, 1962.

R. Eccleshall *et al.*, *Political Ideologies: An Introduction*, Hutchinson, 1984.

F. Fukuyama, *The End of History and the Last Man*, Hamish Hamilton, 1992.

A. Gamble, *An Introduction to Modern Social and Political Thought*, Macmillan, 1981.

A. Heywood, *Political Ideologies: An Introduction*, Macmillan, 1992.

Will Kamenka, *Contemporary Political Philosophy: An Introduction*, OUP, 1990.

R. Leach, *British Political Ideologies*, Philip Allan, 1991.

S. M. Lipset, *Political Man*, Heinemann, 1960.

D. McLellan, *Ideology*, Open UP, 1986.

D. Miller (ed.), *The Blackwell Encyclopaedia of Political Thought*, Blackwell, 1991.

M. A. Riff (ed.), *Dictionary of Modern Political Ideologies*, Manchester University Press, 1987.

S. Schama, *Citizens: A Chronicle of the French Revolution*, Penquin, 1989.

R. Scruton, *A Dictionary of Political Thought*, Macmillan, 1982.

A. K. Thorlby, *The Romantic Movement*, Longman, 1966.

W. Wordsworth, *The Prelude* (Text of 1805), OUP, 19660.

Liberalism and democracy

Anthony Arblaster, *The Rise and Decline of Western Liberalism*, Blackwell, 1984.

E. K. Bramsted & K. J. Melhuish, *Western Liberalism*, Longman, 1978.

A-N. de Condorcet, *Sketch for a Historical Picture of the Progress of the Human Mind*, Nooneday Press, 1955.

F. E. Dowrick, *Human Rights: Problems, Perspectives and Texts*, Saxon House, 1979.

Eccleshall (ed.), *British Liberalism: Liberal Thought from the 1640s to 1980s*, Longman, 1986.

M. Foley, *American Political Ideas: Traditions and Usages*, Manchester University Press, 1991.

L. Hartz, *The Liberal Tradition in America*, Harcourt, Brace & World, 1955.

A. Hamilton *et al.*, *The Federalist Papers*, Mentor, 1961.

D. Heater, *Citizenship: The Civic Ideal in World History, Politics and Education*, Longman, 1990.

D. Held, *Models of Democracy*, Polity, 1987.

R. Hielbroner, *The Worldly Philosophers* (5th ed.), Penguin, 1980.

L. T. Hobhouse, *Liberalism*, OUP, 1964.

R. Hofstadter, *The American Political Tradition*, Cape, 1967.

B. Holden, *The Nature of Democracy*, Nelson, 1974.

W. von Humboldt, *The Limits of State Action*, CUP, 1969.

E. Ions (ed.), *Political and Social Thought in America 1870–1970*, Weidenfeld & Nicholson, 1970.

J. Locke, *Two Treatise of Government*, Mentor, 1965.

D. Manning, *Liberalism*, Dent, 1976.

J. S. Mill, *Utilitarianism, Liberty, Representative Government*, Dent, 1910.

Baron de Montesquieu, *The Spirit of the Laws*, Hafner, 1949.

T. Paine, *The Rights of Man*, Penguin, 1969.

B. Parekh (ed.), *Bentham's Political Thought*, Croom Helm, 1973.

J. Plamenatz, *Readings from Liberal Writers: English and French*, Allen & Unwin, 1965.

J. Rawls, *A Theory of Justice*, OUP, 1973.

J-J. Rousseau, *The Social Contract and Discourses*, Dent, 1973.
A. Sharp (ed.), *Political Ideas of the English Civil Wars 1641–1649*, Longman, 1983.
H. Spencer, *Man versus the State*, Penguin, 1969.
A. de Tocqueville, *Democracy in America* (2 vols.), Fontana, 1968.

Conservatism and the right

E. Burke, *Reflections on the Revolution in France*, Penguin, 1969.
R. Eatwell & N. O'Sullivan (eds.), *The Nature of the Right*, Pinter, 1989.
R. Eccleshall (ed.), *English Conservatism since the Restoration*, Unwin Hyman, 1990.
I. Gilmour, *Inside Right: A Study of Conservatism*, Quartet, 1978.
J. S. McClland (ed.), *The French Right: From de Maistre to Maurras*, Cape, 1970.
F. O'Gorman (ed.), *British Conservatism: Conservative Thought from Burke to Thatcher*, Longman, 1986.
N. O'Sullivan, *Conservatism*, Dent, 1976.
A. Quinton, *The Politics of Imperfection*, Faber, 1978.
H. S. Reiss (ed.), *The Political Thought of the German Romantics 1793–1815*, Blackwell, 1955.
J. Weiss, *Conservatism in Europe*, Thames & Hudson, 1977.

Nationalism and internationalism

P. Alter, *Nationalism*, Edward Arnold, 1985.
E. J. Hobsbawm, *Nations and Nationalism since 1780*, CUP, 1990.
E. Kedourie, *Nationalism* (3rd ed.), Hutchinson, 1966.
J. Mazzini, *The Duties of Man and other essays*, Dent, 1907.
K. R. Minogue, *Nationalism*, Methuen, 1967.
A. D. Smith, *National Identity*, Penguin, 1991.

Varieties of socialism

Tony Benn, *Arguments for Socialism*, Penguin, 1980.
R. N. Berki, *Socialism*, Dent, 1975.
E. Bernstein, *Evolutionary Socialism*, Schocken Books, 1961.

B. Crick, *Socialism*, Open University Press, 1987.

C. A. R. Crossland, *The Future of Socialism*, Cape, 1964.

G. Foote, *The Labour Party's Political Thought: A History*, Croom Helm, 1986.

J. Le Grand & S. Estrin (eds.), *Market Socialism*, OUP, 1989.

J. Ramsay, Macdonald, *The Socialist Movement*, Williams & Norgate, 1991.

N. MacKenzie, *Socialism: A Short History* (2nd ed.), Hutchinson, 1966.

N. & J. MacKenzie, *The First Fabians*, Quartet, 1977.

K. Taylor, *The Political Ideas of the Utopian Socialists*, Frank Cass, 1982.

A. Wright (ed.), *British Socialism: Socialist Thought from the 1880's to 1960's*, Longman, 1983.

A Wright, *Socialisms: Theories and Practices*, OUP, 1986.

Anarchism

D. Apter & J. Joll (eds.), *Anarchism Today*, Macmillan, 1971.

M Bakunin, *Statism and Anarchy*, CUP, 1990.

M. Bookchin, *Post-Scarcity Anarchism*, Wildwood House, 1974.

A. Carter, *The Political Theory of Anarchism*, RKP, 1971.

S. Edwards (ed.), *Selected Writings of Pierre-Joseph Proudhon*, Macmillan, 1969.

D. Friedman, *The Machinery of Freedom*, Harper, 1973.

W. Goodwin, *An Enquiry Concerning Political Justice*, Penguin, 1976.

P. Kropotkin, *Mutual Aid*, Heinemann, 1910.

D. Miller, *Anarchism*, Dent, 1984.

M. Stirner, *The Ego and His Own*, Cape, 1921.

H. D. Thoreau, *Walden* and *Civil Disobedience*, Signet, 1960.

C. Ward, *Anarchy in Action*, Freedman Press, 1982.

J. Warren, *Equitable Commerce*, Fowler & Wells, 1852.

G. Woodcock, *Anarchism*, Penguin, 1963.

G. Woodcock (ed.), *The Anarchist Reader*, Fontana, 1977.

Marxism

S. Avineri, *Karl Marx: Social and Political Thought*, CUP, 1968.

I. Berlin, *Karl Marx* (3rd ed.), OUP, 1963.

T. Bottomore *et al.* (eds.), *A Dictionary of Marxist Thought*, Blackwell, 1983.

I. Deutscher (ed.), *The Age of Permanent Revolution: A Trotsky Anthology*, Del, 1964.

M. Evans, *Karl Marx*, Allen & Unwin, 1975.

D. Held, *Introduction to Political Theory: Horkheimer to Habermas*, Hutchinson, 1980.

V. I. Lenin, *Selected Works*, Lawrence & Wishart, 1968.

G. Lichtheim, *Marxism* (2nd ed.), RKP, 1964.

D. McLellan, *The Thought of Karl Marx* (2nd ed.), Macmillan, 1980.

D. McLellan, *Marxism after Marx* (2nd ed.), 1979.

D. McLellan (ed.), *Karl Marx: Selected Writings*, OUP, 1977.

S. Schram (ed.), *The Political thought of Mao Tse Tung* (2nd ed.), Praeger, 1969.

K. Sward (ed.), *Times Guide to Eastern Europe: The Changing Face of the Warsaw Pact*, 1990.

H. Tudor, *Marxism and Social Democracy: The Revisionist Debate 1896–1898*, 1988.

Racism and Fascism

M. Banton, *Race Relations*, Tavistock, 1967.

J. Barzun, *Race: A Study in Superstition*, Harper & Row, 1965.

R. Benewick, *Gorineau: Selected Political Writings*, Cape, 1970.

S. Carmichael & C. V. Hamilton, *Black Power: The Politics of Liberation in America*, Random House, 1967.

L. Cheles *et al.* (eds.), *Neo-Fascism in Europe*, Longman, 1991.

F. Fanon, *Black Skin, White Masks*, Grove Press, 1982.

G. Harris, *The Dark Side of Europe: The Extreme Right Today*, Edinburgh UP, 1990.

A. Hitler, *Mein Kampf*, Hutchinson, 1969.

M. L. King, *Why We Can't Wait*, Harper & Row, 1964.

A. Lyttleton, *Italian Fascism: From Pareto to Gentile*, Cape, 1973.

E. Nolte, *Three Faces of Fascism*, Mentor, 1965.

N. O'Sullivan, *Fascism*, Dent, 1983.

L. L. Snyder, *The Idea of Racism*, Van Hostrand, 1962.

L. Thompson, *The Political Mythology of Apartheid*, Yale UP, 1985.

P. Wilkinson, *The New Fascists* (2nd ed.), Pan, 1983.

S. J. Woolf (ed.), *Fascism in Europe*, Methuen, 1981.

M. X. *The Autobiography of Malcolm X*, Grove Press, 1966.

The New Right

P. Clarke & G. Graham, *The New Englightenment: The Rebirth of Liberalism*, Macmillan/Channel 4, 1986.

M. & R. Friedman, *Free to Choose*, 1980.

A. Gamble, *The Free Economy and the Strong State: The Politics of Thatcherism*, Macmillan, 1988.

D. G. Green, *The New Right: The Counter Revolution in Political, Social and Economic Thought*, Wheatsheaf, 1987.

F. A. Hayek, *The Road to Serfdom*, RKP, 1944.

W. Keegan, *Mrs Thatchers Economic Experiment*, Penguin, 1985.

D. S. King, *The New Right: Politics, Markets and Citizenship*, Macmillan, 1987.

R. Levitas, *The Ideology of the New Right*, Polity, 1986.

R. Nozick, *Anarchy, State and Utopia*, Blackwell, 1974.

G. Peele, *Revival and Reaction: The Right in Contemporary America*, OUP, 1984.

G. Sampson, *An End to Allegiance: Individual Freedom and the New Politics*, Temple Smith, 1984.

New radicalisms

R. Bahro, *From Red to Green*, Verso, 1984.

S. de Beauvoir, *The Second Sex*, Penguin, 1972.

D. Bouchier, *The Feminist Challenge: The Movement for Women's Liberation in Britain and the United States*, Macmillan, 1983.

S. Brownmiller, *Against Our Will: Men, Women and Rape*, Penguin, 1975.

J. Charvet, *Feminism*, Dent, 1982.

P. Clarke & A. Linzey, *Political Theory and Animal Rights*, Pluto Press, 1990.

A. Dobson, *Green Political Thought*, Unwin, 1984.

H. Eisentein, *Contemporary Feminist Thought*, Unwin, 1984.

S. Firestone, *The Dialectic of Sex: the Case for Feminist Revolution*, Paladin, 1972.

Betty Friedan, *The Feminine Mystique*, Penguin, 1965.

G. Greer, *The Female Eunuch*, Paladin, 1971.

D. Henshaw, *Animal Warfare: The Story of the Animal Liberation Front*, Fontana, 1989.

Maggie Humm (ed.), *Feminisms: A Reader*, Harvester-Wheatsheaf, 1992.

D. Icke, *The Truth Vibrations*, HarperCollins, 1991.

Kate Millett, *Sexual Politics*, Virago, 1977.

R. Mohr, *Gays/Justice*, Columbia UP, 1988.

S. Parkin, *Green Parties: An International Guide*, Heretic Books, 1989.

J. Porritt, *Seeing Green: The Politics of Ecology Explained*, Blackwell, 1984.

J. Porritt & D. Winner, *The Coming of the Greens*, Fontana, 1988.

P. Singer, *Animal Liberation: Towards an End to Man's Inhumanity to Animals*, Thorsons, 1983.

J. Weeks, *Coming Out: Homosexual Politics in Britain, from the Nineteenth Century to the Present*, Quartet, 1977.

Religious fundamentalism

Steve Bruce, *The Rise and Fall of the New Christian Right: Conservative Protestant Politics in America 1978–1988*, OUP, 1988.

Y. M. Choueiri, *Islamic Fundamentalism*, Pinter, 1990.

H. Enayat, *Modern Islamic Political Thought*, Macmillan, 1982.

D. Hiro, *Islamic Fundamentalism*, Paladin, 1988.

M. Ruthven, *Islam in the World* (2nd ed.), Penguin, 1991.

P. Sluglett & M. Farouk-Sluglett (eds.), *The Times Guide to the Middle East: The Arab World and its Neighbours*, Times Books, 1991.

Index